ATLA Bibliography Series
edited by Dr. Kenneth E. Rowe

1. A Guide to the Study of The Holiness Movement, by Charles Edwin Jones. 1974

2. Thomas Merton: A Bibliography, by Marquita E. Breit. 1974

THOMAS MERTON:
A Bibliography

Compiled and edited

by

Marquita Breit

ATLA Bibliography Series, No. 2

The Scarecrow Press, Inc., Metuchen, N. J.
and
The American Theological Library Association
1974

Library of Congress Cataloging in Publication Data

Breit, Marquita E   1942-
  Thomas Merton: a bibliography.

  (ATLA bibliography series, no. 2)
  1. Merton, Thomas, 1915-1968--Bibliography.
I. Series: American Theological Library Association.
ATLA bibliography series, no. 2.
Z8570.6.B73 1974   016.2   73-23092
ISBN 0-8108-0705-X

To

All My Family

and Friends

EDITOR'S FOREWORD

With the accidental death of Thomas Merton in December of 1968, America lost one of her most creative spiritual writers and perceptive social critics. For more than twenty years in the seclusion of his abbey Thomas Merton authored modern classics of the spiritual life. But he was more than the silent mystic who could celebrate the virtues of monastic life in glowing prose and poetry. He also was a social commentator of great skill and imagination who could write freedom songs for the civil rights movement and articles for the anti-war movement of the 1960's.

Merton experienced little tension between his commitment to the monastic life and his commitment to the contemporary world. His entire life was lived with deep concern for the tragic alienations of the real world, passionately aware of both the inward and outward crises confronting mid-twentieth century man. The contemplative life simply gave him a unique perspective from which he could understand the world's anguish and share its joy.

Ms. Marquita Breit's bibliography includes more than 1800 items by and about Thomas Merton published between the years 1957 and 1973. An earlier bibliography compiled by Frank Dell'Isola (<u>Thomas Merton: A Bibliography</u>, Farrar, Straus and Cudahy, 1956) covers the period up to 1956.

The **ATLA** Bibliography Series is designed to stimulate and encourage the preparation and publication of reliable guides to the literature of religious studies in all of its scope and variety. Each compiler is free to define his or her field, make the appropriate selections, and work out internal organization according to the unique demands of the subject chosen.

Ms. Breit studied history at Ursuline College and Library Science at Spalding College, both in Louisville, Kentucky.

She is currently Circulation Librarian at Bellarmine College
in the same city.   We are pleased to publish Ms. Breit's
Merton bibliography as number two in our series.

Drew University Library   Kenneth E. Rowe, Editor
Madison, New Jersey

CONTENTS

Editor's Foreword (Kenneth E. Rowe)   v

Foreword (Brother Patrick Hart, O. C. S. O.)   ix

Introduction   xiii

PRIMARY SOURCES

    Books and Pamphlets by Thomas Merton   1

    Prose Contributions to Books   10

    Prose Contributions to Newspapers and Periodicals   18

    Poetry in Books, Newspapers, and Periodicals   50

    M. A. Thesis   57

    Translations by Thomas Merton   57

    Translations of Merton's Works   63

    Recordings   81

SECONDARY SOURCES

    Books about Thomas Merton   83

    Articles in Books, Newspapers, and Periodicals   84

    Reviews of Thomas Merton's Books   108

    Reviews of Books about Thomas Merton   127

    Selected Theses and Dissertations   129

    Foreign Language Books about Thomas Merton   131

    Films   131

Index   133

FOREWORD

Brother Patrick Hart, O. C. S. O.

Although a cloistered contemplative monk, Thomas Merton was one of the most prolific writers in the history of monasticism. Born of a New Zealand artist father, Owen Merton, and an American mother, Ruth Jenkins, on January 31, 1915, in Prades, a small French town on the Spanish border, his early school was unusually cosmopolitan.

The young Tom Merton moved to the United States with his parents in 1916 and resided in Maryland briefly, and then New York--both in Flushing and Douglaston. After the death of his mother in Bellevue Hospital (New York) in 1921, he went to Bermuda with his father where he attended elementary school. Returning to Douglaston in 1923, he spent two more years in America before departing with his father once again for France (St. Antonin), where he entered the Lycée Ingres at Montauban.

Two years later he left with his father for England, and commenced his studies at Oakham School in Ruthland. Following his father's death at Middlesex Hospital (London) in January of 1931, he continued at Oakham and acquired a Higher Certificate and Scholarship to Clare College at Cambridge. During the summer of 1933 the 18-year-old Merton traveled to Italy, where he experienced a great religious awakening, especially in Rome. He returned to England in the fall and entered Cambridge, concentrating on modern languages.

After a chaotic year at Cambridge, he came to America once again, in 1935, to live with his maternal grandparents and continue his studies at Columbia University where he earned his B. A. in 1938 and his M. A. in 1939 (the master's thesis was on "Nature and Art in William

Blake"). Although he began studies for the doctorate (on
the poetry of Gerard Manley Hopkins) he was unable to complete this work. (In 1963 Columbia University awarded
Thomas Merton their Medal of Excellence, and the same
year the University of Kentucky at Lexington conferred on
him "in absentia" the honorary Litt. D.)

The story of Merton's conversion and his reception
into the Catholic Church is well-known to readers of The
Seven Storey Mountain. After a short teaching career at
Columbia University Extension and St. Bonaventure College
(now a university) in upstate New York, and following a
brief stint of social work with Baroness Catherine de Hueck
Doherty at Friendship House in Harlem, Merton entered the
Abbey of Gethsemani in Trappist, Kentucky, on December
10, 1941. Just twenty-seven years to the day of his en-
trance, December 10, 1968, he met his tragic death in
Bangkok, Thailand, by accidental electric shock.

In the spring of 1968, Father Merton received a
pressing invitation to attend a meeting of Asian monastic
superiors (Benedictine and Cistercian) at Bangkok. He was
also asked to deliver a paper at an interfaith meeting of the
Spiritual Summit Conference, sponsored by the Temple of
Understanding, in Calcutta a few weeks prior to the Bangkok
meeting. Taking advantage of his Eastern journey, several
Trappist Abbots requested him to give retreats to their
communities in Asia before returning to America. On
December 10th he gave what was to be his last message to
the world: a paper entitled "Marxism and Monastic Perspectives." After lunch he retired to his cottage for a mid-
day rest. Apparently he touched a defective fan, either to
turn it on or pull it closer to the bed, received a 220 volt
electric shock, and died.

Looking back on his twenty-seven years as a Trappist
monk at Gethsemani, Merton's writings take on tremendous
proportions and his wide-ranging interests seem incredible--
from early Irish monasticism to Shaker communities--from
the Greek Fathers to nuclear disarmament--from the Chinese
classics to twentieth-century ecumenism. Merton summed
up succinctly the unifying element in his writings for over a
quarter of a century in these words which he wrote for the
opening of the Merton Collection at the Bellarmine College
Library in 1963: "Whatever I may have written, I think it
all can be reduced in the end to this one root truth: that
God calls human persons to union with Himself and with one

another in Christ, in the Church which is His Mystical Body"
(Merton Studies Center, Vol. I, p. 10).

Merton himself describes very well the various phases
of his monastic writings in "First and Last Thoughts: An
Author's Preface" (A Thomas Merton Reader, Harcourt,
Brace, 1962): "I would say that my life at Gethsemani has
fallen roughly into four periods. First, the novitiate. I
was a novice in 1942.... It was a period of training, and
a happy, austere one, during which I wrote little. The best
Gethsemani poems belong to this period."

He speaks then of a second period beginning with his
appointment to translate French books and articles, and a
little biographical writing on Cistercian saints. At the same
time he studied philosophy and theology in preparation for
ordination to the priesthood. He comments: "This second
period extends from 1944, my first vows, to ordination in
1949.... In 1946 I wrote The Seven Storey Mountain, in
1947 Seeds of Contemplation, and in 1948 The Waters of
Siloe."

Thomas Merton was made Master of Scholastics (or
students) in 1951, which begins a third stage. This new
appointment brought with it considerable work in preparing
conferences and classes, as well as giving spiritual direction
to the young students in the monastery. Books of this period included No Man Is an Island, Thoughts in Solitude, The
Silent Life and The Living Bread.

In 1955 Father Merton was appointed Master of Choir
Novices, beginning a fourth period, which resulted in even
greater responsibilities. Very little writing was possible for
the first year or two, but after that short books or collections of essays appeared, such as Disputed Questions, The
Behavior of Titans, The Wisdom of the Desert (with a translation of the Desert Fathers) and New Seeds of Contemplation. In the early sixties he began writing on controversial
social problems, especially racial injustice and nuclear war-
fare. At the same time his interests in classical Chinese
thought and the Zen masters increased, and soon developed
into a fifth stage of writings with works like The Way of
Chuang Tzu, Mystics and Zen Masters, Gandhi and Non-
Violence and Seeds of Destruction.

Merton resigned his position as Novice Master in
August of 1965 and entered upon the final stage of his

monastic life, retiring to a small cinderblock hermitage on
a secluded wooded hill on the monastery property.   Two
long book-length poems were written during this period,
Cables to the Ace and The Geography of Lograire, revealing
Merton's new experiments in language.   Conjectures of a
Guilty Bystander, Faith and Violence and Zen and the Birds
of Appetite also belong to this period.   He spent three
years in the hermitage, leaving it in August of 1968 to be-
gin his extensive Asian trip.   The Asian Journal of Thomas
Merton, which is his last book (chronologically), records
this final journey.

        During the five years since his death, a phenomenal
interest in Thomas Merton and his work is evidenced by
over twenty doctoral, as well as numerous masters'
theses already completed or in the process of completion,
on some aspect of his life, thought and concerns.   In addi-
tion, scholars frequent the Merton Collection at the Bellarmine College Library as a necessary preparation for
their studies of Merton for theological and literary journals.

        In 1956 Frank Dell'Isola published an early bibliogra-
phy of Thomas Merton (Farrar, Straus and Cudahy) which
included Mertoniana up to 1956.   Since that time, however,
an enormous amount of material has been published.   This
includes not only Merton's own writings, but also many
critical studies by scholars and students of his work.   The
present bibliography, professionally compiled and edited by
Miss Marquita Breit of the Bellarmine College Library staff,
lists primary and secondary sources: all the books, pamphlets, poems and articles by Thomas Merton and their
translations into foreign languages, as well as the critical
works on Merton and his writings from 1956 to the present
date of publication.

        With the growing number of students of Thomas Mer-
ton, his life and work, this volume will be an invaluable
tool for continued research.   We are indebted to Miss Breit
and all who have cooperated with her in providing this up-
dated bibliography of Thomas Merton, an important achieve-
ment for which we can only be grateful.

INTRODUCTION

The Thomas Merton Bibliography has been prepared for scholars engaged in research and for anyone interested in the life, works, and thought of Thomas Merton. Here is made available--through collecting, rearranging by type of work, and indexing fully in one source--a listing of the numerous published materials that can be, at present, located only by extensive searching through many indexes, catalogs and bibliographies.

The bibliography covers the period from 1957 to 1973. The period through 1956 is covered by Thomas Merton: A Bibliography, by Frank Dell'Isola (Farrar, Straus, and Cudahy), published in 1956. The present work is intended to be as complete a listing as possible of all published writings by and about Merton that have been indexed or listed in a selected number of the standard bibliographical tools that are readily available in most libraries. Some items published too late to be indexed in the bibliographical tools at the time of publication have also been included. Since there was throughout the years a multitudinous amount of material not indexed, it must be understood by the user that this work is not exhaustive or comprehensive.

All materials listed in the bibliography have been verified in several ways: (1) through use of standard bibliographic reference materials; (2) use of the materials in the Thomas Merton Collection in Bellarmine College Library; (3) communication with Brother Patrick Hart, O. C. S. O. , Thomas Merton's personal secretary at the Abbey of Gethsemani, who has graciously verified numerous items which escaped location through the usual channels; (4) use of the card catalog in the Rare Books Section at the University of Kentucky's Margaret I. King Library; and (5) actual handling of various materials by the editor.

Throughout the bibliography, in citations where a religious has been responsible in some capacity, either as author or as contributor, the identification of Reverend, Brother, Father, or Sister has been omitted if the initials of the order are known. If, however, the order has not been ascertained, then the religious identification, such as Sister, etc., is included.

The first division is PRIMARY SOURCES. In the first section, "Books and Pamphlets by Thomas Merton," only original publications and new editions are listed. Reprints are not included. No paperback volumes are listed unless the original publication was in paperback form. For the most part, this first section cites alphabetically by title those items published in the United States, Canada, England, and Ireland. If a particular title has been published in more than one of these countries, the alphabetizing is then by the cities where the editions have been published. The complete bibliographic information has been cited whenever either it has been located in the standard bibliographic reference materials or the item has been personally handled by the editor.

The following section, "Prose Contributions to Books," is arranged alphabetically by the title of the contribution or, if untitled, by whatever form that contribution is--i.e., foreword to, introduction to, or preface to. The full bibliographic citation is given for the publication being contributed to but the pages given indicate only Thomas Merton's contribution.

"Prose Contributions to Newspapers and Periodicals" consist of book reviews, comments on articles, and excerpts from Merton's works. A complete citation is given in each entry, except in the case of books being reviewed by Merton. In such cases the pagination refers only to Merton's reviews. Many of the articles have no specific titles, and in these instances the title of the book or article being discussed is used in the alphabetizing scheme of the section. Upon observation the user will notice that numerous articles cited appear in Cistercian Studies and its French counterpart Collectanea Cisterciensia. In this particular periodical there is a regular section, "Bulletin of Monastic Spirituality," which has its own separate pagination. Each item in this section is assigned an individual number, beginning with the first issue of the year. To assist the user in avoiding further confusion, we have used the assigned number instead of the page citation when referring to one of these articles.

If the entry is anything other than a regular article, there
is an indication after the title identifying the item as a book
review, excerpt, or comment on an article.

In "Poetry in Books, Newspapers, and Periodicals"
many entries have an additional notation in the form of an
asterisk. These items have been so marked to denote
that they have also appeared in other works by Thomas
Merton published since 1957. At the end of each citation,
marked as such, there is a letter abbreviation of the title
which indicates where that poem appears. All of the titles
used are listed alphabetically at the beginning of the section.
Although this bibliography includes poetry published in
sources copyrighted since 1957, many of these poems had
previously appeared in other sources copyrighted prior to
1957. These sources, prior to 1957, are not included in
the present bibliography.

In "Translations by Thomas Merton," the entries are
arranged alphabetically by the author being translated. Complete citations are given. In cases where other items may
also be included in the same citation, e. g., "The Jaguar
Myth and Other Poems," by Pablo Antonio Cuadra, each
poem is listed with the citation for the convenience of the
user, and each title is also listed in the general index following the bibliography.

All of the book titles, chapters in books, and periodicals by Thomas Merton which have been translated into
foreign language are listed alphabetically by language in
"Works by Thomas Merton in Translation." The original
work is indicated in brackets immediately following the
foreign title and is not underlined or within quotes.

The division, SECONDARY SOURCES, makes up the
second half of the bibliography and includes all works by
other authors on Thomas Merton, his philosophy, his life,
and his literature. Two of these sections, "Reviews of
Thomas Merton's Books," and "Reviews of Books about
Thomas Merton," are alphabetically arranged, first, by the
title of the book by Thomas Merton or about Thomas Merton.
That title is immediately followed by a list of all the reviews listed by name of the periodical. If any of the entries
have definite titles, they have been listed in these sections
and also in the section, "Articles in Books, Newspapers,
and Periodicals," under the name of the author. Checking
the index under the author's name would indicate to the user

if there is more than one entry for a specific author.
Basically the first review section includes only titles by
Merton which have been published since 1957, but in a few
instances titles not readily located in earlier bibliographies
have been included.

Finally, the Index is also arranged alphabetically with
the entry followed by entry number, see, or see also reference. This index includes the following: titles of Merton's
books, pamphlets, titled contributions, poetry, titled articles,
titled reviews; authors and titles of foreign items translated
by Merton; foreign language titles of books by Merton; trans-
lators of books by Merton; authors and titles of books and
pamphlets about Merton; authors and titles of articles about
Merton; authors and titles of reviews of Merton's books;
authors and titles of selected unpublished materials about
Merton; authors and titles of recorded works by and about
Merton; authors, titles, and editors, etc., of collections
containing Merton's writings; all titled chapters and poetry
titles in Merton's books published since 1957; subtitles
essential to the index have been included for the following:
Merton's books, articles, chapter headings in the books by
Merton, poetry titles in the books by Merton, books, articles, and poetry by other authors or editors. All subtitles
are followed by a see reference to the main title of the
entry.

Acknowledgments must be extended to the following
persons who so graciously agreed to assist me in this en-
deavor: Miss Doris J. Batliner, Chemicals Group Librarian,
Chemetron Corporation; the librarians of Bellarmine College:
Miss Betty Delius, Mrs. Ilona Franck, Mrs. Merija Nonacs,
Ms. Rosalind Parnes, and Miss Joan Wettig; Mrs. Charlaine
Hays, assistant in the Thomas Merton Collection, Bellarmine
College; the staff and student assistants of Bellarmine College
Library; Mrs. Carolyn Hammer, Librarian, University of
Kentucky, Special Collections; Brother Patrick Hart, O. C. S. O.,
Abbey of Gethsemani; Mrs. Marian Veath, Librarian, Gener-
al Electric Company, Appliance Park; Professor Leonard
Latkovski, professor of foreign languages, Bellarmine Col-
lege; Mr. Wen-Hwa Yen, Technical Service Engineer, Cata-
lyst Division, Chemetron Corporation.

Since this Bibliography was completed, one major
item has been published by a private press at the University
of Kentucky. The King Library Press has issued a limited
number of copies of Boris Pasternak/Thomas Merton: Six

Letters. This twenty-eight page volume includes three letters
by Merton to Pasternak, and three letters by Pasternak to
Merton, dating from August 22, 1958 to February 7, 1960.
Also included is a Foreword by Naomi Burton Stone, a
Trustee of the Merton Legacy Trust, and an Introduction
by Pasternak's sister, Lydia Pasternak Slater.

BOOKS AND PAMPHLETS BY THOMAS MERTON

1 Adaptation of the Monastic Life: Some Personal Observations--Strictly Confidential. n. p. , 1964. 7p.

2 Albert Camus' 'The Plague': Introduction and Commentary. Religious Dimensions in Literature Series. New York: Seabury Press, 1968. 43p.

3 Asian Journal. Edited by Naomi Burton, Brother Patrick Hart, O. C. S. O. , James Laughlin, and Amiya Chakravarty. New York: New Directions, 1973. 480p.

4 Basic Principles of Monastic Spirituality. London: Burns, Oates and Washbourne, 1957. 71p.

5 Basic Principles of Monastic Spirituality. Trappist, Kentucky: Abbey of Our Lady of Gethsemani, 1957. 35p.

6 The Behavior of Titans. New York: New Directions, 1961. 106p.

7 The Black Revolution. Atlanta: Southern Christian Leadership Conference, 1963.

8 Blessed Are the Meek: The Christian Roots of Nonviolence. Reprinted from Fellowship Magazine (May, 1967) published by the Fellowship of Reconciliation. New York: Catholic Peace Fellowship, 1967. 12p.

9 Breakthrough to Peace. Edited with an Introduction by Thomas Merton. New York: New Directions, 1962. 253p.

10   Cables to the Ace: Or, Familiar Liturgies of Misunder-
     standing.   New York: New Directions, 1968.   60p.

11   Cassian and the Fathers.   Notes for a Conference Given
     in the Choir Novitiate.   Trappist, Kentucky: Abbey
     of Our Lady of Gethsemani, 1960?   54p.

12   Christ in the Desert.   Abiquiu, New Mexico: Monastery
     of Christ in the Desert, 196- .   16p.

13   The Cistercian Order from the Death of St. Benedict to
     the Reform of Benedict XII (1153-1335).   Trappist,
     Kentucky: Abbey of Our Lady of Gethsemani, 1963?

14   The Climate of Monastic Prayer.   London: Ecclesia
     Press, 1969.   156p.

15   The Climate of Monastic Prayer.   Shannon, Ireland:
     Irish University Press, 1969.   154p.

16   The Climate of Monastic Prayer.   Foreword by Douglas
     V. Steere.   Cistercian Studies Series, no. 1.   Spen-
     cer, Massachusetts: Cistercian Publications, 1969.
     154p.

17   Come to the Mountain: New Ways and Living Traditions
     in the Monastic Life.   Snowmass, Colorado: St.
     Benedict's Cistercian Monastery, 1964.

18   Conjectures of a Guilty Bystander.   London: Burns and
     Oates, 1968.

19   Conjectures of a Guilty Bystander.   New York: Double-
     day and Co., 1966.   328p.

20   Contemplation in a World of Action.   Introduction by
     Jean Leclercq, O. S. B.   New York: Doubleday and
     Co., 1965.   384p.

21   Contemplative Prayer.   New York: Herder and Herder,
     1969.   144p.

22   Disputed Questions.   London: Hollis and Carter, 1961.

23   Disputed Questions.   New York: Farrar, Straus and
     Cudahy, 1960.   297p.

24 Disputed Questions.   Toronto: Ambassador Books, 1960.
      297p.

25 Early Poems/1940-42.   Anvil Press Publications, no. 9.
      Lexington, Kentucky: Anvil Press, 1971.   26p.

26 Emblems of a Season of Fury.   A New Directions Paper-
      back, no. 140.   Norfolk, Connecticut: James Laugh-
      lin, 1963.   149p.

27 Examination of Conscience and 'Conversatio Morum. '
      Trappist, Kentucky: Abbey of Our Lady of Geth-
      semani, 1963.

28 Faith and Violence: Christian Teaching and Christian
      Practice.   Notre Dame, Indiana: University of Notre
      Dame Press, 1968.   291p.

29 For a Renewal of Eremitism in the Monastic State.
      Trappist, Kentucky: Abbey of Our Lady of Geth-
      semani, 1965.

30 Gandhi on Non-Violence.   Edited with an Introduction by
      Thomas Merton. New York: New Directions, 1965.
      82p.

31 The Geography of Lograire.   New York: New Directions,
      1969.   153p.

32 Gethsemani: A Life of Praise.   Text by Thomas Mer-
      ton. n. p. , 1966.

33 Hagia Sophia. Lexington, Kentucky: Stamperia del
      Santuccio, 1962.   8p.

34 Honest to God: Letter to a Radical Anglican.   n. p. ,
      1964.   13p.

35 Landscape, Prophet and Wild Dog.   Poem by Thomas
      Merton.   Etchings by Don Cortese. Syracuse, New
      York: 1968.

36 Life and Holiness.   London: Chapman and Hall, 1963.
      162p.

37 Life and Holiness.   Montreal: Palm Publishers Press,
      1963.

38   Life and Holiness.   New York: Herder and Herder,
       1963.   162p.

39   Life at Gethsemani.   Photographs by Shirley Burden,
       Terrell Dickey, and the Monk of Gethsemani.   Trap-
       pist, Kentucky: Abbey of Our Lady of Gethsemani,
       1958.

40   Liturgical Feasts and Seasons.   Conferences Given in
       the Choir Novitiate, Abbey of Gethsemani.   2 volumes.
       Trappist, Kentucky: Abbey of Our Lady of Gethse-
       mani, 1960?

41   Living Bread.   London: Burns, Oates and Washbourne,
       1956.   132p.

42   Living Bread.   Toronto: Ambassador Books, 1956.
       157p.

43   Loretto and Gethsemani.   In Commemoration of the 150th
       Anniversary of the Founding of the Congregation of the
       Sisters of Loretto at the Foot of the Cross, 1812-
       1962.   n.p., n.d.   8p.

44   Marthe, Marie, et Lazare.   Bruges: Desclée de Brouwer,
       1956.   145p.

45   Material for Retreat Conferences.   Given at the Scholas-
       ticate.   Trappist, Kentucky: Abbey of Our Lady of
       Gethsemani, 1951-55.   128p.

46   A Monastic Introduction to Sacred Scripture.   Trappist,
       Kentucky: Abbey of Our Lady of Gethsemani, 1956.

47   Monastic Life at Gethsemani.   Trappist, Kentucky: Ab-
       bey of Our Lady of Gethsemani, 1965.

48   Monastic Orientation.   Lectures Given to the Choir Nov-
       ices at the Abbey of Gethsemani, 1950.   Trappist,
       Kentucky: Abbey of Our Lady of Gethsemani, 1950.

49   Monastic Peace.   Trappist, Kentucky: Abbey of Our
       Lady of Gethsemani, 1958.   57p.

50   Monastic Vocation and the Background of Modern Secular
       Thought.   n.p., 1964.   16p.

51 Monastic Vows: A Memorandum. n. p. , n. d.   3p.

52 Monks Pond. Quarterly edited by Thomas Merton.
    Nos. 1-4, Spring-Winter, 1968.

53 My Argument with the Gestapo: A Macaronic Journal.
    New York: Doubleday and Co. , 1969.   259p.

54 Mystics and Zen Masters. New York: Farrar, Straus
    and Giroux, 1967.   303p.

55 Mystics and Zen Masters. Toronto: Ambassador Books,
    1969.

56 Mystics and Zen Masters. Trappist, Kentucky: Abbey
    of Our Lady of Gethsemani, 1963 ?

57 The Name of the Lord. Trappist, Kentucky: Abbey of
    Our Lady of Gethsemani, 1963.   14p.

58 Nativity Kerygma. St. Paul, Minnesota: North Central
    Publishing Co. , 1958.   16p.

59 Nativity Kerygma. Trappist, Kentucky: Abbey of Our
    Lady of Gethsemani, 1958.   16p.

60 The New Man. London: Burns and Oates, 1961.   175p.

61 The New Man. New York: Farrar, Straus and Cudahy,
    1961.   248p.

62 The New Man. Toronto: Ambassador Books, 1962.

63 New Seeds of Contemplation. London: Burns and Oates,
    1962.   230p.

64 New Seeds of Contemplation. New York: New Directions,
    1961.   297p.

65 Notes by the Artist for an Exhibit of His Drawings.
    Notes written expressively to accompany a showing
    of 26 drawings first displayed privately on Novem-
    ber 13, 1964 at Catherine Spalding College, Louis-
    ville, Kentucky. 5p.

66 Notes on Genesis. For the Choir Novitiate at Gethsemani.

Trappist, Kentucky: Abbey of Our Lady of Gethsemani, 1957. 80p.

67 Notes on Sacred Art. Conference Given the Scholastics,
Abbey of Gethsemani, October and November, 1954.
Trappist, Kentucky: Abbey of Our Lady of Gethsemani,
1954.

68 Opening the Bible. Collegeville, Minnesota: Liturgical
Press, 1970. 84p.

69 Opening the Bible. London: Allen and Unwin, 1972.
84p.

70 Original Child Bomb: Points for Meditation to Be
Scratched on the Walls of a Cave. Abstract Drawings
by Emil Antonucci. New York: New Directions, 1962.

71 Our Monastic Observances. Trappist, Kentucky: Abbey
of Our Lady of Gethsemani, 1960? 159p.

72 Peace in the Post-Christian Era. Trappist, Kentucky:
Abbey of Our Lady of Gethsemani, 1962? 138p.

73 The Poorer Means: A Meditation on Ways to Unity.
Trappist, Kentucky: Abbey of Our Lady of Gethsemani,
1965. 8p.

74 A Prayer of Cassiodorus. From the Treatise 'De Anima.'
Preface and Translation by Thomas Merton. Worcester, England: Stanbrook Abbey Press, 1967. 15p.

75 Praying the Psalms. Collegeville, Minnesota: Liturgical
Press, 1956. 32p.

76 Pre-Benedictine Monachism. Series I: Rufinus, Cassian,
St. Pachomius, St. Basil, etc. Trappist, Kentucky:
Abbey of Our Lady of Gethsemani, 1963. 96p.

77 Pre-Benedictine Monachism. Series II: Syria, Persia,
Palestine. Trappist, Kentucky: Abbey of Our Lady of
Gethsemani, 1964. 87p.

78 Prometheus: A Meditation. Lexington, Kentucky: Margaret I. King Library Press, University of Kentucky,
1958. 10p.

79 The Psalms Are Our Prayer. Paternoster Series, no.
15. London: Burns, Oates and Washbourne, 1957.
42p.

80 Raids on the Unspeakable. New York: New Directions,
1966. 182p.

81 Redeeming the Time. London: Burns and Oates, 1966.
187p.

82 Reflections on Love: Eight Sacred Poems. Trappist,
Kentucky: Abbey of Our Lady of Gethsemani, 1966.

83 "The Root of War," and "Red or Dead." Nyack, New
York: Fellowship Publications. 11p.

84 'Salve Regina.' A Meditation on the Text. Accompani-
ment, Music, and Historical Notes. n.p., 1959.

85 Seasons of Celebration. New York: Farrar, Straus and
Giroux, 1964. 248p.

86 Secular Journal of Thomas Merton. London: Hollis and
Carter, 1959. 132p.

87 Secular Journal of Thomas Merton. New York: Farrar,
Straus and Cudahy, 1959. 270p.

88 Seeds of Destruction. New York: Farrar, Straus and
Giroux, 1964. 328p.

89 Selected Poems. With an Introduction by Mark Van
Doren. New York: New Directions, 1967. 140p.

90 Selections on Prayer. For the Choir Novitiate. Trappist, Kentucky: Abbey of Our Lady of Gethsemani,
1961. 53p.

91 Sign of Jonas. Toronto: Blue Ribbon Books, 1956.
362p.

92 Silence in Heaven: A Book of the Monastic Life. With
90 Photographs and Many Texts from Religious Writings (Selected and Arranged by the Monks of La Pierre-
qui-Vire). Translated by Phyllis Cummins. London:
Thames and Hudson, 1956. 68p.

93   Silence in Heaven: A Book of the Monastic Life. With
       90 Photographs and Many Texts from Religious
       Writings (Selected and Arranged by the Monks of
       La Pierre-qui-Vire). Translated by Phyllis Cum-
       mins. New York: Studio Publications in associa-
       tion with Thomas Y. Crowell, 1956. 68p.

94   Silence in Heaven: A Book of the Monastic Life. With
       90 Photographs and Many Texts from Religious
       Writings (Selected and Arranged by the Monks of
       La Pierre-qui-Vire). Translated by Phyllis Cum-
       mins. Toronto: Longmans, 1956. 152p.

95   Silent Life. Dublin: Clonmore and Reynolds, 1957.
       134p.

96   Silent Life. London: Burns, Oates and Washbourne,
       1957. 134p.

97   Silent Life. New York: Farrar, Straus and Cudahy,
       1957. 178p.

98   Silent Life. Toronto: Ambassador Books, 1957. 178p.

99   The Solitary Life. Lexington, Kentucky: Stamperia del
       Santuccio, 1960. 21p.

100 The Solitary Life: A Letter of Guigo. Introduction and
       Translation from the Latin by Thomas Merton.
       Worcester, England: Stanbrook Abbey Press, 1963.

101 Spiritual Direction and Meditation. Collegeville, Minne-
       sota: Liturgical Press, 1960. 99p.

102 Spiritual Direction and Meditation. Paraclete Books.
       London: Burns and Oates, 1961. 102p.

103 Strange Islands: Poems. London: Hollis and Carter,
       1957. 88p.

104 Strange Islands: Poems. New York: New Directions,
       1957. 102p.

105 Thomas Merton on Peace. Edited with an Introduction
       by Gordon C. Zahn. New York: McCall Publishing
       Co. , 1971. 269p.

106 A Thomas Merton Reader. New York: Harcourt,
       Brace and World, 1962. 553p.

107 Thoughts in Solitude. London: Burns, Oates and
       Washbourne, 1958. 101p.

108 Thoughts in Solitude. New York: Farrar, Straus and
       Cudahy, 1958. 124p.

109 The Tower of Babel. Printed and Illustrated by Ger-
       hard Marcks for James Laughlin. Hamburg, Ger-
       many: 1957.

110 The Tower of Babel. Illustrations by Gerhard Marcks.
       New York: New Directions, 1958. 32p.

111 The Tragedy of Father Perrin. Trappist, Kentucky:
       Abbey of Our Lady of Gethsemani, 1964? 8p.

112 The True Solitude: Selections from the Writings of
       Thomas Merton. Selected by Dean Wally. Kansas
       City: Hallmark Editions, 1969. 61p.

113 The Way of Chuang Tzu. Free Renderings of Selections
       from the Works of Chuang Tzu, Taken from Var-
       ious Translations. New York: New Directions,
       1965. 159p.

114 The Way of Chuang Tzu. Trappist, Kentucky: Abbey
       of Our Lady of Gethsemani, 1965.

115 What Ought I to Do? Sayings from the Desert Fathers
       of the Fourth Century (Verba Seniorum). Trans-
       lated by Thomas Merton. Lexington, Kentucky:
       Stamperia del Santuccio, 1959. 35p.

116 Wisdom of the Desert: Sayings from the Desert Fathers
       of the Fourth Century (Verba Seniorum). Trans-
       lated by Thomas Merton. London: Hollis and
       Carter, 1961.

117 Wisdom of the Desert: Sayings from the Desert Fathers
       of the Fourth Century (Verba Seniorum). Trans-
       lated by Thomas Merton. New York: New Direc-
       tions, 1960. 81p.

118   <u>Zen and the Birds of Appetite</u>. New York: New Direc-
       tions, 1968. 141p.

PROSE CONTRIBUTIONS TO BOOKS

119   "Albert Camus and the Church," in <u>A Penny a Copy:</u>
       <u>Readings from the 'Catholic Worker.</u>' Edited by
       Thomas C. Cornell and James H. Forest. New
       York: Macmillan, 1968. 254-71.

120   "Art and Morality," in <u>The New Catholic Encyclopedia</u>,
       1967, I, 864-67.

121   "The Art of William Congdon," in <u>In My Disc of Gold</u>,
       by William Congdon. New York: Reynal and Co.,
       1962, book jacket.

122   "Atlas Watches Every Evening," in <u>New Directions in</u>
       <u>Prose and Poetry, 18</u>. Edited by James Laughlin.
       New York: New Directions, 1964, 10-15.

123   " 'Baptism in the Forest': Wisdom and Initiation in
       William Faulkner," in <u>Mansions of the Spirit</u>.
       Edited by George A. Panichas. New York: Haw-
       thorn, 1967, 19-44.

124   "A Christian Looks at Zen," an introduction in <u>The</u>
       <u>Golden Age of Zen</u>, by John C. H. Wu. National
       War College in cooperation with the Committee on
       the Compilation of the Chinese Library, 1967, 1-27.

125   "Christian Perfection," in <u>The Catholic Encyclopedia for</u>
       <u>School and Home</u>, 1965, VIII, 328-32.

126   "Clement of Alexandria," in <u>Clement of Alexandria:</u>
       <u>Selections from the 'Protreptikos,</u>' by Titus Flavius
       Clemens. Norfolk, Connecticut: New Directions,
       1963, 1-13.

127   "Concerning the Collection in the Bellarmine College
       Library--A Statement, November 10, 1963," in
       <u>The Thomas Merton Studies Center</u>, by Thomas
       Merton, John Howard Griffin, and Msgr. Alfred

F. Horrigan. Vol. I. Santa Barbara: Unicorn
Press, 1971, 13-15.

128 "Contemplation," in <u>The Catholic Encyclopedia for
School and Home</u>, 1965, III, 228-30.

129 "The Council and Monasticism," in <u>Impact of Vatican II</u>.
Edited by Jude P. Dougherty. Bellarmine College
Studies Series. Saint Louis: B. Herder Co., 1966,
44-60.

130 "Death," in <u>Prophetic Voices: Ideas and Words in
Revolution</u>. Edited by Ned O'Gorman. New York:
Random House, 1969, 230-38.

131 "A Devout Meditation in Memory of Adolf Eichmann,"
in <u>New Directions in Prose and Poetry, 18</u>. Edited
by James Laughlin. New York: New Directions,
1964, 16-18.

132 "Distractions in Prayer," in <u>Springs of Devotion</u>. Kan-
sas City: Hallmark, 1969, 31-32.

133 "The Early Legend," in <u>New Directions in Prose and
Poetry, 18</u>. Edited by James Laughlin. New
York: New Directions, 1964, 1-9.

134 "Easter: The New Life," in <u>Harvest, 1960</u>. Edited by
Dan Herr and Paul Cuneo. Westminster, Maryland:
Newman Press, 1960, 159-70.

135 "Extemporaneous Remarks at the First Summit Conference of World Religions, Calcutta, October 22-26,
1968," in <u>The World Religions Speak on the Relevance of Religion in the Modern World</u>. Edited by
Finley P. Dunne, Jr. World Academy of Art and
Science Series, publication 6. Hague: Dr. W.
Junk, N.V. Publishers, 1970, 79-81.

136 Foreword to <u>Bernard of Clairvaux</u>, by Henri Daniel-
Rops. Translated from the French, <u>Saint Bernard
et Ses Fils</u>, by Elisabeth Abbott. First American
Edition. New York: Hawthorn, 1964, 5-7.

137 Foreword to <u>Notes on the Lord's Prayer</u>, by Raissa
Maritain. New York: P. J. Kenedy, 1964, 7-11.

138   Foreword to <u>The Psalms of Struggle and Liberation</u>, by
        Ernesto Cardenal.   New York: Herder and Herder,
        1971,   7-8.

139   Foreword to <u>Vietnam: Lotus in a Sea of Fire</u>, by Thich
        Nhat-Hanh.   New York: Hill and Wang, 1967, vii-x.

140   <u>Four Freedom Songs</u>.   For baritone solo, mixed chorus,
        and chamber orchestra or piano.   Words by Thomas
        Merton.   Music by Charles Alexander Peloquin.
        Chicago: GIA Publications, 1968.   60p.

141   "Gandhi and the One-Eyed Giants," an introduction in
        <u>Gandhi on Non-Violence</u>.   Selected Texts from
        Mohandas K. Gandhi's <u>Non-Violence in Peace and
        War</u>.   Edited by Thomas Merton.   New York:
        New Directions, 1964, 1-20.

142   "Gethsemani, Abbey of," in <u>The New Catholic Encyclo-
        pedia</u>, 1967, IV, 457-58.

143   "The Glass of His Humanity."   Excerpt from <u>Seeds of
        Contemplation</u>, in <u>Come, South Wind: A Collection
        of Contemplatives</u>.   Edited by M. L. Shrady.   New
        York: Pantheon Books, 1957, 40-41.

144   "God Speaks His Name in the Center of Our Soul."   Ex-
        cerpt from <u>Seeds of Contemplation</u>, in <u>Come, South
        Wind: A Collection of Contemplatives</u>.   Edited by
        M. L. Shrady.   New York: Pantheon Books, 1957,
        28-29.

145   "Guigo the Carthusian," an introduction in <u>The Solitary
        Life: A Letter of Guigo</u>.   Translated from the
        Latin by Thomas Merton.   Worcester, England:
        Stanbrook Abbey Press, 1963, 1-4.

146   "Hermit Life," in <u>The Catholic Encyclopedia for School
        and Home</u>, 1965, V, 160-61.

147   "The Holiness of Created Things."   Excerpt from <u>Seeds
        of Contemplation</u>, in <u>Come, South Wind: A Collec-
        tion of Contemplatives</u>.   Edited by M. L. Shrady.
        New York: Pantheon Books, 1957, 57-58.

148   "In Silentio," in <u>Silence in Heaven: A Book of the
        Monastic Life</u>.   With 90 Photographs and Many

Texts from Religious Writings (Selected and Ar-
ranged by the Monks of La Pierre-qui-Vire).
Translated by Phyllis Cummins. New York:
Studio Publications in association with Thomas
Y. Crowell, 1956, 17-30.

149 Introduction to <u>Breakthrough to Peace</u>. Edited with an
Introduction by Thomas Merton. New York: New
Directions, 1962, 7-14.

150 Introduction to <u>God Is My Life: The Story of Our Lady</u>
<u>of Gethsemani</u>, by Shirley Burden. With 69 Photo-
graphs by Shirley Burden. New York: Reynal and
Co., 1960, unpaged.

151 Introduction to <u>No More Strangers,</u> by Philip Berrigan,
S.S.J. New York: Macmillan, 1965, vi-xx.

152 Introduction to <u>Religion in Wood: A Book of Shaker</u>
<u>Furniture,</u> by Edward Deming Andrews and Faith
Andrews. Bloomington, Indiana: Indiana University Press, 1966, vii-xv.

153 Introduction to <u>The Monastic Theology of Aelred of</u>
<u>Rievaulx: An Experimental Theology</u>, by Amedee
Hallier. Translated by Columban Heaney. Translations from Aelred's Works by Hugh McCaffery.
Cistercian Studies Series, no. 2. Spencer, Massachusetts: Cistercian Publications, 1969, vii-xiii.

154 Introduction to <u>The Prison Meditations of Father Alfred</u>
<u>Delp</u>. New York: Herder and Herder, 1963, vii-
xxx.

155 Introduction to <u>The Simple Steps to God</u> [Présence à
Dieu et a soi-même] by Rev. François de Sainte
Marie Buffevent. Translated by Harold Evans.
First American Edition. The Carmel Series on
Christian Life, vol. I. Wilkes-Barre, Pennsyl-
vania: Dimension Books, 1963, 11-15.

156 Introduction to <u>The Soul of the Apostolate</u> by Jean Baptiste Chautard, O.C.S.O. Introduction and Trans-
lation from the Latin by Thomas Merton. New
York: Doubleday and Co., 1961, 1-3.

157 Introduction to <u>To Live Is to Love</u>, by Ernesto Cardenal.

Translated by Kurt Reinhardt. New York: Herder
and Herder, 1972, 7-18.

158 Introductory Essay in The Christmas Sermons of Blessed
Guerric of Igny. Sermons translated by Sister Rose
of Lima. Trappist, Kentucky: Abbey of Our Lady
of Gethsemani, 1959, 1-25.

159 "It Was a Moment of Crisis ... a Moment of Searching
... a Moment of Joy," in Turning Point: Fateful
Moments That Revealed Men and Made History.
Edited by Philip Dunaway and George de Kay.
New York: Random House, 1958, 34-38.

160 "Learning to Live," in University on the Heights.
Edited by Wesley First. New York: Doubleday
and Co. , 1969, 187-99.

161 "Letter from Thomas Merton-February, 1962," in A
Penny a Copy: Readings from the 'Catholic
Worker.' Edited by Thomas C. Cornell and
James H. Forest. New York: Macmillan, 1968,
207-9.

162 "Letters to Che: Canto Bilinque," in !Viva Che! Con-
tributions in Tribute to Ernesto "Che" Guevara.
Edited by Marianne Alexandre. Third World Series.
London: Lorrimer Publishing, 1968, 85.

163 "A Life of Prayer," an introduction to A Catholic
Prayer Book. Edited by Dale Francis. New
York: Dell Publishing Co. , 1958, 9-12.

164 "Marxism and Monastic Perspectives," in A New Charter for Monasticism. Proceedings of the Meeting
of Monastic Superiors in the Far East, Bangkok,
December 9-15, 1968. Edited with an Introductory
Essay by John Moffitt. South Bend, Indiana: University of Notre Dame Press, 1970, 69-81.

165 "Monastic Experience and the East-West Dialogue," in
The World Religions Speak on the Relevance of
Religion in the Modern World. Edited by Finley P.
Dunne, Jr. World Academy of Art and Science
Series, publication 6. Hague: Dr. W. Junk, N.V.
Publishers, 1970, 72-78.

166 "Morte D'Urban: Two Celebrations," in J. F. Powers.
      Compiled by Fallon Evans. The Christian Critic
      Series. Saint Louis: B. Herder Co., 1968, 95-
      100.

167 "The Ox Mountain Parable of Meng Tzu," an introduc-
      tion to The Ox Mountain Parable, by Meng Tzu.
      After the translation of I. A. Richards. Lexington,
      Kentucky: Stamperia del Santuccio, 1960.

168 "Peace: A Religious Responsibility," in Breakthrough
      to Peace. Edited with an Introduction by Thomas
      Merton. New York: New Directions, 1962, 88-
      116.

169 "Poetry and Contemplation," in Essays in the American
      Catholic Tradition. Edited by Pierre Albert Duha-
      mel. New York: Holt, Rinehart and Winston,
      1960, 214-228.

170 "Poetry, Symbolism and Typology." Excerpt from
      Bread in the Wilderness, in Catholic Critics.
      Edited by Philip H. Vitale, vol. 2. Chicago:
      Auxiliary University Press, 1961, 13-26.

171 "Pope of the Virgin Mary," in Pio XII, Pontifex Maxi-
      mus, Postridie Kalendas Martias, 1876-1956, by
      the Pontificia Accademia delle Scienze. Rome:
      Typis Polygottis Vaticanis, 1956, 30-45.

172 Preface to Alone with God [Seul avec Dieu] by Jean
      Leclercq, O. S. B. Translation by Elizabeth
      McCabe. New York: Farrar, Straus and Cudahy,
      1961, xxiii-xxvii.

173 Preface to L'Attende dans le silence: Le Père Marie-
      Joseph Cassant, O. C. S. O., by Marie-Etienne
      Chenevière, O. C. S. O. Brussells: Desclée de
      Brouwer, 1961, 9-13.

174 Preface to In Search of a Yogi, by Denys Rutledge.
      New York: Farrar, Straus and Cudahy, 1962,
      vii-xii.

175 Preface to Non-Violence and the Christian Conscience,
      by Raymond Régamey. With a Foreword by

Stanley Windass.   New York: Herder and Herder,
1966, 7-14.

176   Preface to the French Edition of The Black Revolution
[La révolution noire: lettre à un blanc libéral suivie
de la légende de Tucker Caliban] Translated by
Marie Tadié.   Tournai: Casterman, 1964, 9-24.

177   Preface to the Japanese Edition of The New Man
[Atarashii hito] Translated by Yasuwo Kikama.
Tokyo: Veritas Publishing Co. , 1968, 6-18.

178   Preface to the Japanese Edition of Seeds of Contemplation [Kanso no tane] Translated by Yasuwo Kikama.
Kyoto: Veritas Publishing Co. , 1965, 1-13.

179   Preface to the Japanese Edition of Seven Storey Mountain
[Nanae no yama] Translated by Kudo Tadishi.   Tokyo: Toyo Publishing Co. , 1965, 9-13.

180   Preface to the Japanese Edition of Thoughts in Solitude
[Kodoku no naka no shisaku] Translated by Yasuwo
Kikama.   Kyoto: Veritas Publishing Co. , 1966,
1-24.

181   Preface to the Korean Edition of Life and Holiness
[Hyeondaeineui sinang saenghwal] Translated by
Jeong-Jin Kim.   Seoul: Kaetoric Chulpansa,
1965, 9-14.

182   Preface to the Vietnamese Edition of No Man Is an
Island [Không ai là một hòn đảo] Translated by
Thanh-Bàng.   Saigon: Phong Trào Văn Hóa,
1967, 15-25.

183   Prólogo dos Vida en el amor, de Ernesto Cardenal.
Buenos Aires: Cuardernos Latinoamericanos,
1970, 9-22.

184   Prólogo para Boom!!! Poemo de Ludovico Silva.
Caracas: Esta edición fue realizada con la
colaboración del Ateneo, 1965, 3.

185   "Purity," in Prophetic Voices: Ideas and Words in
Revolution.   Edited by Ned O'Gorman.   New York:
Random House, 1969, 164-72.

186 "The Recovery of Paradise," in New Directions in Prose
     and Poetry, 17. Edited by James Laughlin. New
     York: New Directions, 1961, 81-101.

187 "Reflections on the Character and Genius of Fénelon,"
     in Fénelon Letters, by François de Salignac de la
     Mothe-Fénelon. Chosen and Translated by John
     McEwen. London: Harvill Press, 1964, 9-30.

188 "Reflections on the Character and Genius of Fénelon,"
     in Letters of Love and Counsel, by François de
     Salignac de la Mothe-Fénelon. Selected and Trans-
     lated by John McEwen. New York: Harcourt,
     Brace and World, 1964, 9-30.

189 "Saint Bernard, moine et apôtre," preface to Bernard
     de Clairvaux. Edited by Commission histoire de
     l'ordre de Citeaux. Paris: Editions Alsatia, 1953,
     vii-xv.

190 "The Significance of the Bhagavad Gita," in The Bhaga-
     vad Gita As It Is. With an Introduction, Transla-
     tion, and Authorized Purport by A. C. Bhaktiven-
     danta Swami. New York: Macmillan, 1968, 18-22.

191 "Solitude and Love," in Spirit of Man: Great Stories
     and Experiences of Spiritual Crisis, Inspiration,
     and the Joy of Life by Forty Famous Contempor-
     aries. Edited by Whit Burnett. New York: Haw-
     thorn, 1958, 113-19.

192 "Spiritual Life," in The Catholic Encyclopedia for
     School and Home, 1965, X, 318-20.

193 "Statement," in Authors Take Sides on Vietnam: Two
     Questions on the War in Vietnam Answered by the
     Authors of Several Nations. Edited by Cecil Woolf
     and John Bagguley. New York: Simon and Schuster,
     1967, 51.

194 "Symbolism: Communication or Communion?" in New
     Directions in Prose and Poetry, 20. Edited by
     James Laughlin. New York: New Directions, 1968,
     1-15.

195 Treasury of the World's Great Diaries. Edited by

Philip Dunaway and Melvin Evans. With an Introduction by Louis Untermeyer. New York: Doubleday and Co. , 209-17.

196 "Ut Sint Consummati in Unum." Excerpt from <u>Seeds of</u>
<u>Contemplation</u>, in <u>Come, South Wind: A Collection</u>
<u>of Contemplatives</u>. Edited by M. L. Shrady. New
York: Pantheon Books, 1957, 47-48.

197 "War and the Crisis of Language," in <u>The Critique of</u>
<u>War: Contemporary Philosophical Explorations</u>.
Edited by Robert Ginsberg. Chicago: Henry
Regnery Co. , 1969, 99-119.

198 <u>War Within Man</u>. Edited by Erich Fromm. The Beyond
Deterrance Series. Philadelphia: Peace Literature
Service of American Friends Service Committee,
1963, 44-50.

199 "The Wild Places," in <u>The Ecological Conscience:</u>
<u>Values for Survival</u>. Edited by Robert Disch.
New York: Prentice-Hall, 1970, 37-43.

200 "Wisdom in Emptiness," by Thomas Merton and Daisetz
Teitaro Suzuki, in <u>New Directions in Prose and</u>
<u>Poetry, 17</u>. Edited by James Laughlin. New
York: New Directions, 1961, 65-101.

PROSE CONTRIBUTIONS TO
NEWSPAPERS AND PERIODICALS

201 "Absurdity in Sacred Decoration." <u>Worship</u> 34 (April
1960): 248-55.

202 "The Advent Mystery." <u>Worship</u> 38 (December 1963):
17-25.

203 "Advice to a Young Prophet." <u>Catholic Worker</u> 28
(January 1962): 4.

204 "Albert Camus and the Church." <u>Catholic Worker</u> 33
(December 1966): 1, 4-5, 8.

205 Review of <u>Anglican Devotion</u>, by C. S. Stranks. Lon-
     don: Student Christian Movement Press, 1961, in
     <u>Collectanea Ordinis Cisterciensium Reformatorum</u>
     26 (1964): no. 4, article no. 171.

206 "Anglicanisme." Review of <u>English Spirituality</u>, by
     Martin Thornton. London: Society for Promoting
     Christian Knowledge, 1963, in <u>Collectanea Ordinis
     Cisterciensium Reformatorum</u> 26 (1964): no. 4,
     article no. 170.

207 "Answers on Art and Freedom." <u>Lugano Review</u> 1
     (1965): 43-45.

208 "An Anti-Poem: Plessy vs. Ferguson: Theme and
     Variations." <u>Commonweal</u> 89 (7 February 1969):
     592-93.

209 "Art and Worship." <u>Sponsa Regis</u> 31 (December 1959):
     114-17.

210 Review of <u>L'Art irlandais</u>, by Françoise Henry. Photos
     inédites de Pierre Belziaux. 3 volumes. La
     Pierre-qui-Vire (Yonne): Zodiaque, 1963-64, in
     <u>Collectanea Cisterciensia</u> 27 (1965): no. 4, article
     no. 76.

211 "As Man to Man." <u>Cistercian Studies</u> 4 (1969): no. 1,
     90-94.

212 Review of <u>Ascetismo e monachesimo prebenedittino</u>, by
     Guiseppe Turbessi. Rome: Editrice Studium, 1961,
     in <u>Monastic Studies</u> 3 (1965): 269-71.

213 "Ash Wednesday." <u>Worship</u> 33 (February 1959): 165-70.

214 "Asian Letter I." <u>Cistercian Studies</u> 3 (1968): no. 4,
     272-76.

215 "Auschwitz: A Family Camp." Review of <u>Auschwitz:
     A Report on the Proceedings against Robert Karl
     Ludwig Mulka and Others before the Court at Frank-
     fort</u>, by Bernd Naumann. Translated from the Ger-
     man by Jean Steinbert with an Introduction on Han-
     nah Arendt. London: Pall Mall, 1966, in <u>Catholic
     Worker</u> 33 (November 1967): 4-5+.

216 Review of <u>The Awakening of a New Consciousness in</u>
     <u>Zen</u>, by Daisetz Teitaro Suzuki. Paree dans <u>Man</u>
     <u>and Transformation</u>. Papers from the <u>Eranos</u>
     <u>Yearbook</u>, vol. 5, Bollingen Series XXX. New
     York: Pantheon Books, 1964, pp. 179-202, in
     <u>Collectanea Cisterciensia</u> 29 (1967): no. 3, 183-84.

217 " 'Baptism in the Forest': Wisdom and Initiation in
     William Faulkner." Excerpt from his Introductory
     Essay in <u>Mansions of the Spirit</u>, edited by George
     A. Panichas. New York: Hawthorn, 1967, pp. 19-
     44, in <u>Catholic World</u> 207 (June 1968): 124-30.

218 "Barth's Dream." <u>Motive</u> 25 (March 1965).

219 "Barth's Dream and Other Conjectures." <u>Sewanee Re-</u>
     <u>view</u> 73 (Winter 1965): 1-18.

220 "The Benedictines." Review of <u>The Benedictines: A</u>
     <u>Digest for Moderns</u>, by David Knowles, O. S. B.
     Saint Leo, Florida: Abbey Press, 1962, in <u>Mon-</u>
     <u>astic Studies</u> 1 (1963): 137-41.

221 "The Benedictines of Galicia." Comment on article,
     "Los monasterios de Benedictinos de Galicia," by
     Maximino Arias. <u>Studia Monastica</u> 8 (1966): 35-
     69, in <u>Cistercian Studies</u> 3 (1968): no. 4, article
     no. 204.

222 "Beyond the Sacred: A Letter to the Editor." <u>Common-</u>
     <u>weal</u> 87 (19 January 1968): 479.

223 "<u>The Black Revolution--Letters to a White Liberal</u>."
     Excerpt. <u>Albert Magnus Alumna</u> 1 (Spring 1964):
     8-13.

224 "<u>The Black Revolution--Letters to a White Liberal</u>."
     <u>Motive</u> 24 (March 1964): 3-16.

225 "<u>The Black Revolution--Letters to a White Liberal</u>."
     <u>Negro Digest</u> 13 (August 1964): 60-84.

226 "<u>The Black Revolution--Letters to a White Liberal</u>."
     <u>Ramparts</u> 2 (Christmas 1963): 4-8+.

227 "Blake and the New Theology." <u>Sewanee Review</u> 76
     (Autumn 1968): 673-82.

228 "Blessed Are the Meek: The Roots of Christian Non-
     violence. " Fellowship 33 (May 1967): 18-22.

229 "Boris Pasternak and the People with Watch Chains. "
     Jubilee 7 (July 1959): 17-31.

230 "Brothers and Aggiornamento. " Brothers' Newsletter 7
     (Summer 1965): no. 2, pp. 8-11.

231 "Buddhism and the Modern World. " Cross Currents 16
     (Fall 1966): 495-99.

232 "Building Community on God's Love. " Edited by Naomi
     Burton Stone. Sisters Today 42 (December 1970):
     185-93.

233 "The Burning of Papers, the Human Conscience and the
     Peace Movement. " By Paul Salstrom, Mulford Q.
     Sibley, George Lakey, and Thomas Merton. Fel-
     lowship 35 (March 1969): 5-9, 30.

234 "A Buyer's Market for Love?" Ave Maria 104 (24 De-
     cember 1966): 7-10, 27.

235 "Called Out of Darkness. " Sponsa Regis 33 (November
     1961): 61-71.

236 "Camus: Journals of the Plague Years. " Sewanee Re-
     view 75 (Autumn 1967): 717-30.

237 "Can We Choose Peace?" Excerpt from Seeds of De-
     struction. The Seraphic 24 (July-August 1967):
     no. 1, pp. 4-7.

238 "Can We Survive Nihilism?" Saturday Review 50
     (15 April 1967): 16-19.

239 "Canon Law. " Comment on article, "Proposed Canon
     on Monastic Life," by Louis Meyer, O.S.B.
     American Benedictine Review 17 (Autumn 1966):
     354-61, in Cistercian Studies 4 (1969): no. 3,
     article no. 295.

240 "Carta a un poèta sobre Vallejo [Letter to a Poet about
     Vallejo]. " La prensa literaria (Nicaragua)
     (18 August 1963): 1.

241 "A Catch of Anti-Letters." Correspondence between
     Thomas Merton and Robert Lax. Voyages 11
     (Winter-Spring 1968): nos. 1 and 2, pp. 44-56.

242 "The Catholic and Creativity: Theology of Creativity."
     Three-part article by Thomas Merton, William
     Davidson, M. D. , and Brother Antoninus, O. P.
     American Benedictine Review 11 (September-Decem-
     ber 1960): 197-213.

243 "The Cell." Sobornost 5 (Summer 1967): no. 5, pp.
     332-38.

244 "Challenge of Responsibility." Saturday Review 48 (13
     February 1965): 28-30.

245 Review of Les chrétientés celtiques, by Olivier Loyer.
     Collection mythes et religions, 56. Paris: Presses
     universitaires de France, 1965, in Collectanea Cis-
     terciensia 29 (1967): no. 3, article no. 140.

246 "Christ, the Way." Sponsa Regis 33 (January 1962):
     144-53.

247 "Christian Action in World Crisis." Blackfriars 43
     (June 1962): 256-68.

248 "The Christian as Peacemaker." Fellowship 29 (March
     1963): 7-9.

249 Review of Christian Commitment: Essays in Pastoral
     Theology, by Karl Rahner. Translated by Cecily
     Hastings. New York: Sheed and Ward, 1963, in
     Ramparts 3 (October 1964): 56-61.

250 "Christian Culture Needs Oriental Wisdom." Catholic
     World 195 (May 1962): 72-79.

251 "Christian Ethics and Nuclear War." Catholic Worker
     28 (March 1962): 2+; (April 1962): 2.

252 "Christian Freedom and Monastic Formation." Ameri-
     can Benedictine Review 13 (September 1962): 289-
     313.

253 "Christian Humanism." Spiritual Life 13 (Winter 1967):
     219-30.

254 "The Christian in Time of Change." The Rambler
     (Ladycliff College, Highland Falls, New York) 10
     (15 October 1965): 1.

255 "The Christian Message in a Changing World." UMC
     News 1 (Summer (1964): no. 1, pp. 1-2.

256 "Christian Morality and Nuclear War." The Way (U.S.)
     19 (June 1963): 12-22.

257 "Christian Solitude: Notes on an Experiment." Cross
     Currents 7 (February 1967): 14-28.

258 Review of Christianisme Russe, by Divo Barsotti.
     Traduzione de l'italien par Ch. Roux de Bezieux
     et Y. Moubarac. Tournai: Casterman, 1963, in
     Collectanea Ordinis Cisterciensium Reformatorum
     26 (1964): no. 4, article no. 164.

259 "Christianity and Mass Movements." Cross Currents 9
     (Summer 1959): 201-11.

260 "Church and Bishop." Worship 37 (January 1963): 110-
     20.

261 "The Church in World Crisis." Katallagete (Summer
     1967): 30-36.

262 "Cistercians and Study." A Transcription. Cistercian
     Studies 6 (1971): no. 2, pp. 180-83.

263 "Classic Chinese Thought." Jubilee 8 (January 1961):
     26-32.

264 "The Climate of Mercy." Cord 15 (April 1965): 89-96.

265 "The Climate of Monastic Prayer." Collectanea Cister-
     ciensia 27 (1965): 273-87.

266 Review of The Collected Works of Ramana Maharsi.
     Edited and Annotated by Arthur Osborne. London:
     Rider and Co., 1959, in Collectanea Cisterciensia
     27 (1965): no. 1, pp. 79-80.

267 "Comment on Charlotte Buhler, Tom Stonier, Walter A.
     Weisskopf." Forum for Correspondence and Con-
     tact 1 (March 1968): no. 2, pp. 11-13.

268 "Comments on Dr. Prince's and Dr. Savage's Paper on
     Mystical States and Regression." The R. M.
     Bucke Memorial Society Newsletter (Montreal) 1
     (January 1966): no. 1, pp. 4-5.

269 "Community." Comment on article, "Community: A
     Monastic Witness," by Sister Agnes Shaw, O. S. B.
     American Benedictine Review 17 (Winter 1966):
     409-35, in Cistercian Studies 4 (1969): no. 2,
     article no. 267.

270 "Community, Politics, and Contemplation." Edited by
     Naomi Burton Stone. Sisters Today 42 (January
     1971): 241-46.

271 "The Concept of Acedia." Review of The Sin of Sloth:
     Acedia in Medieval Thought and Literature, by
     Siegfried Wenzel. Chapel Hill, North Carolina:
     University of North Carolina Press, 1967, in
     Cistercian Studies 4 (1969): no. 3, article no. 347.

272 "A Conference on Prayer, Calcutta, October 27, 1968."
     Sisters Today 41 (April 1970): 449-56.

273 "Conjectures of a Guilty Bystander." Excerpts. Life
     61 (5 August 1966): 60-73.

274 "The Conquest of France: Speech and Testimonials,
     1941." Monks Pond 1 (Fall 1968): 71-78.

275 "Conquistador, Tourist, and Indian." Good Work 25
     (Summer 1962): 90-94.

276 "Contemplation and Ecumenism." Season 3 (Fall 1965):
     133-42.

277 "Contemplation in a World of Action." Excerpt. Edited
     by Naomi Burton Stone. Sisters Today 42 (March
     1971): 345-51.

278 "The Contemplative and the Atheist." Schema XIII
     1 (January 1970): 11-18.

279 "The Contemplative Life in the Modern World." The
     Mountain Path (October 1965): 223-27.

280 "Contemplatives and the Crisis of Faith." Cistercian

Studies 2 (1967): no. 4, pp. 269-73.

281 "Conversatio Morum." Cistercian Studies 1 (1966):
     no. 2, pp. 130-44.

282 "Correspondence: Note on Joyce's Ulysses." Sewanee
     Review 76 (October-December 1968): 694.

283 "The Council and Religious Life." New Blackfriars 47
     (October 1965): 5-17.

284 "Creative Silence." The Baptist Student 48 (February
     1969): 18-22.

285 "Cross Fighters--Notes on a Race War." Unicorn
     Journal 1 (1968): 26-40.

286 "Cuba Project: Letter to the Editor." Liberation 3
     (April 1963): 30.

287 "The Cultural Cold War: Comments." Nation 205
     (9 October 1967): 340.

288 "D. T. Suzuki: The Man and His Work." Eastern
     Buddhist (New Series) 2 (August 1967): 1-5.

289 "Dance of Death." Pax Bulletin (London) (September
     1962): no. 90, pp. 1-3.

290 "Day of a Stranger." Hudson Review 20 (Summer 1967):
     211-18.

291 "The Death of a Holy Terror: The Strange Story of
     Frère Pascal." Jubilee 15 (June 1967): 35-38.

292 "The Death of God, I: The Death of God and the End
     of History." Theoria to Theory 2 (October 1967):
     3-16.

293 "Demythologizing Bishop Robinson: The 'Honest to God'
     Debate." Commonweal 80 (21 August 1964): 573-
     74+.

294 "A Devout Meditation in Memory of Adolf Eichmann."
     Peace News (London) (19 May 1967): 12.

295 "A Devout Meditation in Memory of Adolf Eichmann."

Ramparts 5 (October 1966): 8-9+.

296   "Dialogue and Renewal in the Contemplative Life."
      Spiritual Life 14 (Spring 1968): 41-52.

297   Review of La doctrine spirituelle de Théophane le
      Reclus: le coeur et l'esprit, by Thomas Spidlik,
      S. J.   Orientalia Christiana Analecta, 172.   Rome:
      Pont. Institum Orientalium Studiorum, 1965, in
      Collectanea Cisterciensia 28 (1966): no. 4, article
      no. 280.

298   "Dom Vitalis to Gethsemani."   Abdijleven (March-
      April 1967): no. 2, pp. 26-35.

299   "Don Gaspar Melchor de Jovellanos."   Comment on
      article, "Monasterior y monjes en los Diarios de
      Jovellanos," by Isabel Mateo Gomez.   Yermo 4
      (1966): 107-213, in Cistercian Studies 3 (1968):
      no. 4, article no. 252.

300   "The Drawings of Thomas Merton--A Note by the Ar-
      tist."   Voyages 1 (Fall 1967): no. 1, pp. 53-60.

301   "Dream of the Rood."   Comment on article, "The
      Dream of the Rood and Anglo-Saxon Monasticism,"
      by J. Fleming.   Tradito 22 (1966): 43-72, in
      Cistercian Studies 3 (1968): no. 4, article no. 190.

302   "Du Bouddhisme au Catholicisme."   Collectanea Cister-
      ciensia 29 (1967): 151-63.

303   "Easter: The New Life."   Worship 33 (April 1959):
      276-84.

304   "Ecclesiastical Baroque."   Commonweal 79 (7 February
      1964): 573-74.

305   "Ecumenism and Monastic Renewal."   Journal of Ecu-
      menical Studies 5 (Spring 1968): 268-83.

306   "Elegy for a Trappist."   Commonweal 85 (9 December
      1966): 294.

307   "Elias: Variations on a Theme."   Thought 31 (Summer
      1956): 245-50.

308 "An Enemy of the State." Review of <u>In Solitary Wit-
     ness: The Life and Death of Franz Jagerstatter</u>.
     New York: Holt, Rinehart and Winston, 1964, in
     <u>Pax Bulletin</u> (London) (May 1965), no. 97, pp. 3-5.

309 "The English Mystics." <u>Collectanea Ordinis Cistercien-
     sium Reformatorum</u> 23 (1961): 362-67.

310 "The English Mystics." <u>Jubilee</u> 9 (September 1961):
     36-40.

311 "Epitaph for a Public Servant: In Memoriam-Adolf
     Eichmann." <u>Motive</u> 27 (May 1967): 16-17.

312 "Eremitism." Comment on article, "L'Eremitisme a
     la catalunya nova," by Fort I. Cogul. <u>Studia
     Monastica</u> 7 (1965): 63-126, in <u>Cistercian Studies</u>
     3 (1968): no. 4, article no. 241.

313 "Eremitism in Mallorca." Review of <u>Mallorca
     Eremitica</u>, por un Ermitaño. Palma de Mallorca:
     Imp. Sagrados Corazones, 1965, in <u>Cistercian
     Studies</u> 3 (1968): no. 4, article no. 248.

314 "Ethics and War: A Footnote." <u>Catholic Worker</u> 28
     (April 1962): 2.

315 "Events and Pseudo-Events." <u>Katallagete</u> (Summer
     1966): 10-17.

316 "Examination of Conscience and 'Conversatio Morum.' "
     <u>Collectanea Ordinis Cisterciensium Reformatorum</u>
     25 (1963): 355-59.

317 "The Extremists, Black and White: The Mystique of
     Violence." <u>Peace News</u> (London) (18 September
     1964): 6.

318 "The Face: Tertullian and St. Cyprian on Virgins."
     Abridged transcription of a taped conference given
     in 1962. Transcribed and annotated by Brother
     Robert McGregor, Mt. St. Bernard. <u>Cistercian
     Studies</u> 6 (1971): no. 4, pp. 334-42.

319 "Few Questions and Fewer Answers: Extracts from a
     Monastic Notebook." <u>Harpers</u> 231 (November 1965):
     79-81.

320   Comment on article, "Final Integration in the Adult
       Personality," by A. Reza Arasteh. American
       Journal of Psychoanalysis 25 (1965): no. 1, pp. 61-
       73.

321   "Final Integration: Toward a 'Monastic Therapy.' "
       Monastic Studies 6 (1968): 87-99.

322   "Flannery O'Connor." Jubilee 12 (November 1964): 49-
       53.

323   "For a Renewal of Eremitism in the Monastic State."
       Collectanea Cisterciensia 27 (1965): 121-49.

324   Review of For the Union Dead, by Robert Lowell. New
       York: Farrar, Straus and Cudahy, 1964, in Com-
       monweal 81 (4 December 1964): 357-59.

325   "La formation monastique selon Adam de Perseigne."
       Translated from the English by Charles Dumont,
       O. C. S. O. Collectanea Ordinis Cisterciensium
       Reformatorum 19 (1957): 1-17.

326   "Franciscan Eremitism." Cord 16 (December 1966):
       356-64.

327   "From Pilgrimage to Crusade." Cithara (St. Bonaven-
       ture University) 4 (November 1964): 3-21.

328   "From the Abbey of Gethsemani." Letter from Thomas
       Merton to Lorraine Karpowich. Blueprint (Holy
       Angels Academy, Fort Lee, New Jersey) 7 (June
       1964): no. 3, pp. 12-13.

329   "The Function of Monastic Review." Collectanea Cis-
       terciensia 27 (1965): no. 1, pp. 9-13.

330   "Galician Nuns." Comment on article, "Los monasterios
       de monjas en Galicia," by G. Martinez. Yermo 4
       (1966): 51-78, in Cistercian Studies 3 (1968): no. 4,
       article no. 188.

331   "Gandhi and the One-Eyed Giant." Jubilee 12 (January
       1965): 12-17.

332   "Gandhi on Non-Violence." Diakonia 2 (1967): no. 4,
       pp. 380-85.

333 Review of Gebete, by Anselm von Canterbury. Über-
     setzt und eingeleitet von Leo Heibling, O.S.B. Col-
     lection Sigillum, 24. Einsiedeln: Johannes Verlag,
     1965, in Collectanea Cisterciensia 28 (1966): no. 4,
     article no. 213.

334 "The General Dance." Jubilee 9 (December 1961): 8-11.

335 "The Gentle Revolutionary." Ramparts 3 (December
     1964): 28-32.

336 "Gethsemani (chronique de nos Abbayes: Annual Report-
     Gethsemani, written in French) N.D. de Gethse-
     mani." Collectanea Ordinis Cisterciensium Re-
     formatorum 12 (1950): 132-34; 13 (1951): 141-42;
     14 (1952): 143-44; 15 (1953): 223; 16 (1954): 145.

337 "Godless Christianity?" Katallagete (Winter 1967-1968):
     15-21.

338 "The Good News of the Nativity: A Monastic Reading of
     the Christmas Gospels." Bible Today 21 (Decem-
     ber 1965): 1367-75.

339 "The Grandmontines." Comment on article, "The
     Grandmontines--A Forgotten Order," by Desmond
     Seward. Downside Review 83 (July 1965): 249-64,
     in Cistercian Studies 3 (1968): no. 4, article no.
     205.

340 "Growth in Christ." Sponsa Regis 33 (March 1962):
     197-210.

341 "Guerric of Igny's Easter Sermons." Cistercian
     Studies 7 (1972): no. 1, pp. 85-95.

342 "Guigo the Carthusian." Comment on article, "Le
     'meditationes' del Beato Guigo Certosino," by
     M. E. Cristofolini. Aevum 39 (1965): 201-17,
     in Cistercian Studies 2 (1967): no. 4, article no.
     110.

343 "A Handbook for Hermits." Comment on article, "Un
     manual de ermitaños," by G. M. Colombas.
     Yermo 3 (1965): 317-33, in Cistercian Studies 3
     (1968): no. 4, article no. 257.

344 "Herakleitos, the Obscure." <u>Jubilee</u> 8 (September 1960):
     24-29.

345 Comment on article, "The Heritage of Celtic Monas-
     ticism," by Patrick Hart, O.C.S.O. <u>Cistercian
     Studies</u> 1 (1966): no. 1, 39-53, in <u>Collectanea
     Cisterciensia</u> 29 (1967): no. 3, pp. 79-80.

346 "Hesychasm." Review of <u>Heschasme et prière</u>, by
     Irenee Hausherr, S. J. Orientalia Christiana
     Analecta, 176. Rome: Pont. Institum Orientalium
     Studiorum, 1966, in <u>Cistercian Studies</u> 3 (1968):
     no. 2, article no. 141.

347 "The Historical Consciousness." <u>Contemplative Review</u>
     1 (May 1968): 2-3.

348 "Holy Camp." Review of <u>Monks, Nuns, and Monas-
     teries</u>, by Sacheverell Sitwell. New York: Holt,
     Rinehart and Winston, 1965, in <u>The Critic</u> 24
     (February-March 1966): 68-70.

349 "A Homily on Light and on the Virgin Mother." <u>Wor-
     ship</u> 37 (October 1963): 572-80.

350 Review of <u>Honest to God</u>, by J. A. T. Robinson.   Lon-
     don: Student Christian Movement Press, 1963, in
     <u>Collectanea Ordinis Cisterciensium Reformatorum</u>
     26 (1964): no. 4, article no. 172.

351 "How It Is: Apologies to an Unbeliever." <u>Harpers</u> 233
     (November 1966): 36+.

352 "The Humanity of Christ in Monastic Prayer." <u>Monas-
     tic Studies</u> 2 (1964): 1-27.

353 "I Have Chosen You." <u>Sponsa Regis</u> 30 (September
     1958): 1-6.

354 Review of <u>In Tune with the World: A Theory of Fes-
     tivity</u>, by Josef Pieper. Translated from the Ger-
     man by Richard and Clara Winston. New York:
     Harcourt, Brace and World, in <u>Cistercian Studies</u>
     1 (1966): no. 1, pp. 108-9.

355 "Introducing a Book." Introduction to the Japanese
     Edition of <u>Seven Storey Mountain</u>. <u>Queen's Work</u>

56 (January 1964): 9-10.

356 "Is Man a Gorilla with a Gun?" Review of African
     Genesis, by Robert Ardrey. New York: Dell
     Publishing Co. , 1963, in Negro Digest 14 (March
     1965): 8-14.

357 "Is the Contemplative Life an Evasion?" Comment on
     article, "Aphorisms for a Contemplative," by J.
     Carmody, S. J. American Benedictine Review 17
     (Winter 1966): 519-22, in Cistercian Studies 4
     (1969): no. 2, article no. 264.

358 "Is the Contemplative Life Finished?" Monastic Studies
     7 (1969): 11-62.

359 "Is the World a Problem? Ambiguities of the Secular."
     Commonweal 84 (3 June 1966): 305-9.

360 "Isaac de l'Etoile." Review of Sermons, by Isaac de
     l'Etoile. Texte et introduction critiques par A.
     Hoste, O. S. B. Introduction, traduction et notes
     par G. Salet, S. J. Collection Sources Chrétiennes,
     130. Série des textes monastiques d'Occident, 20.
     Paris: Cerf, 1967, in Cistercian Studies 3 (1968):
     no. 4, article no. 230.

361 "Isaac of Stella: An Introduction to Selections from His
     Sermons. " Cistercian Studies 2 (1967): no. 3,
     pp. 243-51.

362 "Ishi: A Meditation. " Review of Ishi, Last of His
     Tribe, by Theodora K. B. Kroeber. Drawings
     by Ruth Robbins. Berkeley, California: Parnassus
     Press, 1964, in Catholic Worker 33 (March 1967):
     5-6.

363 "Ishi: A Meditation. " Review of Ishi, Last of His
     Tribe, by Theodora K. B. Kroeber. Drawings by
     Ruth Robbins. Berkeley, California: Parnassus
     Press, 1964, in Peace News (London) (30 June
     1967): 6.

364 "Itinerary to Christ." Liturgical Arts 30 (February
     1962): 60.

365 "The Japanese Tea Ceremony. " Good Work 32 (Spring
     1969): 6-7.

366 "The Jesuits in China." Jubilee 10 (September 1962):
      34-39.

367 "Journal of Thomas Merton." Excerpt from "The Night
      Spirit and the Dawn Air," published in Conjectures
      of a Guilty Bystander. New Blackfriars 46 (Septem-
      ber 1965): 687-93.

368 Comment on Chapitre 1 (Par Otto Karrer), dans The
      Kingdom of God Today. Traduit par Rosaleen
      Ockenden. New York: Herder and Herder, 1964,
      in Collectanea Cisterciensia 29 (1967): no. 1, pp.
      180-81.

369 "Lactantius." Transcribed and annotated by Brother
      Robert McGregor, Mt. St. Bernard. Cistercian
      Studies 7 (1972): no. 4, pp. 243-55.

370 "The Ladder of Divine Ascent." Jubilee 7 (February
      1960): 37-40.

371 "Let the Poor Man Speak." Catholic Mind 60 (January
      1962): 47-52.

372 "Let the Poor Man Speak." Jubilee 8 (October 1960):
      18-21.

373 "Letter from Father Thomas Merton." Excerpt. The
      Center Letter 3 (1968): 7; 4 (1968): 7.

374 "Letter to a Bishop--August 1968." Peace (New York)
      3 (Fall-Winter 1968): 11-12.

375 "Letter to a Papal Volunteer." Motive 25 (November
      1964): 4-8.

376 "Letter to Pablo Antonio Cuadra concerning Giants."
      Blackfriars 43 (February 1962): 69-81.

377 "Letter to the Editor." Nation 205 (9 October 1967):
      340.

378 "Letters to a White Liberal (Black Revolution)." Black-
      friars 44 (November 1963): 464-77; 44 (December
      1963): 503-16.

379 "A Life Free from Care." A transcription. Cistercian

<u>Studies</u> 5 (1970): no. 3, pp. 217-26.

380   Comment on article, "Life Is Tragic: The Diary of
      Nishida Kitaro," by Lothar Knauth.   <u>Monumenta</u>
      <u>Nipponica</u> 20 (1965): nos. 3-4, p. 335+, in <u>Col-</u>
      <u>lectanea Cisterciensia</u> 29 (1967): no. 3, pp. 184-85.

381   "The Life of Faith." <u>Sponsa Regis</u> 33 (February 1962):
      167-71.

382   "The Life That Unifies." <u>Sisters Today</u> 42 (October
      1970): 65-73.

383   "Liturgical Renewal: The Open Approach." <u>The Critic</u>
      23 (December 1964-January 1965): 10-15.

384   "Liturgy and Spiritual Personalism." <u>Worship</u> 34
      (October 1960): 494-506.

385   "Love and Maturity." <u>Sponsa Regis</u> 32 (October 1960):
      44-53.

386   "Love and Person." <u>Sponsa Regis</u> 32 (September 1960):
      6-11.

387   "Love and Solitude."   Preface to the Japanese Edition
      of <u>Thoughts in Solitude</u>. <u>The Critic</u> 25 (October-
      November 1966): 30-37.

388   "Man Is a Gorilla with a Gun: Reflections on an Amer-
      ican Best Seller."   Review of <u>African Genesis</u>, by
      Robert Ardrey.   New York: Dell Publishing Co.,
      1963, in <u>New Blackfriars</u> 46 (May 1965): 452-57.

389   "Man Is a Gorilla with a Gun: Reflections on a Best
      Seller."   Review of <u>African Genesis</u>, by Robert
      Ardrey.   New York: Dell Publishing Co., 1963,
      in <u>Quest</u> Monograph 3 (December 1964): 67-70.

390   "Manifestation of Conscience and Spiritual Direction."
      <u>Sponsa Regis</u> 30 (July 1959): 277-82.

391   Foreword to "Marcel and Buddha: A Metaphysics of
      Enlightenment," by Sally Donnelly. <u>Journal of</u>
      <u>Religious Thought</u> 24 (1967-1968): no. 1, pp. 51-57.

392   "Martyr to the Nazis." Excerpt from Thomas Merton's

Introduction to The Prison Meditations of Father
Delp. Jubilee 10 (March 1963): 32-35.

393   Review of The Matter of Zen: A Brief Account of
Zazen, by Paul Wienpaha. New York: New York
University Press, 1964, in Collectanea Cisterciensia
27 (1965): no. 1, pp. 78-79.

394   "The Meaning of Malcolm X. " Continuum 5 (Summer
1967): 432-35.

395   "The Meaning of Satyagraha. " Gandhi Marg 10 (April
1966): 108-10.

396   "Meditation. " L'Osservatore Romano (English Edition)
(2 October 1969): no. 40, [79] 6.

397   "Meditation: Action and Union. " Sponsa Regis 31
(March 1960): 191-98.

398   "Meditation in the Woods. " Condensed from "Day of a
Stranger. " Catholic Digest 32 (January 1968): 20-
24.

399   "A Meditation on Adolf Eichmann. " Condensed from
Raids on the Unspeakable. Catholic Digest 31
(November 1966): 18-20.

400   "Merton: Regain the Old Monastic Charism: Letter to
the Editor. " National Catholic Reporter 4 (11 January 1968): 11.

401   "Merton View of Monasticism: Seeking God through Total Love Is Goal. " Extemporaneous talk delivered
at the Spiritual Summit Conference in Calcutta,
October 22-26, 1968. Washington Post (18 January
1969): 9 C.

402   "Merton's View on Nonviolence. " World Campus 11
(February 1968): 11-12.

403   "Message to Poets from Thomas Merton. " Excerpts.
Americas 16 (April 1964): 29.

404   "Mircea Eliade: A Critical Observer of the Archetypal
Myth. " Review of From Primitives to Zen: A
Thematic Sourcebook of the History of Religions,

by Mircea Eliade. New York: Harper and Row,
1967, in National Catholic Reporter 3 (23 August
1967): 9.

405 "Mississippi y Auschwitz." La liberacion por la non-
violence 4 (March 1967): no. 3, pp. 3-4.

406 "Modern War: Letter to the Editor." Commonweal 81
(2 April 1965): 62-63.

407 "Monachesimo del futuro: quale?" Vita monastica 96
(1969): 3-15.

408 "Monachisme bouddhique: Le Zen." Collectanea Cisterciensia 29 (1967): 132-50.

409 Comment on article, "Los monasterios de monjas en
Galicia," by G. Martinez. Yermo 4 (1966): 51-78,
in Collectanea Cisterciensia 29 (1967): no. 3, article no. 135.

410 Comment on article, "Monasterium Carcer," by Gregorio
Penco. Studia Monastica 8 (1966): 133-43, in Collectanea Cisterciensia 29 (1967): no. 3, article no.
108.

411 "Monastery at Midnight." Catholic Digest 17 (May 1953):
112-16.

412 "Monastic Attitudes: A Matter of Choice." Cistercian
Studies 2 (1967): no. 1, pp. 3-14.

413 "Monastic Vocation and Modern Thought." Monastic
Studies 4 (1966): 17-54.

414 "The Monk and Sacred Art." Sponsa Regis 28 (May
1957): 231-34.

415 "Monk as a Slave." Comment on article, "Civil Rights
of the Monk in Roman and Canon Law: The Monk
as 'Servus,' " by P. M. Blecker, O. S. B. American Benedictine Review 17 (June 1966): 185-98, in
Cistercian Studies 4 (1969): no. 4, article no. 377.

416 "Monk as Marginal Man." Center Magazine 2 (January
1969): 33.

417   "The Monk in the Diaspora." Blackfriars 45 (July-
         August 1964): 290-302.

418   "The Monk in the Diaspora." Commonweal 79 (20
         March 1964): 741-45.

419   "The Monk Today." Latitudes 2 (Spring 1968): 10-14.

420   "Morte D'Urban: Two Celebrations." Worship 36
         (November 1962): 645-50.

421   "Mount Athos." Jubilee 7 (August 1959): 8-16.

422   "A Mountain of Monks." Condensed from 'Mount Athos'
         published in Disputed Questions. Catholic Digest
         25 (December 1960): 100-3.

423   "Mystics and Zen Masters." Chinese Culture 6 (March
         1965): 1-18.

424   "The Name of the Lord." Worship 38 (February 1964):
         142-51.

425   "Nativity Kerygma." Worship 34 (December 1959): 2-9.

426   "The Negro Revolt." Review of A Different Drummer,
         by William M. Kelley. New York: Doubleday and
         Co., 1962, in Jubilee 11 (September 1963): 39-43.

427   "Negro Violence and White Non-Violence: Letter to
         Dr. Martin E. Marty." National Catholic Reporter
         3 (6 September 1967): 8.

428   "Neither Caliban nor Uncle Tom." Liberation 8 (June
         1963): 20-22.

429   "A New Christian Conscience." Excerpt. Theoria to
         Theory 3 (January 1969): 5-8.

430   "The New Man." Excerpts. Tablet 216 (27 January
         1962): 79-80; (3 February 1962): 102-3; (10 Feb-
         ruary 1962): 127-28; (17 February 1962): 151-52.

431   "News of the Joyce Industry." Sewanee Review 77
         (Summer 1969): 543-54.

432   "Nhat Hanh Is My Brother." Inward Light 29 (Fall
         1966): 20-23.

433 "Nhat Hanh Is My Brother." Jubilee 14 (August 1966): 11.

434 "The Night Spirit and the Dawn Air." New Blackfriars 46 (September 1965): 687-93.

435 Review of Non-Violence: A Christian Interpretation, by William Robert Miller. New York: Association Press, 1964, in Commonweal 81 (4 December 1964): 357-59.

436 "Non-Violence Does Not, Cannot Mean Passivity." Ave Maria 108 (7 September 1968): 9-10.

437 "Note on the New Church at Gethsemani." Liturgical Arts 36 (August 1968): 100-101.

438 "Notes on Contemplation." Spiritual Life 7 (Fall 1961): 196-204.

439 "Notes on Love." Frontier 10 (Autumn 1967): 211-14.

440 "Notes on Prayer and Action." The Light 1 (April-May 1967): 1, 3.

441 "Notes on Sacred and Profane Art." Jubilee 4 (November 1956): 25-32.

442 "Notes on Spiritual Direction." Sponsa Regis 31 (November 1959): 86-94.

443 "Notes on the Future of Monasticism." Monastic Exchange 1 (Spring 1969): 9-13.

444 "Nuclear War and Christian Responsibility." Commonweal 75 (9 February 1962): 509-13.

445 "On Aid to Civilian War Victims in Vietnam." Fellowship (January 1968): 15, 29.

446 Review of One Hundred Poems of Kabir. Translated by Rabindranath Tagore, Assisted by Evelyn Underhill. London: Macmillan and Co., 1962, in Collectanea Cisterciensia 27 (1965): no. 1, pp. 80-82.

447 "Opening the Bible?" Bible Today 50 (November 1970): 104-13.

448   "Openness and Cloister. " Cistercian Studies 2 (1967):
        no. 4, pp. 312-23.

449   "Openness and Cloister. " Spiritual Life 15 (Spring
        1969): 26-36.

450   "Orthodoxy and the World. " Review of Ultimate Ques-
        tions: An Anthology of Modern Russian Religious
        Thought, by Alexander Schmemann. New York:
        Holt, Rinehart and Winston, 1965, and Sacraments
        and Orthodoxy, by Alexander Schmemann. New
        York: Herder and Herder, 1965, in Monastic
        Studies 4 (1966): 105-15.

451   "The Other Side of Despair: Notes on Christian Existen-
        tialism. " The Critic 24 (October-November 1965):
        12-23.

452   "The Ox Mountain Parable of Meng Tzu. " Commonweal
        74 (12 May 1961): 174.

453   "Paradise Bugged. " Review of All the Collected Short
        Poems, 1956-1964, by Louis Zukofsky. New York:
        W. W. Norton, 1966, in The Critic 25 (February-
        March 1967): 69-71.

454   "Passivity and the Abuse of Power. " Continuum 1
        (Autumn, 1963): 403-6.

455   "The Pasternak Affair in Perspective. " Thought 34
        (Winter 1959): 485-517.

456   "Peace and Protest. " Continuum 3 (Winter 1966): 509-
        12.

457   "Peace and Revolution: A Footnote from Ulysses. "
        Peace (New York) 3 (Fall 1968-Winter 1969): 5-10.

458   "Peril of Nuclear Hell Spurs Peace Seekers. " Reprint
        of Thomas Merton's Introduction to Breakthrough to
        Peace. Los Angeles Times (9 December 1962):
        1, 16-17.

459   "The Place of Obedience in Monastic Renewal. " Ameri-
        can Benedictine Review 16 (September 1965): 359-
        68.

460   "Poetry and Contemplation: A Reappraisal." Common-
      weal 69 (24 October 1958): 87-92.

461   "The Poorer Means." Cord 15 (September 1965): 243-
      47.

462   "The Poorer Means." Sobornost 5 (Winter-Spring 1966):
      no. 2, pp. 74-79.

463   "The Pope of the Virgin Mary." Marian Reprint (1958):
      no. 62, pp. 1-15.

464   "Prayer and Conscience." Edited by Naomi Burton
      Stone. Sisters Today 42 (April 1971): 409-18.

465   "Prayer for Guidance (in Art)." Liturgical Arts 27
      (May 1959): 64.

466   "Prayer for Peace." U.S. Congressional Record 108
      (18 April 1962): Part 5, 6937.

467   "Prayer, Personalism, and the Spirit." Sisters Today
      42 (November 1970): 129-36.

468   "Prayer, Tradition, and Experience." Edited by Naomi
      Burton Stone. Sisters Today 42 (February 1971):
      285-93.

469   "Preghiera al Sacro Cruore." Convivium 2 (1957): 46.

470   "Presuppositions to Meditation." Sponsa Regis 31
      (April 1960): 231-40.

471   "Prison." Comment on article, "Monasterium Carcer,"
      by Gregorio Penco. Studia Monastica 8 (1966):
      133-43, in Cistercian Studies 3 (1968): no. 3,
      article no. 170.

472   "Protestant Monasticism." Review of Der monastische
      Gedanke, by F. Parpert. Munich: Reinhardt
      Verlag, 1966, in Cistercian Studies 4 (1969): no. 2,
      article no. 284.

473   "Rafael Alberti and His Angels." Continuum 5 (Spring
      1967): 175-79.

474   "Rain and the Rhinoceros." Holiday 37 (May 1965): 8,
      10, 12, 15-16.

475   "Raissa Maritain's Poems." Commentary and transla-
      tions of the following items: "Prisoner," "Lake,"
      "Chagall," "Pillars," "Autumn," "Mosaic: St.
      Praxed's," "Glass Orchard," "The Glove," "Re-
      cipe," "Eurydice," "The Cloud," "The Restoration
      of the Pictures." Jubilee 10 (April 1963): 24-27.

476   Review of La rectitudo chez saint Anselme: un itiné-
      raire augustinien de l'âme à Dieu, by Robert
      Pouchet. Paris: Etudes Augustiniennes, 1964,
      in Collectanea Cisterciensia 28 (1966), no. 4,
      article no. 215.

477   "Red or Dead: The Anatomy of a Cliché." Nyack,
      New York: Fellowship Publications.

478   "Reflections on Some Recent Studies of Saint Anselm."
      Monastic Studies 3 (1965): 221-34.

479   "The Relevancy of RB." Comment on article, "Rele-
      vancy of the Rule Today," by Sister M. W.
      McPherson, O. S. B. American Benedictine Review
      17 (March 1966): 41-51, in Cistercian Studies 4
      (1969): no. 4, article no. 367.

480   "Religion and Race in the United States." New Black-
      friars 46 (January 1965): 218-25.

481   "Religion and the Bomb." Jubilee 10 (May 1962): 7-13.

482   "Renewal and Discipline in the Monastic Life." Cister-
      cian Studies 5 (1970): no. 1, pp. 3-18.

483   "Renewal in Monastic Education." Cistercian Studies 3
      (1968): no. 3, pp. 247-52.

484   "Reply to Dom Kucera." Comment on article, "Monas-
      tic Renewal Revisited: Resourcement Aggiorna-
      mento," by Claude Peifer, O. S. B. American
      Benedictine Review 17 (Winter 1966): 448-66, in
      Cistercian Studies 4 (1969): no. 3, article no. 294.

485   "Reply to Martin E. Marty." National Catholic Reporter
      3 (6 September 1967): 8.

486   "Rites for the Extrusion of a Leper." Kentucky Review 2 (February 1968): 26.

487   "Rites for the Extrusion of a Leper." Peace News (London) (30 August 1968): 6.

488   "The Root of War." Catholic Worker 28 (October 1961): 1, 7, 8.

489   "The Root of War." Pax Bulletin (London) (January 1962): no. 88, pp. 5-6.

490   "Sacred Art and the Spiritual Life." Sponsa Regis 31 (January 1960): 133-40.

491   "The Sacred City." Catholic Worker 34 (January 1968): 4-6.

492   "The Sacred City." The Center Magazine 1 (March 1968): 72-77.

493   "Saint Anselm and His Argument." American Benedictine Review 17 (June 1966): 238-62.

494   "Saint Bruno." Review of Saint Bruno, le premier des ermites de Chartreuse, by A. Ravier, S. J.   Paris: Lethielleux, 1967, in Cistercian Studies 3 (1968): no. 4, article no. 203.

495   "Saint Francis and Peace." Saint Anthony Messenger 73 (October 1965): 39.

496   "Saint Gertrude." Review of Oeuvres spirituelles, by (Saint) Gertrude d'Helfta.   Texte latin, introduction, traduction et notes par Jacques Hourlier et Albert Schmitt.   Collection Sources Chrétiennes, 127. Serié des textes monastiques d'Occident, 19. Paris: Cerf, 1967, in Cistercian Studies 3 (1968): no. 4, article no. 237.

497   "Saint Peter Damian and the Medieval Monk." Jubilee 8 (August 1960): 39-44.

498   "Schema XIII: An Open Letter to the American Hierarchy." Unity (Montreal) 2 (July-August 1965): no. 4, pp. 1, 3-4.

499 "Schema XIII: An Open Letter to the American Hier-
        archy. " Vox Regis (Christ the King Seminary,
        Saint Bonaventure, New York) 31 (December 1965):
        5-7.

500 "Schema XIII: An Open Letter to the American Hier-
        archy. " Worldview 8 (September 1965): 4-7.

501 "Second Coming. " Jubilee 3 (April 1956): 6-9.

502 "The Secular Journals of Thomas Merton: Excerpts
        from the Famous Trappist's Pre-Monastic Note-
        books. " Jubilee 6 (February 1959): 16-20.

503 "Secular Saint. " Comment on article, "The Secular
        Saint," by Michael Novak. The Center Magazine
        1 (May 1968): 50-59, in The Center Magazine 1
        (July 1968): 93-94.

504 "Seeking God. " Sponsa Regis 28 (January 1957): 113-21.

505 "Seeking Our Redeemer. " Sponsa Regis 28 (February
        1957): 141-49.

506 "The Self of Modern Man and the New Christian Con-
        sciousness. " The R. M. Bucke Memorial Society
        Newsletter-Review 2 (April 1967): no. 1, pp. 17-
        21.

507 "O sentido de nossa doação. " Sponsa Christi (Petropo-
        lis, Brazil) (August 1964): 346-47.

508 Review of Seraphim von Sarow, by Valentine (Vera)
        Zander. Dusseldorf: Patmos Verlag, 1965, in
        Collectanea Cisterciensia 28 (1966): no. 4, article
        no. 278.

509 "Seven Qualities of the Sacred. " Good Work 27 (Winter
        1964): 15-20.

510 "The Shakers. " Jubilee 11 (January 1964): 36-41.

511 "The Shelter Ethic. " Catholic Worker 28 (November
        1961): 1+.

512 "The Shoshoneans. " Review of The Shoshoneans: The
        People of the Basin-Plateau, by Edward Dorn.

Photographs by Leroy Lucas. New York: W.
Morrow, 1966, in Catholic Worker 33 (June 1967):
5-6.

513 "Signed Confession of Crimes against the State." Carle-
ton Miscellany (Northfield, Minnesota) 1 (Fall 1960):
no. 4, pp. 21-23.

514 "Sincerity in Art and Life." Selection from a letter of
Owen Merton. Good Work 30 (Spring 1967): 58-59.

515 "The Solitary Life." A transcription. Cistercian
Studies 4 (1969): no. 3, pp. 213-17.

516 "Solitude." Spiritual Life 14 (Fall 1968): 171-78.

517 "Sonship and Espousals." Sponsa Regis 28 (March
1957): 169-78.

518 "The Sounds Are Furious." Review of Faulkner: A
Collection of Critical Essays. Edited by Robert
Penn Warren. Englewood Cliffs, New Jersey:
Prentice-Hall, 1966, in Critic 25 (April-May 1967):
76-80.

519 Review of Spiritual Consciousness in Zen from a
Thomistic Theological Point of View, by Augustin
Hideshi Kishi. Theologia Montis Regii, 46, University of Montreal, 1966, in Collectanea Cisterciensia 29 (1967): no. 3, pp. 181-82.

520 Review of The Spiritual Dialogue of East and West, by
Jacques-Albert Cuttat. New Delhi: Mueller
Bhavan Publications, 1961, in Collectanea Cister-
ciensia 27 (1965): no. 1, p. 77.

521 "Spiritual Direction." Sponsa Regis 30 (June 1959):
249-54.

522 "The Spiritual Father in the Desert Tradition." Cistercian Studies 3 (1968): no. 1, pp. 3-23.

523 "The Spiritual Father in the Desert Tradition." Monastic Studies 5 (1968): 87-111.

524 "Spiritualité psychédélienne." Collectanea Cisterciensia
29 (1967): no. 3, pp. 191-94.

525 "Spirituality for the Age of Overkill." Continuum 1
      (Spring 1963): 9-12.

526 "The State of Letters--A Letter from Thomas Merton."
      Sewanee Review 77 (Summer 1969): 555-56.

527 Review of The Story of a Life, by Konstantin Paustovsky.
      Translated from the Russian by Joseph Barnes.
      New York: Pantheon Books, 1964, in Commonweal
      81 (4 December 1964): 357-59.

528 "The Stranger: Poverty of an Anti-Hero." Unicorn
      Journal 2 (Fall 1968): 10-19.

529 "The Street Is for Celebration." The Mediator (Boston)
      20 (Summer 1969): 2-4.

530 Review of A Study of Good, par Nishida Kitaro. Tra-
      duit par V. H. Viglielmo. Preface de D. T. Su-
      zuki. Printing Bureau, Japanese Government,
      Japanese National Commission for UNESCO, 1960,
      in Collectanea Cisterciensia 29 (1967): no. 3,
      pp. 185-88.

531 "The Subject of Meditation." Sponsa Regis 31 (May
      1960): 268-74.

532 "Symbolism: Communication or Communion?" Monas-
      tic Exchange 2 (Summer 1970): 1-10 (articles sec-
      tion).

533 "Symbolism: Communication or Communion?" The
      Mountain Path (India) 3 (October 1966): 339-48.

534 Comment on "Technique and Personal Devotion in the
      Zen Exercise," par Heinrich Dumoulin, S. J. , dans
      Studies in Japanese Culture. Edité par Joseph
      Raggendorf. Tokyo: Universite Sophia, 1963, in
      Collectanea Cisterciensia 29 (1967): no. 3, p. 183.

535 Review of The Technological Society, by Jacques Ellul.
      Translated from the French by John Wilkinson.
      With an Introduction by Robert K. Merton. New
      York: Alfred A. Knopf, 1964, in Commonweal 81
      (4 December 1964): 357-59.

536 "Teilhard's Gamble: Betting on the Whole Human

Species." Commonweal 87 (27 October 1967): 109-11.

537 "Temperament and Meditation." Sponsa Regis 31 (June 1960): 296-99.

538 "Terror and the Absurd: Violence and Nonviolence in Albert Camus." Motive 29 (February 1969): 5-15.

539 "The Testing of Ideals." Sponsa Regis 33 (December 1961): 95-100.

540 "This Is God's Work." Sisters Today 42 (August-September 1970): 1-7.

541 Comment on article, "Thomas Merton: An Appraisal," by Clifford Stevens. American Benedictine Review 18 (June 1967): 223-26, in Cistercian Studies 4 (1969): no. 4, article no. 464.

542 "Thomas Merton, 1915-1968." Excerpts from Merton's articles in Commonweal. Commonweal 89 (27 December 1968): 435-37.

543 "Thomas Merton on the Peace Strike: Letter to Jim Forest." Catholic Worker 28 (February 1962): 7.

544 "Thomas Merton Replies to a Perceptive Critic." National Catholic Reporter 3 (18 January 1967): 4.

545 "Three Letters: To a Papal Volunteer; To a Brazilian Friend; To Dorothy Day." Motive 15 (November 1964): 4-8.

546 Review of Three Muslim Sages, by Seyyed Hossein Nasr. Harvard Studies in World Religions Series. Cambridge, Massachusetts: Harvard University Press, 1964, in Collectanea Cisterciensia 27 (1965): no. 1, p. 83.

547 "Three Saviors in Camus." Thought 43 (Spring 1968): 5-23.

548 "Time and the Liturgy." Worship 31 (December 1956): 2-10.

549 "Time of the End Is the Time of No Room." Motive 15 (December 1965): 4+.

550   "Time of the End Is the Time of No Room." Peace
       News (London) (22 December 1967): 6-7.

551   "To Each His Darkness: Some Paradoxes of Julian
       Green." Charlatan 1 (Spring 1964): unpaged.

552   "To Live Is to Love." Introduction to To Live Is to
       Love, by Ernesto Cardenal. Translated by Kurt
       Reinhardt. New York: Herder and Herder, 1972,
       in U.S. Catholic 37 (March 1972): 19-23.

553   "Tradition occidentale." Comment on article, "Saint
       Augustine as Psychotherapist," by Martin Versfeld.
       Blackfriars 45 (March 1964): 98-110, in Collectanea
       Cisterciensia 27 (1965): no. 4, article no. 38.

554   Review of Transformation of Man: A Study of Conver-
       sion and Community, by Rosemary Haughton.
       Springfield, Illinois: Templegate, 1967, in Book
       News (Templegate Publishers, Springfield) (Fall-
       Winter 1967): 1.

555   Comment on "The Transformation of Man in Mystical
       Islam," by Fritz Meier, which appeared in Man
       and Transformation. Papers from the Eranos
       Yearbook, Vol. 5, Bollingen Series XXX. New
       York: Pantheon Books, 1964, pp. 37-68, in
       Collectanea Cisterciensia 27 (1965): no. 1, pp. 83-
       84.

556   "A Tribute to Flannery O'Connor." Reprint from
       Jubilee 12 (November 1964): 49-53, in Catholic
       Mind 63 (March 1965): 43-45.

557   "A Tribute to Gandhi." Unicorn Journal 3 (1969):
       endsheets.

558   "The True Legendary Sound: The Poetry and Criticism
       of Edwin Muir." Sewanee Review 75 (Spring 1967):
       317-24.

559   "Truth and Crisis: Pages from a Monastic Notebook."
       Gandhi Marg (India) 9 (October 1965): 294-98.

560   "Truth and Violence." Continuum 2 (Summer 1964):
       268-81.

561 "Two Chinese Classics." Chinese Culture Quarterly 4
     (June 1962): no. 2, pp. 34-41.

562 "Two Letters of the Late Thomas Merton: On the
     Future of Monasticism; Buddhist Monasticism and
     Meditation." L'Osservatore Romano 4 (23 January
     1969): 5, 10.

563 "Two Meditations for Our Members: The Priest in
     Union with Mary Immaculate." Convivium (Rome)
     1 (1956): 27-37.

564 "Unamuno." Comment on article, "Unamuno y la vida
     monástica," by J. Alvarez Arrayo. Yermo 4
     (1966): 1-50, in Cistercian Studies 4 (1969): no. 2,
     article no. 285.

565 Comment on Article, "L'Utilisation de l'écriture Sainte
     chez Anselm de Canterbery," by R. Gregoire,
     O. S. B. Revue d'Ascetique et de Mystique 39
     (1963): 273-93, in Collectanea Cisterciensia 28
     (1966): no. 4, article no. 214.

566 Review of Varieties of Unbelief, by Martin E. Marty.
     New York: Holt, Rinehart and Winston, 1964, in
     Commonweal 81 (8 January 1965): 490-91.

567 "La vie solitaire a l'ombre d'un monastère cistercien."
     Lettre de Ligué (Lettre de l'Abbaye Saint Martin)
     (January-February 1967): no. 129, pp. 30-36.

568 "Vietnam and Pacifism: Letter to the Editor." Com-
     monweal 82 (7 May 1965): 202.

569 "The Vietnam War: An Overwhelming Atrocity."
     Catholic Worker 34 (March 1968): 1, 6-7.

570 "Virginity and Humanism in the Latin Fathers."
     Sponsa Regis 34 (January 1963): 131-44.

571 "Vision of Peace: Some Reflections on the Monastic
     Way of Life." Jubilee 6 (August 1958): 24-27.

572 "War and Vision: The Autobiography of a Crow Indian."
     Review of Two Leggings: The Making of a Crow
     Warrior, by Peter Nabokov. New York: Thomas

Y. Crowell, 1967, in Catholic Worker 33 (December 1967): 4+.

573 "War and Vision." Review of Two Leggings: The Making of a Crow Warrior, by Peter Nabokov. New York: Thomas Y. Crowell, 1967, in Theoria to Theory 2 (July 1968): 336-42.

574 "We Have to Make Ourselves Heard." Catholic Worker 28 (May 1962): 4-6; (June 1962): 4-5.

575 "What Is Meditation?" Sponsa Regis 31 (February 1960): 180-87.

576 "Where the Religious Dimension Enters In." The Center Letter (1968): no. 3, p. 6.

577 "Who Is Nat Turner?" Review of The Confessions of Nat Turner, by William Styron. New York: Random House, 1966, in Katallagete (Spring 1968): 20-23.

578 "The Wild Places." Review of Wilderness and the American Mind, by Roderick Nash. New Haven, Connecticut: Yale University Press, 1967, in Catholic Worker 34 (June 1968): 4+.

579 "The Wild Places." Review of Wilderness and the American Mind, by Roderick Nash. New Haven, Connecticut: Yale University Press, 1967, in The Center Magazine 1 (July 1968): 40-44.

580 "Wilderness and Paradise." Review of Christ in the Wilderness: The Wilderness Theme in the Second Gospel and Its Basis in the Biblical Tradition, by Ulrich Mauser. Naperville, Illinois: A. R. Allenson, 1963, and Wilderness and Paradise in Christian Thought, by George H. Williams. New York: Harper and Row, 1962, in Cistercian Studies 2 (1967): no. 1, pp. 83-89.

581 "William Congdon." Liturgical Arts 30 (February 1962): 60.

582 Review of Word and Revelation, by Hans Urs von Balthasar. Translated by A. V. Littledale in cooperation with Alexander Dru. New York: Herder and

Herder, 1964, in Commonweal 81 (4 December
1964): 357-59.

583   "Writing as Temperature." Review of Writing Degree
       Zero, by Roland Barthes. New York: Hill and
       Wang, 1968, in Sewanee Review 77 (Summer 1969):
       535-42.

584   Review of "Zen and Christian Mysticism," by William
       Johnston, S. J. in The Japan Missionary Bulletin
       (Tokyo) (November 1966): 608-15, in Collectanea
       Cisterciensia 29 (1967): no. 3, p. 182.

585   Review of Zen in Japanese Art: A Way of Spiritual Ex-
       perience, by Toshimitsu Hasumi. Traduit de
       l'allemand par John Petrie. London: Routledge
       and Kegan Paul, 1962, in Collectanea Cisterciensia
       29 (1967) no. 3, pp. 188-90.

586   Review of Zen in Japanese Art: A Way of Spiritual
       Experience, by Toshimitsu Hasumi. Translated
       from the German by John Petrie. London:
       Routledge and Kegan Paul, 1962, in Catholic
       Worker 33 (July-August 1967): 8.

587   "The Zen Koan." Review of The Three Pillars of Zen:
       Teaching, Practice, and Enlightenment. Compiled
       and Edited, with Translations, Introductions, and
       Notes by Philip Kapleau. Foreword by Huston
       Smith. New York: Harper and Row, 1966, in
       The Lugano Review 1 (1966): 126-39.

588   "The Zen Revival." Continuum 1 (Winter 1964): 523-38.

589   "Zen: Sense and Sensibility." Review of Zen Catholi-
       cism: A Suggestion, by Aelred Graham. New York:
       Harcourt, Brace and World, 1963, in America 108
       (25 May 1963): 752-54.

590   Review of Zen, Weg zur Erleuchtung, by H. M.
       Enomiya-Lasalle, S. J. Vienna: Verlag Herder,
       1960, in Collectanea Cisterciensia 28 (1965):
       no. 1, pp. 77-78.

591   "Zukofsky: The Paradise Ear." Review of All the
       Collected Short Poems, 1956-1964, by Louis
       Zukofsky. New York: W. W. Norton, 1966, in
       Peace News (London) (28 July 1967): 8+.

POETRY IN BOOKS,
NEWSPAPERS, AND PERIODICALS

The entries in the following section marked with an
asterisk may also be located in the six books listed immediately below. Each entry marked with an asterisk will have
an initial abbreviation of the title to indicate where that poem
appears. The initial title abbreviation will appear immediately after the citation. If a poem has also appeared in one
of Thomas Merton's earlier volumes, which has been listed
in Thomas Merton: A Bibliography by Frank Dell'Isola, it
has not been so indicated in this present bibliography.

CTTA	Cables to the Ace
EOASOF	Emblems of a Season of Fury
GOL	Geography of Lograire
SP	Selected Poems
SI	Strange Islands
TMR	Thomas Merton Reader

592   *"And the Children of Birmingham." Saturday Review
        46 (10 August 1963): 32. (EOASOF)

593   *"An Argument--of the Passion of Christ," in The
        Criterion Book of Modern American Verse.   Edited
        by Wystan Hugh Auden. New York: Criterion
        Books, 1956, 284-86. (TMR)

594   "A Baroque Gravure." Commonweal 79 (1 November
        1963): 167.

595   "A Baroque Gravure," in A Controversy of Poets: An
        Anthology of Contemporary American Poetry.
        Edited by Paris Leary and Robert Kelly. New
        York: Doubleday and Co. (Anchor Book), 1965,
        279-80.

596   "Blessed Virgin Mary Compared to a Window," in I
        Sing of a Maiden: The Mary Book of Verse.
        Edited by M. Therese Lentfoehr, S.D.S. New
        York: Macmillan, 1947, 354-55.

597   "Cables to the Ace." Excerpt from Cables to the Ace
        with four poems and a calligraphy. Latitudes 2
        (Spring 1968): 16-20.

598   *"The Candlemas Procession," in <u>A New Directions</u>
          <u>Reader</u>. Edited by Hayden Carruth and James
          Laughlin. A New Directions Paperback, 135.
          New York: New Directions, 1964, 133. (SP)

599   *"Carol," in <u>Kentucky Authors</u>, by Mary Carmel Brown-
          ing, O.S.U. Evansville, Indiana: Keller-Crescent
          Co., 1968, 219. (SP)

600   "A Carol," in <u>Unicorn Folio</u>. Series one, number four.
          Santa Barbara, California: Unicorn Press, 1967.

601   "Ceremony for Edward Dahlberg." <u>Tri-Quarterly</u> (Fall
          1970): no. 19, pp. 138-39.

602   *"Chant to Be Used in Processions Around a Site with
          Furnaces." <u>Blackfriars</u> 43 (April 1962): 180-82.
          (EOASOF) (TMR)

603   *"Chant to Be Used in Processions Around a Site with
          Furnaces." <u>Catholic Worker</u> 28 (August 1961): 4.
          (EOASOF) (TMR)

604   *"Duns Scotus," in <u>A Controversy of Poets: An Anthol-</u>
          <u>ogy of Contemporary American Poetry</u>. Edited by
          Paris Leary and Robert Kelly. New York: Double-
          day and Co. (Anchor Book): 1965, 273-74. (SP)

605   *"Early Blizzard." <u>Sewanee Review</u> 75 (Summer 1967):
          385-86. (CTTA)

606   *"An Elegy for Ernest Hemingway." <u>Commonweal</u> 74
          (22 September 1961): 513. (EOASOF) (TMR)

607   *"An Elegy for Five Old Ladies." <u>Pax</u> (1968): no. 7.
          (EOASOF) (SP)

608   *"An Elegy for James Thurber." <u>Commonweal</u> 76
          (13 July 1962): 396. (EOASOF)

609   *"An Elegy for James Thurber." <u>Pilot</u> (Norfolk, Vir-
          ginia) (15 December 1963). (EOASOF)

610   *"Elegy for the Monastery Barn," in <u>A Controversy of</u>
          <u>Poets: An Anthology of Contemporary American</u>
          <u>Poetry</u>. Edited by Paris Leary and Robert Kelly.
          New York: Doubleday and Co. (Anchor Book), 1965,
          275-76. (SP) (SI) (TMR)

611   *"Elegy for the Monastery Barn," in A New Directions
      Reader. Edited by Hayden Carruth and James
      Laughlin. A New Directions Paperback, 135. New
      York: New Directions, 1964, 134. (SP) (SI) (TMR)

612   "Evening of the Visitation," in I Sing of a Maiden: The
      Mary Book of Verse. Edited by M. Therese Lent-
      foehr, S.D.S. New York: Macmillan, 1947, 356.

613   *"The Fall." Continuum 1 (Autumn 1963): 386.
      (EOASOF)

614   "Figures for an Apocalypse," in The Criterion Book of
      Modern American Verse. Edited by Wystan Hugh
      Auden. New York: Criterion Books, 1956, 286-
      87.

615   "First Lesson about Man," in Homenaje a Merton, In
      Memoriam Ludovici to Merton the Magician.
      Honolulu: Mele, 1969? unpaged.

616   "First Lesson about Man." Saturday Review 52 (11
      January 1969): 21.

617   "For the Spanish Poet Miguel Hernandez." Sewanee
      Review 74 (Autumn 1966): 897-98.

618   "Found Macaronic Antipoem." Monks Pond (Summer
      1968): no. 2, opposite 16.

619   *"Gloss on the Sin of Ixion." Saturday Review 46
      (21 September 1963): 29. (EOASOF)

620   *"Guns of Fort Knox." Sign 37 (August 1957): 39 (SI)
      (SP)

621   *"Hagia Sophia." A prose poem. Ramparts 1 (March
      1963): 65-71. (EOASOF)

622   *"Harmonies of Excess." Sewanee Review 75 (Summer
      1967): 389-90. (CTTA)

623   "Holy Child's Song." Vogue 156 (December 1970): 111-
      12.

624   "If You Seek a Heavenly Light." Approach (Spring
      1962): no. 43, p. 2.

625 "Lion." Sewanee Review 75 (Summer 1967): 387-88.

626 *"Love Winter When the Plant Says Nothing." Catholic
       Worker 26 (June 1960): 4. (EOASOF)

627 "Man the Master," in New Directions in Prose and
       Poetry, 19. Edited by James Laughlin. New
       York: New Directions, 1966, 296-98.

628 *"Messenger from the Horizon." Saturday Review 44
       (11 February 1961): 40. (EOASOF)

629 "The Moment of Truth." Critic 20 (February-March
       1962): 21.

630 *"The Moslems' Angel of Death: Algeria 1961."
       Commonweal 76 (1 June 1962): 255. (EOASOF)

631 "My Lord God; a prayer." Critic 30 (September-
       October 1971): 76.

632 *"Night-Flowering Cactus." Poet 5 (March 1964): 21-
       22. (EOASOF)

633 "Night of Destiny." Mele (Carta International de
       Poesia) (Honolulu) (March 1966): unpaged.

634 *"Notes for a New Liturgy." Poetry 112 (July 1968):
       254-55. (GOL)

635 "Origen." Monastic Studies 8 (1972): 117-18.

636 "Origen," in New Directions in Prose and Poetry, 19.
       Edited by James Laughlin. New York: New
       Directions, 1966, 288-89.

637 "The Originators," in Unicorn Folio. Series one,
       number three. Santa Barbara, California: Uni-
       corn Press, 1967.

638 "Picture of a Black Child with a White Doll," in New
       Directions in Prose and Poetry, 19. Edited by
       James Laughlin. New York: New Directions,
       1966, 290-91.

639 "Picture of a Negro Child with a White Doll." New
       Blackfriars 46 (October 1964): 32.

640   "Planet over Eastern Parkway." Sewanee Review 75
        (Summer 1967): 390-92.

641   "Plessy vs. Ferguson: Theme and Variation," in New
        Directions in Prose and Poetry, 21. Edited by
        James Laughlin. New York: New Directions,
        1969, 201-3.

642   *"A Practical Program for Monks," in A Controversy
        of Poets: An Anthology of Contemporary American
        Poetry. Edited by Paris Leary and Robert Kelly.
        New York: Doubleday and Co. (Anchor Book),
        1965, 277-79. (SP) (TMR)

643   *"A Practical Program for Monks." Pax (1958): no. 7.
        (SP) (TMR)

644   *"Prelude: For the Feast of Saint Agnes." Common-
        weal 63 (23 December 1955): 304. (SI) (TMR)

645   *"A Psalm." Commonweal 69 (24 October 1958): 89.
        (SP) (TMR)

646   "Rain and Vision." Sewanee Review 75 (Summer 1967):
        388-89.

647   "Rilke's Epitaph." Mele (Carta International de Poesia)
        (Honolulu) (August 1966): unpaged.

648   "A Round and a Hope for Smithgirls." Tennessee
        Poetry Journal 1 (Winter 1968): 25.

649   "Ruben Dario." Continuum 4 (Autumn 1966): 469-70.

650   *"Saint Agnes: A Responsory," in The Mentor Book of
        Religious Verse. Edited by Horace Gregory and
        Marya Zaturenska. New York: New American Li-
        brary, 1956. (SP)

651   *"Saint Malachy," in A Controversy of Poets: An
        Anthology of Contemporary American Poetry.
        Edited by Paris Leary and Robert Kelly.   New
        York: Doubleday and Co. (Anchor Book), 1965,
        274-75. (SP) (TMR)

652   "Le Secret," in Homenaje a Merton, In Memoriam
        Ludovici to Merton the Magician. Honolulu: Mele,
        1969? unpaged.

653 "Le Secret." La table ronde (Paris) (July-August 1966):
      nos. 222-223, pp. 88-90.

654 "Secular Signs." Tennessee Poetry Journal 1 (Fall
      1967): 15.

655 "Seneca," in A Controversy of Poets: An Anthology
      of Contemporary American Poetry. Edited by
      Paris Leary and Robert Kelly. New York:
      Doubleday and Co. (Anchor Book), 1965, 280-81.

656 "Seneca," in Homenaje a Merton, In Memoriam Ludovici
      to Merton the Magician. Honolulu: Mele, 1969?
      unpaged.

657 "Seneca," in New Directions in Prose and Poetry, 19.
      Edited by James Laughlin. New York: New Di-
      rections, 1966, 292-93.

658 "Seneca." Poetry 103 (March 1964): 381.

659 *"Seven Archaic Images." Saturday Review 45
      (4 August 1962): 24. (EOASOF)

660 *"Sincerity." Poetry 89 (December 1956): 140-41.
      (TMR)

661 *"Song," in Kentucky Authors, by Mary Carmel Brown-
      ing, O.S.U. Evansville, Indiana: Keller-Crescent
      Co., 1968, 219-20. (TMR)

662 *"Song for Nobody." Pilot (Norfolk, Virginia) (15 De-
      cember 1963). (EOASOF)

663 *"Song for Nobody." Saturday Review 44 (22 July 1961):
      21. (EOASOF)

664 *"Song for the Death of Averroes." Texas Quarterly 5
      (Winter 1962): 61-63. (EOASOF)

665 *"Song from Crossportion's Pastoral," in A New Direc-
      tions Reader. Edited by Hayden Carruth and James
      Laughlin. A New Directions Paperback, 135. New
      York: New Directions, 1964, 133. (SP) (TMR)

666 "A Song: Sensation Time at Home," in New Directions
      in Prose and Poetry, 19. Edited by James

Laughlin.   New York: New Directions, 1966, 291-
92.

667   *"Sports Without Blood: A Letter to Dylan Thomas,"
        in A Garland for Dylan Thomas.   Gathered and
        With a Preface by George J. Frimage.   New York:
        Clarke and Way, Inc. , 1963, 86-90.   (SI)

668   *"Stranger," in The Earth Is the Lord's: Poems of the
        Spirit.   Compiled by Helen Plotz.   Illustrated with
        Wood Engravings by Clare Leighton.   New York:
        Thomas Crowell, 1965, 14-15.   (SI) (TMR)

669   "Sweetgum Avenue Leads to a College of Charm. "
        Sewanee Review 75 (Summer 1967): 386-87.

670   *"To a Severe Nun," in A Controversy of Poets: An
        Anthology of Contemporary American Poetry.
        Edited by Paris Leary and Robert Kelly.   New
        York: Doubleday and Co. (Anchor Book), 1965,
        276-77.   (SI) (SP)

671   *"To Sons: Not to Be Numb," in The Bread Is Rising.
        New York: Emmaus House, 1967, unpaged.   (CTTA)

672   "Tonight There Is a Showing of Champion Lights," in
        New Directions in Prose and Poetry, 19.   Edited
        by James Laughlin.   New York: New Directions,
        1966, 294-96.

673   *"The Trappist Abbey: Matins," in Poetry for Pleasure:
        The Hallmark Book of Poetry.   Selected and Ar-
        ranged by the Editors.   New York: Doubleday and
        Co. , 1960, 360-61.   (SP) (TMR)

674   "A Tune for Festive Dances in the Nineteen Sixties," in
        New Directions in Prose and Poetry, 19.   Edited by
        James Laughlin.   New York: New Directions, 1966,
        293-94.

675   "Western Fellow Students Salute with Calypso Anthems:
        The Movie Career of Robert Lax. "   Latitudes 1
        (February 1967): 8-9.

676   *"Why Some Look Up to Planets and Heroes. "   America
        108 (30 March 1963): 433.   (EOASOF)

677   *"Wisdom," in Kentucky Authors, by Mary Carmel
          Browning, O.S.U.   Evansville, Indiana: Keller-
          Crescent Co. , 1968, 220.   (SI) (SP) (TMR)

678   *With the World in My Bloodstream. "   Florida Quarterly
          1 (Summer 1967): 19-21.

M. A. THESIS

679   "Nature and Art in William Blake: An Essay in Inter-
          pretation. "   Submitted in partial fulfillment of the
          requirements for the degree of Master of Arts in
          the Department of English and Comparative Litera-
          ture.   New York: Columbia University, February,
          1939, 98p.

TRANSLATIONS BY THOMAS MERTON

680   Alberti, Rafael.   "Roman Nocturnes. "   Kayak (1968):
          no. 15, pp. 18-21.

681   Andrade, Carlos Drummond de.   "Two Poems: 'Song
          of Purification'; 'Memories of the Ancient World.' "
          The Spokesman (Loras College, Dubuque, Iowa) 62
          (1964-65): 41-44.

682   Cardenal, Ernesto.   "Drake in the Southern Sea, " in
          Emblems of a Season of Fury, by Thomas Merton.
          A New Directions Paperback, no. 140.   Norfolk,
          Connecticut: James Laughlin, 1963, 122-24.

683   _____.   "Drake in the Southern Sea, " in New Direc-
          tions in Prose and Poetry, 17.   Edited by James
          Laughlin.   New York: New Directions, 1961, 102-
          4.

684   _____.   "Drake in the Southern Sea. "   Pax (1958):
          no. 7.

685 _____. "Selections from 'Gethsemani, Kentucky,' "
      in Emblems of a Season of Fury, by Thomas Mer-
      ton. A New Directions Paperback, no. 140. Nor-
      folk, Connecticut: James Laughlin, 1963, 117-21.

686 _____. "Three Epigrams," in Emblems of a Season
      of Fury, by Thomas Merton. A New Directions
      Paperback, no. 140. Norfolk, Connecticut: James
      Laughlin, 1963, 116-17.

687 Carrera Andrade, Jorge. "Cocoa Tree," in Emblems
      of a Season of Fury, by Thomas Merton. A New
      Directions Paperback, no. 140. Norfolk, Connecti-
      cut: James Laughlin, 1963, 129.

688 _____. "A Man from Ecuador Beneath the Eiffel
      Tower," in Emblems of a Season of Fury, by
      Thomas Merton. A New Directions Paperback,
      no. 140. Norfolk, Connecticut: James Laughlin,
      1963, 131-32.

689 _____. "Mirror's Mission," in Emblems of a Season
      of Fury, by Thomas Merton. A New Directions
      Paperback, no. 140. Norfolk, Connecticut: James
      Laughlin, 1963, 132-33.

690 _____. "Notes of a Parachute Jumper," in Emblems
      of a Season of Fury, by Thomas Merton. A New
      Directions Paperback, no. 140. Norfolk, Connecti-
      cut: James Laughlin, 1963, 133-34.

691 _____. "Six Poems," in New Directions in Prose
      and Poetry, 17. Edited by James Laughlin. In-
      cludes: "Cocoa Tree," "Weathercock on the Cathe-
      dral of Quito," "A Man from Ecuador Beneath the
      Eiffel Tower," "Radicals," "Mirror's Mission,"
      "Notes of a Parachute Jumper." New York: New
      Directions, 1961, 115-23.

692 _____. "Weathercock on the Cathedral of Quito," in
      Emblems of a Season of Fury, by Thomas Merton.
      A New Directions Paperback, no. 140. Norfolk,
      Connecticut: James Laughlin, 1963, 129-31.

693 Cassiodorus Senator, Flavius Magnus Aurelius. A
      Prayer from the Treatise 'De Anima.' Preface
      and Translation from Latin by Thomas Merton.

Worcester, England: Stanbrook Abbey Press, 1967.

694   Char, René. "Seven Poems from Retour Amont." Uni-
        corn Journal 3 (1969): 53-58. Includes: "Come
        Dance in Baronies," "Fighters," "At the Gates of
        Aerea," "Celebrating Giacometti," "Septentrion,"
        "Faction du Muet," "Convergence of the Many."

695   Chautard, Jean Baptiste, O. C. S. O.   The Soul of the
        Apostolate. Introduction and Translation from the
        Latin by Thomas Merton. New York: Doubleday
        and Co. , 1961.

696   Clemens, Titus Flavius Alexandrinus.   Clement of
        Alexandria: Selections from the 'Protreptikos. '
        An Essay "Clement of Alexandria" and Transla-
        tion from Latin by Thomas Merton. Worcester,
        England: Stanbrook Abbey Press, 1967.

697   Cortes, Alfonso. "Aegeus in Prison," in Emblems of
        a Season of Fury, by Thomas Merton. A New
        Directions Paperback, no. 140. Norfolk, Connec-
        ticut: James Laughlin, 1963, 147.

698   _____. "Air," in Emblems of a Season of Fury,
        by Thomas Merton. A New Directions Paperback,
        no. 140. Norfolk, Connecticut: James Laughlin,
        1963, 147.

699   _____. "Flower of the Fruit," in Emblems of a
        Season of Fury, by Thomas Merton. A New Di-
        rections Paperback, no. 140. Norfolk, Connecti-
        cut: James Laughlin, 1963, 144.

700   _____. "Flower of the Fruit." Sewanee Review 71
        (Summer 1963): 466.

701   _____. "Great Prayer," in Emblems of a Season of
        Fury, by Thomas Merton. A New Directions Paper-
        back, no. 140. Norfolk, Connecticut: James
        Laughlin, 1963, 145.

702   _____. "Space Song," in Emblems of a Season of
        Fury, by Thomas Merton. A New Directions
        Paperback, no. 140. Norfolk, Connecticut: James
        Laughlin, 1963, 143-144.

703   _____. "Space Song." Sewanee Review 71 (Summer
          1963): 467.

704   _____. "Sundown," in Emblems of a Season of Fury,
          by Thomas Merton. A New Directions Paperback,
          no. 140. Norfolk, Connecticut: James Laughlin,
          1963, 148.

705   _____. "Three Sisters," in Emblems of a Season
          of Fury, by Thomas Merton. A New Directions
          Paperback, no. 140. Norfolk, Connecticut: James
          Laughlin, 1963, 145-46.

706   _____. "Truth," in Emblems of a Season of Fury,
          by Thomas Merton. A New Directions Paperback,
          no. 140. Norfolk, Connecticut: James Laughlin,
          1963, 146.

707   _____. "When You Point Your Finger," in Emblems
          of a Season of Fury, by Thomas Merton. A New
          Directions Paperback, no. 140. Norfolk, Connec-
          ticut: James Laughlin, 1963, 148.

708   Cuadra, Pablo Antonio. "Birth of the Sun," in Emblems
          of a Season of Fury, by Thomas Merton. A New
          Directions Paperback, no. 140. Norfolk, Connecti-
          cut: James Laughlin, 1963, 98-99.

709   _____. "Cup with a Jaguar for the Drinking of
          Health," in Emblems of a Season of Fury, by
          Thomas Merton. A New Directions Paperback,
          no. 140. Norfolk, Connecticut: James Laughlin,
          1963, 98.

710   _____. "Despairing Man Draws a Serpent," in
          Emblems of a Season of Fury, by Thomas Merton.
          A New Directions Paperback, no. 140. Norfolk,
          Connecticut: James Laughlin, 1963, 99.

711   _____. "Eye Is a Dog Howling in the Distance," in
          Emblems of a Season of Fury, by Thomas Merton.
          A New Directions Paperback, no. 140. Norfolk,
          Connecticut: James Laughlin, 1963, 101.

712   _____. "Jaguar Myth," in Emblems of a Season of
          Fury, by Thomas Merton. A New Directions
          Paperback, no. 140. Norfolk, Connecticut: James
          Laughlin, 1963, 96-97.

713 _____. "The Jaguar Myth and Other Poems," in
New Directions in Prose and Poetry, 17.   Edited
by James Laughlin.   Includes: "Cup with a Jaguar
for the Drinking of Health," "Birth of the Sun,"
"Despairing Man Draws a Serpent," "Secret of the
Burning Stars," "Faces of Girls Looking at Them-
selves in the River," "Meditation before an Ancient
Poem," "Pain Is an Eagle Clinging to Your Name,"
"Eye Is a Dog Howling in the Distance," "Nahoa
Urn, for a Woman," "Urn with a Political Profile,"
"World Is a Round Earthenware Plate," "Lament of
a Maiden for the Warrior's Death," "Written Next
to a Blue Flower." New York: New Directions,
1961, 105-14.

714 _____. "Lament of a Maiden for the Warrior's
Death," in Emblems of a Season of Fury, by
Thomas Merton. A New Directions Paperback,
no. 140. Norfolk, Connecticut: James Laughlin,
1963, 102-3.

715 _____. "Pain Is an Eagle Clinging to Your Name,"
in Emblems of a Season of Fury, by Thomas Merton. A New Directions Paperback, no. 140. Norfolk, Connecticut: James Laughlin, 1963, 100.

716 _____. "Secret of the Burning Stars," in Emblems
of a Season of Fury, by Thomas Merton. A New
Directions Paperback, no. 140. Norfolk, Connecticut: James Laughlin, 1963, 99-100.

717 _____. "Urn with a Political Profile," in Emblems
of a Season of Fury, by Thomas Merton. A New
Directions Paperback, no. 140. Norfolk, Connecticut: James Laughlin, 1963, 101.

718 _____. "World Is a Round Earthenware Plate," in
Emblems of a Season of Fury, by Thomas Merton.
A New Directions Paperback, no. 140. Norfolk,
Connecticut: James Laughlin, 1963, 102.

719 Guigo the Carthusion. The Solitary Life: A Letter of
Guigo. Introduction and Translation from the Latin
by Thomas Merton. Worcester, England: Stanbrook Abbey Press, 1963.

720 Nicholas of Cusa. "Dialogue about the Hidden God."

Lugano Review 1 (Summer 1966): 67-70.

721   Maritain, Raissa. "Autumn," in Emblems of a Season
      of Fury, by Thomas Merton. A New Directions
      Paperback, no. 140. Norfolk, Connecticut: James
      Laughlin, 1963, 112.

722   _____. "Chagall," in Emblems of a Season of Fury,
      by Thomas Merton. A New Directions Paperback,
      no. 140. Norfolk, Connecticut: James Laughlin,
      1963, 109-10.

723   _____. "Lake," in Emblems of a Season of Fury,
      by Thomas Merton. A New Directions Paperback,
      no. 140. Norfolk, Connecticut: James Laughlin,
      1963, 108.

724   _____. "Mosaic: Saint Praxed's," in Emblems of
      a Season of Fury, by Thomas Merton. A New
      Directions Paperback, no. 140. Norfolk, Connec-
      ticut: James Laughlin, 1963, 113.

725   _____. "Pillars," in Emblems of a Season of Fury,
      by Thomas Merton. A New Directions Paperback,
      no. 140. Norfolk, Connecticut: James Laughlin,
      1963, 108.

726   _____. "Prisoner," in Emblems of a Season of
      Fury, by Thomas Merton. A New Directions
      Paperback, no. 140. Norfolk, Connecticut: James
      Laughlin, 1963, 106-7.

727   _____. "Raissa Maritain's Poems." Translation and
      commentary by Thomas Merton. Jubilee 10 (April
      1963): 24-27. Includes: "Prisoner," "Lake,"
      "Chagall," "Pillars," "Autumn," "Mosaic: Saint
      Praxed's," "Glass Orchard," "The Glove," "Re-
      cipe," "Eurydice," "The Cloud," "The Restoration
      of the Pictures."

728   _____. "The Restoration of the Pictures," in Em-
      blems of a Season of Fury, by Thomas Merton. A
      New Directions Paperback, no. 140. Norfolk, Con-
      necticut: James Laughlin, 1963, 111-12.

729   Pessoa, Fernando. Keeper of the Flocks. Trappist,
      Kentucky: Abbey of Our Lady of Gethsemani, 1965.

730 _____. Twelve Poems. Trappist, Kentucky: Abbey
of Our Lady of Gethsemani, 1965.

731 Vallejo, Cesar Abraham. "Anger," in Emblems of a
Season of Fury, by Thomas Merton. A New Direc-
tions Paperback, no. 140. Norfolk, Connecticut:
James Laughlin, 1963, 140.

732 _____. "Black Stone on Top of a White Stone," in
Emblems of a Season of Fury, by Thomas Merton.
A New Directions Paperback, no. 140. Norfolk,
Connecticut: James Laughlin, 1963, 137-38.

733 _____. "Estais Muertos," in Emblems of a Season
of Fury, by Thomas Merton. A New Directions
Paperback, no. 140. Norfolk, Connecticut: James
Laughlin, 1963, 136-37.

734 _____. "Peace, the Wasp," in Emblems of a Season
of Fury, by Thomas Merton. A New Directions
Paperback, no. 140. Norfolk, Connecticut: James
Laughlin, 1963, 138-39.

735 Verba Seniorum. English. What Ought I to Do? Sayings of the Desert Fathers. Lexington, Kentucky:
Stamperia del Santuccio, 1959.

736 _____. Wisdom of the Desert. Sayings from the
Desert Fathers of the Fourth Century. New York:
New Directions, 1960.

TRANSLATIONS OF WORKS
BY THOMAS MERTON

BELGIAN

737 Levend brood. [The Living Bread] Translated by J.
Boosman. Bruges: Desclée de Brouwer, 1957.
153p.

738 Oplettende toeschouwer. [Conjectures of a Guilty By-
stander] Translated by Martha van de Walle.
Bruges: Desclée de Brouwer, 1969. 411p.

739 Het stille leven. [The Silent Life] Translated by
     Reguliere Kanunnikessen van de Prioij H. Graf,
     Doornburgh, Maarssen. Bruges: Desclée de
     Brouwer, 1958. 160p.

CEYLONESE
     (Sinhalese)
740 Gita vaduma. [Praying the Psalms] Kandy, Ceylon:
     Bible Society of India and Ceylon, Ceylon Cateche-
     tical Service, 1964, 5-40.

     (Tamil)
741 Sangita pustakam. [Praying the Psalms] Trincomalee,
     Ceylon: Ceylon Catechetical Service, 1965, 5-37.

CHINESE

742 Mê kuan shêng huo t'an pi. [Seeds of Contemplation]
     Translated by Chiang Ping-Lun. Taichung: Kuang
     Chi Press, 1959. 130p.

CZECHOSLOVAKIAN

743 Hora sedmi stupňů. [Seven Storey Mountain] Rome:
     Křest'anská akademie, 1968. 715p.

DUTCH

744 Beschouwend gebed. [Climate of Monastic Prayer]
     Antwerp/Utrecht: Patmos, 1972. 115p.

745 Brood in de woestijn. [Bread in the Wilderness]
     Antwerp: Sint-Norbertus-Boekh, 1957. 160p.

746 Overpeinzinten van een christen. [Life and Holiness]
     Translated by Cyprianus van den Bogaard. Utrecht:
     Uitgeverij Het Spectrum, N. V. , 1965. 158p.

747 Uw naaste als uzelf. [No Man Is an Island] Translated
     by J. K. van den Brink. Antwerp: Uitgeverij Het
     Spectrum, N. V. , 1956. 253p.

748 De weg van Tsjwang-Tze. [The Way of Chuang Tzu]
     Bilthoven: Amboboeken, 1972. 144p.

FRENCH

749 "A la reconquête du paradis." [The Recovery of Para-
    dise] Translated from the English by Françoise
    Piponnier. Bulletin du cercle Saint Jean-Baptiste
    (March 1963): no. 21, pp. 21-33.

750 Les chemins de la joie. [Thoughts in Solitude] Collec-
    tion traditions monastiques. Paris: Editions d'his-
    toire et d'art, Librairie Plon, 1961. 135p.

751 "Les chrétiens et guerre atomique." [Excerpts from
    The Root of War] Action civique non-violente
    (February 1965): no. 22, p. 3.

752 "Christianisme et question raciale aux Etats-Unis."
    [Christianity and Race in the United States] Frères
    du monde (Bordeaux) (1964): no. 31, pp. 50-65.

753 "Le climat de la prière monastique." [Excerpt from
    Climate of Monastic Prayer] Translated from the
    English by Thibaud Maze. Les Amis du Bec-
    Hellouin (July 1966): no. 18, pp. 9-17.

754 "Dieu n'est pas un problème." [As Man to Man] Col-
    lectanea Cisterciensia 31 (1969): 19-23.

755 Direction spirituelle et méditation. [Spiritual Direction
    and Meditation] Translated by Marie Tadié. Paris:
    Editions Albin Michel, 1962. 135p.

756 Foi et violence. [Faith and Violence] Translated by
    Marie Tadié. Paris: Eds de L'Ep, 1969.

757 La formation monastique selon Adam de Perseigne.
    [Monastic Formation According to Adam Perseigne]
    Translated by Charles Dumont, O. C. S. O. Rome:
    Scourmont, 1957. 17p.

758 "Heureux les doux-les racines de la non-violence
    chrétienne." [Blessed Meek: The Roots of
    Christian Nonviolence] Cahiers de la reconcil-
    iation (Paris) (January 1968): no. 1, pp. 30-40.

759 "Huit chants de liberté." [Eight Freedom Songs]
    Adapted by Hervé Chaigne. Frères du monde
    (Bordeaux) (1964): no. 31, pp. 67-75.

760   Journal d'un laïc. [Secular Journal of Thomas Merton]
         Translated by Marie Tadié. Paris: Editions Albin
         Michel, 1964. 223p.

761   "Lettre d'asie." [Asian Letter] Collectanea Cister-
         ciensia 31 (1969): 14-18.

762   Marthe, Marie, et Lazare. [Marthe, Marie, et Lazare]
         Translated by Juliette Charles Du-Bos. Collection
         présence chrétienne. Paris: Desclée de Brouwer,
         1956. 145p.

763   "Le moine dans la diaspora." [The Monk in the
         Diaspora] Bulletin de liaison des monastères
         d'Afrique 3 (1965): 23-31.

764   La montée vers la lumière. [The Ascent to Truth]
         Translated by Marie Tadié. Paris: Editions Albin
         Michel, 1958. 229p.

765   Mystique et zen. [Abridged version of Mystics and Zen
         Masters] Translated by C. Tunmer. Paris: Les
         Editions du Cerf, 1972. 236p.

766   "Le nom du seigneur." [The Name of the Lord] Bible
         et vie chrétienne (Paris) no. 59, pp. 59-70.

767   Le nouvel homme. [The New Man] Translated by
         Marie Tadié. Paris: Editions du Seuil, 1969.
         192p.

768   Nouvelles semences de contemplation. [New Seeds of
         Contemplation] Translated by Marie Tadié. Paris:
         Editions du Seuil, 1963. 224p.

769   La nuit privée d'étoiles. [The Seven Storey Mountain]
         Collection libre de vie, 2-3. Paris: Editions du
         Seuil, 1961.

770   "Ouverture et clôture." [Openness and Cloister]
         Collectanea Cisterciensia 31 (1969): 24-35.

771   Le pain vivant. [The Living Bread] Translated by
         Marie Tadié. Paris: Editions Alsatia, 1957.
         160p.

772   La paix monastique. [Monastic Peace] Translated by

Marie Tadié. Illustrations by Frank Kacmarcik.
Paris: Éditions Albin Michel, 1961. 143p.

773 "Pâques, une vie nouvelle." [Easter, a New Life]
Vie spirituelle 100 (April 1959): 345-59.

774 "Le père spirituel dans la tradition du desert." [The
Spiritual Father in the Desert Tradition] Trans-
lated by Marie Tadié. La vie spirituelle (Paris)
(November 1969): no. 565, pp. 438-63.

775 "La place de l'obeissance dans le renouveau monastique."
[The Place of Obedience in Monastic Renewal]
Lettre de Ligugé (Lettre de L'Abbaye Saint Martin)
(September-October 1966): no. 119, pp. 8-19.

776 Prions les psaumes. [Praying the Psalms] Translated
by Carmen Bernos de Gasztold. Illustrations by
Sister Geneviève Gallois. Paris: Éditions du
Cloître, n. d. 42p.

777 Questions disputées. [Disputed Questions] Translated
by Marie Tadié. Paris: Éditions Albin Michel,
1963. 272p.

778 Réflexions d'un spectateur coupable. [Conjectures of a
Guilty Bystander] Translated by Marie Tadié.
Paris: Éditions Albin Michel, 1970. 397p.

779 "Renouveau de la formation monastique." [Renewal in
Monastic Education] Collectanea Cisterciensia 30
(1968): 211-18.

780 La révolution noire: lettre à un blanc libéral suivie de
la légende de Tucker Caliban. [The Black Revolu-
tion] Translated by Marie Tadié. Tournai: Casterman, 1964. 128p.

781 La sagesse du désert: apophtegmes des pères du désert
du IVᵉ siècle. [The Wisdom of the Desert] Translated by Marie Tadié. Paris: Éditions Albin
Michel, 1967. 125p.

782 "Sagesse et vacuité: Dialogue entre Daizetz T. Suzuki
et le R. P. Thomas Merton." [Wisdom in Emptiness: A Dialogue between Daizetz T. Suzuki and
Thomas Merton] Hermès (Les amis d'Hermès-
Paris) 6 (1969): 170-97.

783   Semences de destruction. [Seeds of Destruction] Translated by Marie Tadié. Paris: Editions Albin
Michel, 1965. 164p.

784   "Seneque." [Seneca] Translated by Jacques Borel.
Homenaje a Merton, in Memoriam Ludovici to
Merton, the Magician. Honolulu: Mele, 1969.
unpaged.

785   Le temps des fêtes. [Seasons of Celebration] Translated by Marie Tadié. Tournai: Casterman, 1968.
230p.

786   Les titans. [Selections from The Behavior of Titans
and Raids on the Unspeakable] Translated by
Marie Tadié. Paris: Editions de Seuil, 1971.
123p.

787   Vie et sainteté. [Life and Holiness] Translated by
Marie Tadié. Paris: Editions du Seuil, 1966.
154p.

788   La vie silencieuse. [The Silent Life] Collection la
vigne de Carmel. Translated by Marie Tadié.
Paris: Editions du Seuil, 1957. 189p.

789   Les voies de la vraie prière. [Climate of Monastic
Prayer] Translated by C. Tunmer. Paris:
Editions du Seuil, 1970.

790   Zen, Tao et Nirvâna: esprit et contemplation en
Extreme-Orient. [Selections from Zen and the
Birds of Appetite and The Way of Chuang Tzu]
Preface by Marco Pallis. Translated by F.
Ledoux. Paris: Librairie Artheme Fayard,
1970. 172p.

GERMAN

791   Apokalypse der neuen Welt. [Apocalypse of the New
World] Translated by Alfred Kuoni. Zürich:
Die Arche Verlag, 1956. 64p.

792   "Bisschop Robinson zonder Mythe: Het Debate over
'Eerlijk voor God.' " [Demythologizing Bishop
Robinson: The Honest to God Debate] Tijdschrift
voor Ascese en Mystiek (Tilburg) 41: no. 5,
pp. 298-308.

793 Grazias Haus: Gedichte. [Grace's House: Poems]
Epilogue by Hans Urs von Balthasar. Poems from
Selected Poems (1944) and Emblems of a Season of
Fury (1961) translated by Marta Gisi; Figures for
an Apocalypse translated by Lili Sertorius.
Einsiedeln: Johannes Verlag, 1966. 100p.

794 Heilig in Christus. [Life and Holiness] Translated by
Eugen Kende. Freiburg im Breisgau: Herder
Freiburg, 1965. 152p.

795 "Der heilige Johannes vom Krenz." [Saint John of the
Cross] Perspektiven (Frankfurt-S. Fischer Verlag)
(Summer 1953): no. 4, pp. 53-62.

796 Lebendige stille [The Silent Life] Translated by Irene
Marinoff. Einsiedeln: Benziger, 1959. 189p.

797 Der mit dir lebt: Betrachtungen ueber die Eucharistie.
[The Living Bread] Translated by Irene Marinoff.
Einsiedeln: Benziger Verlag, 1958. 185p.

798 Die schwarze Revolution. [The Black Revolution]
Translated by Hans Schmidthus. Freiburg im
Breisgau: Herder Freiburg, 1965. 125p.

799 "Die schwarze Revolution in Amerika." [Excerpt from
The Black Revolution] Dokumente (Zeitschrift für
übernationale Zusammenarbeit) (April 1964): no. 2,
pp. 132-38.

800 Schweigen im Himmel. [Silence in Heaven] Translated
by Erna Melchers. Wiesbaden: Rheinische
Verlagsanstalt, 1957. 72p.

801 Verheissungen der Stille. [New Seeds of Contemplation]
Translated by Magda Larsen and Paul F. Portmann.
Lucerne: Räber Verlag, 1963. 285p.

802 Vom Sinn der Kontemplation. [What is Contemplation?]
Translated by Alfred Kuoni. Zürich: Die Arche
Verlag, 1955. 64p.

803 "Von den Wurzeln des Krieges." [The Root of War]
Basler Volksblatt (4 October 1963).

804 Weltliches Tagebuch 1939-1941. [The Secular Journal

of Thomas Merton] Translated by Alfred Kuoni.
Einsiedeln: Benziger Verlag, 1960. 180p.

805 Wir Suchen Jesus den Christus: Grundlegungen monas-
tischer Spiritualität. [Basic Principles of Monastic
Spirituality] Translated by Margret Meilwes.
Trier, West Germany: Johann Josef Zimmer
Verlag, 1972. 83p.

GREEK

806 Exomologēseis tou anthrōpou eikostou aiōnos. [Confes-
sions of the Man of the Twentieth Century] Trans-
lated by Helen Kapita. Selections from The Seven
Storey Mountain, No Man Is an Island, Life and
Holiness, Seeds of Destruction, Conjectures of a
Guilty Bystander, Thirty Poems, The Tears of the
Blind Lions. Athens: Ekdoseis Theos, 1969. 96p.

807 O kainourgios anthrōpos. [The New Man] Translated
by Antonius Bakardios. Introduction by Johannos
Th. Papabasileios. Athens: Kalos Typos, n. d.
184p.

ITALIAN

808 "Apertura e vita claustrale." [Openness and Cloister]
Ora et labora (January-March 1968): 11-21.

809 Cablogrammi e profezie. [Cables to the Ace and Geography of Lograire] Translated by Romeo Lucchese.
Milan: Garzanti, 1972. 437p.

810 Il clima della preghiera monastica. [The Climate of
Monastic Prayer] Milan: Garzanti, 1970.

811 "Il concilio e la vita dei religiosi." [The Council and
Religious Life] Humanitas (Brescia) anno 20 (November 1965): no. 11, pp. 1097-1115.

812 "Il contemplativo e l'àteo." [Excerpt from Message of
Contemplatives to the Modern World] Studi Cattolici
(Milan) anno 12 (March 1968): no. 84, pp. 202-7.

813 Diario di un testimòne colpevole. [Conjectures of a
Guilty Bystander] Translated by Gino Rampini.
Milan: Garzanti, 1968.

814 Diario secolare. [The Secular Journal of Thomas Mer-
     ton] Translated by Lucia P. Rodocanachi. Milan:
     Garzanti, 1960. 204p.

815 Direzione spirituale e meditazione. [Spiritual Direction
     and Meditation] Translated by Elena Lante Ros-
     pigliosi. Milan: Garzanti, 1965. 124p.

816 Emblemi di un'età di violenza. [Emblems of a Season
     of Fury] Translated by Romeo Lucchese. Milan:
     Garzanti, 1971. 174p.

817 Fede e violenza. [Abridged edition of Faith and Vio-
     lence] Translated by Maria Teresa Galleani
     D'Agliano. Brescia: Morcelliana, 1965. 118p.

818 Fede, resistènza, protesta. [Faith and Violence] Trans-
     lated by Maria Teresa Galleani D'Agliano. Brescia:
     Morcelliana, 1969. 272p.

819 "Gandhi e il ciclope." [Gandhi and the One-Eyed Giants]
     Translated by L. da Schio. Humanitas (Brescia)
     anno 21 (August 1966): no. 8, pp. 785-803.

820 I Salmi. [Praying the Psalms] Translated by Rienzo
     Colla. Vicenza: La Locusta, 1961. 55p.

821 Mistici e maèstri zen. [Mystics and Zen Masters]
     Translated by Franco Bernardini Marzolla. Milan:
     Garzanti, 1969. 261p.

822 Nessun uomo è un'isola. [No Man Is an Island] Trans-
     lated by Emanuel a Moretti. Milan: Garzanti,
     1956. 272p.

823 Nuovi semi di contemplazione. [New Seeds of Contem-
     plation] Translated by Bruno Tasso and Elena
     Lante Rospigliosi. Milan: Garzanti, 1968. 224p.

824 Il pane nel desèrto. [Bread in the Wilderness] Milan:
     Garzanti, 1957.

825 Il pane vivo. [The Living Bread] Milan: Garzanti,
     1958. 183p.

826 Pasternak. [The Pasternak Affair] Translated by
     Antonio Barbieri. Vicenza: La Locusta, 1961.
     87p.

827   Pensieri nella solitudine.   [Thoughts in Solitude]   Milan:
        Garzanti, 1959.   123p.

828   Poesie.   [Selected Poems]   Translated by Romeo
        Lucchese.   Milan: Garzanti, 1962.   243p.

829   Problèmi dello spirito.   [Disputed Questions]   Translated
        by Franco Bernardini.   Milan: Garzanti, 1960.
        348p.

830   La rivoluzione negra.   [The Black Revolution]   Trans-
        lated by Franco Onorat.   Vicenza: La Locusta,
        1965.   94p.

831   Semi di distruzione.   [Seeds of Destruction]   Translated
        by Franco Bernardini Marzolla.   Milan: Garzanti,
        1966.   248p.

832   Têmpo di celebrazione.   [Seasons of Celebration]   Trans-
        lated by Gino Rampini.   Milan: Garzanti, 1967.
        204p.

833   L'Uomo nuovo.   [The New Man]   Translated by Franco
        Bernardini.   Milan: Garzanti, 1963.   206p.

834   Vita e santità.   [Life and Holiness]   Translated by
        Franco Bernardini.   Milan: Garzanti, 1964.   170p.

835   Vita nel silênzio.   [The Silent Life]   Brescia: Morcel-
        liana, 1957.   150p.

836   Vita nel silênzio.   [The Silent Life]   Translated by
        M. R. Cimnaghi.   Brescia: Morcelliana, 1963.
        186p.

837   Lo zen e gli uccèlli rapaci.   [Zen and the Birds of
        Appetite]   Translated by Franco Bernardini Mar-
        zolla.   Milan: Garzanti, 1970.   143p.

JAPANESE

838   Atarashii hito.   [The New Man]   Translated by Yasumo
        Kikama.   Tokyo: Veritas Publishing Co. , 1970.
        301p.

839   Gendai no seijin towa.   [Life and Holiness]   Translated
        by Mezuo Kobayashi.   Tokyo: Enderle (Herder),
        1964.   177p.

840 Kansō no tane. [Seeds of Contemplation] Translated by
Yasuwo Kikama. Kyoto: Veritas Publishing Co.,
1965. 235p.

841 Kirisuto kyō to zen taiken. [Christian Faith and Zen
Experience] Extracts from Mystics and Zen Masters and Zen and the Birds of Appetite. Translated
by Takashi Ikemoto and Yuji Nakata. Tokyo:
Enderle (Herder), 1969. 238p.

842 Kodoku no naka no shisaku. [Thoughts in Solitude]
Translated by Yasuwo Kikama. Kyoto: Veritas
Publishing Co., 1966. 168p.

843 Meisō no shushi. [Seeds of Contemplation] Translated
by Junji Nagasawa. Tokyo: Chuō Shuppansha,
1966. 238p.

844 Nanae no yama. [Seven Storey Mountain] Translated
by Kudō Tadashi. Tokyo: Chuō Shuppansha, 1966.
556p.

845 Shudō reishū no kompon. [Basic Principles of Monastic
Spirituality] Translated by Fujisaburo Kiuchi.
Sapporo: Kōmei sha, 1962. 82p.

KOREAN

846 Hyeondaeineui sinang saenghwal. [Life and Holiness]
Translated by Jeong-Jin Kim. Seoul: Kaetoric
Chulpansa, 1965. 150p.

POLISH

847 "Czas i liturgia." [Time and the Liturgy] Znak
miesiecznik (Cracow) 10 (1958): no. 53, pp. 1218-
21.

848 "Czy przetrwamy nihilism?" [Can We Survive Nihilism?]
Tematy 7 (Winter 1968): no. 25, pp. 24-35.

849 "Mnich i mysliwi." [Monks and Hunters] Kultura-
szkice, opowiadania, sprawozdania (Paris) (1953):
99-102.

850 "Modlimy sie slowami psalmou." [Praying the Psalms]
Przewodnik katolicki (Warsaw) (1967): no. 39,
pp. 346-49.

851   Nikt nie jest samotna wyspa. [No Man Is an Island]
      Translated by Maria Morstin-Gorska.   Cracow:
      Znak, 1960. 182p.

852   "Odpowiedzialność wystawiona na próbę. " [Christian in
      World Crisis] Tematy 4 (Winter 1965): no. 14,
      pp. 21-35.

853   Znak Jonaska. [The Sign of Jonas] Translated by
      Krystyna Poborska.   Cracow: Znak, 1962.   333p.

PORTUGUESE

854   Aguas de Siloe. [The Waters of Siloe] Translated by
      Oscar Mendes.   Belo Horizonte, Brazil: Livraria
      Itatiaia, 1957.   380p.

855   Ascensão para verdade.   [Ascent to Truth] Translated
      by Timoteo Amoroso Anastacio, O. S. B.   Belo
      Horizonte, Brazil: Livraria Itatiaia, 1958.   258p.

856   Bernardo de Claraval.   [The Last of the Fathers]
      Petrópolis, Brazil: Editorial Vozes Limitada,
      1958.   123p.

857   Diário secular.   [Secular Journal of Thomas Merton]
      Translated by Paulo Alceu Amoroso Lima.
      Petrópolis, Brazil: Editorial Vozes Limitada,
      1961.   244p.

858   Direcão espiritual e meditacão.   [Spiritual Direction and
      Meditation] Preface by Basilo Penido, O. S. B.
      Petrópolis, Brazil: Editorial Vozes Limitada,
      1962.   127p.

859   Gandhi e a não-violência.   [Gandhi on Non-Violence]
      Edited with an Introduction by Thomas Merton.
      Petrópolis, Brazil: Editorial Vozes Limitada,
      1967.   125p.

860   Homem algum e uma ilha.   [No Man Is an Island]
      Translated by Timoteo Amoroso Anastacio, O. S. B.
      Rio de Janeiro: Livraria Editorial Agir, 1957.
      251p.

861   O homem nova.   [The New Man] Rio de Janeiro:
      Livraria Editorial Agir, 1966.   187p.

862 A igreja e o mundo sem Deus. [The Church and the
     "Godless World"] Translated by João Morris and
     Edmir Viana, O. F. M. Petrópolis, Brazil: Edi-
     torial Vozes Limitada, 1969. 102p.

863 Na liberdade da solidão. [Thoughts in Solitude] Intro-
     duction by Timoteo Amoroso Anastacio, O. S. B.
     Rio de Janeiro: Editorial Vozes Limitada, 1958.
     111p.

864 Marta, Maria e Lázaro. [Marthe, Marie et Lazare]
     Introduction by Paulo Alceu Amoroso Lima.
     Petrópolis, Brazil: Editorial Vozes Limitada,
     1963. 127p.

865 Noite sem estrelas. [Seven Storey Mountain] Translated
     by Susana Vasques. Lisbon: Livraria Bertrand,
     n. d. 499p.

866 Novas sementes de contemplacão. [New Seeds of Contem-
     plation] Preface by Basilo Penido, O. S. B. Pe-
     trópolis, Brazil: Editorial Vozes Limitada, 1963.
     293p.

867 O pão no deserto. [Bread in the Wilderness] Presen-
     tation by Estêvao Bettencourt, O. S. B. Petrópolis,
     Brazil: Editorial Vozes Limitada, 1963. 175p.

868 O pão vivo. [The Living Bread] Introduction by Paulo
     Alceu Amoroso Lima. Petrópolis, Brazil: Editorial
     Vozes Limitada, 1960. 175p.

869 "Páscoa: uma vitória." [Easter: The New Life] Sponsa
     Christi (Petrópolis, Brazil) 11 (February-March
     1967): 70-79.

870 Questões abertas. [Disputed Questions] Rio de Janeiro:
     Livraria Editorial Agir, 1963. 319p.

871 Reflexoes de um espectador culpado. [Conjectures of a
     Guilty Bystander] Petrópolis, Brazil: Editorial
     Vozes Limitada, 1970. 407p.

872 Sementes de destruição. [Seeds of Destruction] Trans-
     lated by Paulo Alceu Amoroso Lima. Petrópolis:
     Editorial Vozes Limitada, 1966. 327p.

873   Tempo e liturgia. [Seasons of Celebration] Petrópolis,
        Brazil: Editorial Vozes Limitada, 1968.   254p.

874   A via de Chuang Tzu. [The Way of Chuang Tzu] Trans-
        lated by Paulo Alceu Amoroso Lima.   Petrópolis,
        Brazil: Editorial Vozes Limitada, 1965.   203p.

875   Vida e santidade. [Life and Holiness] Preface by
        Paulo Alceu Amoroso Lima.   São Paulo, Brazil:
        Herder Editora, 1965.   176p.

876   A vida silenciosa. [The Silent Life] Preface by
        Basilo Penido, O. S. B.   2nd edition.   Petrópolis,
        Brazil: Editorial Vozes Limitada, 1964.   191p.

877   Vinho dó silêncio. [Selected poems by Thomas Merton
        from his various published volumes plus transla-
        tions of the Castilian Poesias by Ernesto Cardenal]
        Translated by Carmen de Mello.   Belo Horizonte,
        Brazil: Universidade Federal de Minas Gerais,
        1969.   118p.

878   Zen e as aves de rapina. [Zen and the Birds of Ap-
        petite] Rio de Janeiro: Editora Civilização
        Brasileira, 1968.   130p.

SPANISH

879   "El absurdo de la decoración sagrada." [Absurdity in
        Sacred Decoration] Hogar y arquitectura (Madrid)
        (March-April 1965): no. 57, pp. 21-23.

880   "Albada-Harlem." [Aubade-Harlem] Translated by
        Ernesto Cardenal.   La prensa literaria (Nicaragua)
        (28 May 1967): 1 B.

881   "El arte sacro y la vida espiritual." [Sacred Art and
        the Spiritual Life] Hogar y arquitectura (Madrid)
        (March-April 1965): no. 57, pp. 17-20.

882   "Carta a Pablo Antonio Cuadra con respecto a los
        gigantes." [Letter to Pablo Antonio Cuadra con-
        cerning Giants] Translated by Maria Raquel
        Bengolea.   Sur (Revista Bimestral Sumario-Buenos
        Aires) (March-April 1962): no. 275, pp. 1-13.

883   "Carta a Pablo Antonio Cuadra sobre los gigantes."

[Letter to Pablo Antonio Cuadra concerning Giants]
Cultura (San Salvador, El Salvador) (October-November-December 1962): no. 26, pp. 65-74.

884 "Centinela del fuego." [Excerpt from Fire Watch-July 4, 1952] Translated by Napoleon Chow.
Ventana (University of Nicaragua) ano 2, series 2, no. 11, pp. 5, 12.

885 "Cinco poemas." [Song for Our Lady of Cobre, Elegy for Five Old Ladies, In Memory of the Spanish Poet Federico Garcia Lorca, The Ohio River-Louisville, The Reader] Abside (Mexico) 22 (1958): no. 3, pp. 290-94.

886 Conjeturas de un espectador culpable. [Conjectures of a Guilty Bystander] Translated by José Maria Valverde. Barcelona: Editorial Pomaire, 1967. 323p.

887 "Pensamientos de Merton: conjeturas de un espectador culpable." [Excerpt from Conjectures of a Guilty Bystander] La prensa literaria (Nicaragua) (28 May 1967): 1 B, 6 B.

888 "Crucifixión en Harlem." [Aubade-Harlem] Translated by Ernesto Cardenal. La prensa literaria (Nicaragua) (22 March 1964): 5 B.

889 "Cuando en el alma del sereno discípulo." [When in the Soul of the Serene Disciple] La prensa literaria (Nicaragua) (28 May 1967): 1 B.

890 Cuestiones discutidas. [Disputed Questions] Translated by Maria Josefina Martinez Alinari. Barcelona: Editora y Distribuidora, Hispano Americano, 1962. 263p.

891 Cuestiones discutidas. [Disputed Questions] Translated by Juana Martinez Alinari. Buenos Aires: Editorial Sudamericana, 1962. 402p.

892 "D. T. Suzuki: el hombre y su obra." [D. T. Suzuki: The Man and His Work] Translated by Maria Raquel Bengolea. Sur (Revista Bimenstral Sumario-Buenos Aires) (May-June 1967): no. 306, pp. 26-31.

893   El exilio y la gloria. [Exile Ends in Glory] Translated
        by Maria Espiñeira. Barcelona: Editorial Pomaire,
        1969.

894   "Los gigantes. " [Excerpt from Letter to Pablo Antonio
        Cuadra concerning Giants] La revista (Caracas,
        Venezuela) (December 1964): no. 1, pp. 2-4.

895   El hombre nuevo. [The New Man] Translated by José
        Maria Valverde. Barcelona: Editorial Pomaire,
        1966.   229p.

896   Los hombres no son islas. [No Man Is an Island]
        Translated by Gonsalo Meneses Ocón.   Buenos
        Aires: Editorial Sudamericana, 1956.   239p.

897   Incursiónes en lo indecible. [Raids on the Unspeakable]
        Translated by José Maria Valverde.   Santiago,
        Chile: Editorial Pomaire, 1967.   145p.

898   "Mensaje a los poetas. " [Message to Poets] Eco con-
        temporáneo (Argentina (1965): no. 8-9, pp. 60-62.

899   La muntanya dels set cercles. [Seven Storey Mountain]
        Translated by Guillem Colom. 2 vols.   Biblioteca
        selecta, 341, 342. Barcelona: Editorial Selecta,
        1963.   600p.

900   Niña bomba original. [Original Child Bomb] Translated
        by Mary-Lu Sananes and Jaime Lopez Sanz.   Draw-
        ings by Mateo Manaure. Edicions LAM, 1965.

901   Ningún no es una isla. [No Man Is an Island] Trans-
        lated by Herminia Grau de Durán. Barcelona:
        Edicions 62, 1966.   222p.

902   "Notas sobre arte sagrado y profano. " [Notes on
        Sacred and Profane Art] Revista de teología
        (La Plate, Buenos Aires) ano 8 (1959): no. 28-
        29, pp. 24-40.

903   Nuevas semillas de contemplación. [New Seeds of Con-
        templation] Translated by Maria Josefina Martinez
        Alinari. Buenos Aires: Editorial Sudamericana,
        1963.   248p.

904   Obras completas. [Complete Works: vol. 1.   Seven

Storey Mountain. Seeds of Contemplation. The
Waters of Siloe. Exile Ends in Glory. What Are
These Wounds? The Way of Contemplation (Includes
the following: Self-Denial and the Christian, A
Balanced Life of Prayer, What Is Contemplation?
Poetry and the Contemplative Life). Bread in the
Wilderness.] Colección Diamante. Buenos Aires:
Editorial Sudamericana, 1960-. 1693p.

905 "Ocho cantos de libertad." [Eight Songs of Freedom]
Translated by Ceferino Santos, S. J. Humanidades
(Universidad Pontificia, Comillas, Spain) 17 (Sep-
tember-December 1965): no. 42.

906 La oración en la vida religiosa. [Climate of Monastic
Prayer] Bilbao: Mensajero, 1970. 158p.

907 Pensamientos de la soledad y la paz monástica.
[Thoughts in Solitude and Monastic Peace] Trans-
lated by Maria Josefina Martinez Alinari. Buenos
Aires: Editorial Sudamericana, 1960. 147p.

908 Poemas. [Poems] Translated by Ernesto Cardenal.
Illustrated by Armando Morales. Mexico: Im-
prenta Universitaria, 1961. 108p.

909 La revolución negra. [The Black Revolution] Translated by Angeles Maragall. Presentation by José
Verde y Aldea. Colección Cristianismo y tiempo,
24. Barcelona: Editorial Estela, 1965. 97p.

910 "La revolución negra." [Excerpt from The Black Revolu-
tion] La revista (Cuaderno de ensayos literatura y
análisis cultural) (April 1966): no. 4, pp. 17-18.

911 "La revolutión negra." [Excerpt from The Black Revo-
lution] Mensaje (Santiago, Chile) (August 1964):
no. 131, pp. 346-52.

912 Semillas de destrucción. [Seeds of Destruction] Translated by José Maria Valverde. Barcelona: Editorial Pomaire, 1966. 287p.

913 La senda de la contemplación. [The Way of Contemplation:
Self-Denial and the Christian, A Balanced Life of
Prayer, What is Contemplation? Poetry and the Con-
templative Life] Trans. by A. Ugalde and M. del

Pozo.   2nd ed.   Madrid: Ediciónes Rialp, 1958.   166p.

914   "Siete cualidades del arte sagrado. "   [Seven Qualities
         of the Sacred]   Translated by José Coronel Urtecho.
         La prensa literaria (Nicaragua) (22 August 1965): 1B.

915   Tiempos de celebración.   [Seasons of Celebration]
         Translated by José Maria Valverde.   Barcelona:
         Editorial Pomaire, 1966.   251p.

916   Vida i santedat.   [Life and Holiness]   Translated by
         Josep Vallverdu Aixala.   Barcelona: Editorial
         Herder, 1965.   176p.   (Catalan edition)

917   La vida silenciosa.   [The Silent Life]   Translated by
         Maria Josefina Martinez Alinari.   Buenos Aires:
         Editorial Sudamericana, 1958.   220p.

918   "La vida solitaria al amparo de un monasterio Cister-
         ciense. "   [Solitary Life in the Shadow of a Cister-
         cian Monastery]   Cistercium ano 22 (July-September
         1970): no. 119, pp. 205-13.

919   Vida y santidad.   [Life and Holiness]   Translated by
         Josep Vallverdu Aixala.   Barcelona: Editorial
         Herder, 1964.   175p.   (Castilian edition)

920   "Virginidad y humanismo en los santos padres. "   [Vir-
         ginity and Humanism in the Latin Fathers]   Human-
         idades (Palencia) 17 (1965): no. 40, pp. 5-19.

921   "La vocación monástica y el ambiente del pensiamento
         seglar moderno. "   [Monastic Vocation and Modern
         Thought]   Cuadernos monásticos 4-5 (1967): 69-91.

SWEDISH

922   Brōd I odemarken.   [Bread in the Wilderness]   Trans-
         lated by Marianne Pauchard and Kajsa Rootzén.
         Stockholm: Petrus de Dacia, 1959.   133p.

923   Den heliga tystnaden.   [Silence in Heaven]   Translated
         by Erik Cinthio.   Malmo, Sweden: Allhem, 1956.   149p.

924   Kalled till tystand.   [Elected Silence]   Lund, Sweden:
         Gleerupska University Bookstore, 1956.   308p.

VIETNAMESE

925 Hạt giống chiêm niệm. [Seeds of Contemplation] Trans-
     lated by Thanh-Bằng.   Saigon: Phong Trào Văn
     Hóa, 1966.   271p.

926 Không ai là một hòn đảo.   [No Man Is an Island] Trans-
     lated by Thanh-Bằng.   Saigon: Phong Trào Văn
     Hóa, 1967.   274p.

RECORDINGS

927 The Merton Tapes.   12 hour-long cassettes.   Chappaqua,
     New York: Electronic Paperbacks, 1972.
          TM-1   Life and Prayer: The Desert Source.
          TM-2   Life and Prayer: Journey in Christ.
          TM-3   Life and Prayer: The Jesus Prayer.
          TM-4   Life and Contemplation.
          TM-5   Life and the Holy Spirit.
          TM-6   Life and God's Love.
          TM-7   Life and Truth
          TM-8   Life and Solitude.
          TM-9   Life and Prophecy.
          TM-10   Life and Work.
          TM-11   Life and Community.
          TM-12   Life and Celebration.

SECONDARY SOURCES

BOOKS ABOUT THOMAS MERTON

928 Baker, James T. Thomas Merton, Social Critic: A
Study. Lexington, Kentucky: University Press of
Kentucky, 1971. 173p.

929 Dell'Isola, Frank. Thomas Merton: A Bibliography.
New York: Farrar, Straus and Cudahy, 1956.
116p.

930 Griffin, John Howard. A Hidden Wholeness: The
Visual World of Thomas Merton. Photographs
by Thomas Merton and John Howard Griffin.
Text by John Howard Griffin. Boston: Houghton
Mifflin Co. , 1970. 147p.

931 _____. Thomas Merton: A Biography. Boston:
Houghton Mifflin Co. , forthcoming.

932 Higgins, John J. , S. J. Merton's Theology of Prayer.
Cistercian Studies Series, 18. Spencer, Massachusetts: Cistercian Publications, 1971. 160p.

933 Nouwen, Henri J. M. Pray to Live--Thomas Merton:
A Contemplative Critic. [Bidden om het leven]
Notre Dame, Indiana: Fides Publishers, 1972.
157p.

934 Pennington, M. Basil, O. C. S. O. (editor) The Cistercian
Spirit: A Symposium in Memory of Thomas Merton.
Cistercian Studies Series, 3. Spencer, Massachu-
setts: Cistercian Publications, 1970. 284p.

935   Rice, Edward. Man in the Sycamore Tree: The Good
      Times and Hard Life of Thomas Merton. New
      York: Doubleday and Co. , 1970. 144p.

936   Voigt, Robert J. Thomas Merton: A Different Drum-
      mer. Liguori, Missouri: Liguori Publications,
      1972. 127p.

                   ARTICLES IN BOOKS,
             NEWSPAPERS, AND PERIODICALS

937   Abdelnour, M. Madeline, S. C. N. , "Le point vierge in
      Thomas Merton. " Cistercian Studies 6 (1971):
      no. 2, pp. 153-71.

938   Abele, Carl. "Count from Sun to Tree.... " Poem in
      memory of Thomas Merton. Homenaje a Merton
      in Memoriam Ludovici to Merton, the Magician.
      Honolulu: Mele, 1969? unpaged.

939   Allchin, A. M. "A Liberator, a Reconciler. " Con-
      tinuum 7 (Summer 1969): 363-65.

940   _____. "La tradition monastique et la réforme. "
      Collectanea Cisterciensia 32 (1970): 67-74.

941   Andrews, James F. "Was Merton a Critic of Renewal?"
      National Catholic Reporter 6 (11 February 1970): 1+.

942   Atkins, Anselm. "Reflections on Merton's Notes. "
      Monastic Exchange 1 (Summer 1969): article sec-
      tion, pp. 81-84.

943   Baciu, Stefan. "Latin America and Spain in the Poetic
      World of Thomas Merton. " Revue de littérature
      comparée 41 (1967): 288-300.

944   _____. "The Literary Catalyst. " Continuum 7
      (Summer 1969): 295-305.

945   Bail, Jay. "Spiritual Revolution. " The Book Review
      (San Francisco) (1971): no. 18, pp. 6-9, 32-33,
      38.

946 Baird, M. Julien, R. S. M. "Blake, Hopkins and
       Thomas Merton." Catholic World 183 (April 1956):
       46-49.

947 Baker, James T. "An Image in the Making: Thomas
       Merton's Early Interpreters." Mississippi Valley
       Collection Bulletin (Memphis State University) (Fall
       1972): no. 5, pp. 20-28.

948 _____. "The Social Catalyst." Continuum 7 (Summer
       1969): 255-64.

949 _____. "Thomas Merton's Response to America, the
       Grim Reaper of Violence." Religion in Life 40
       (Spring 1971): 52-63.

950 _____. "Thomas Merton's World: View from a
       Monastic Window." Western Kentucky University-
       Faculty Research Bulletin 2 (1971): 43-61.

951 _____. "The Two Cities of Thomas Merton."
       Catholic World 211 (July 1970): 151-55.

952 Ball, John. "Christ in the Demented Inn." Editorial.
       Peace News (London) (23 June 1967): 4.

953 Bamberger, John Eudes, O. C. S. O. "Bernardo prope
       par, Thomas noster." Cistercian Studies 7 (1972):
       no. 2, p. 155.

954 _____. "The Cistercian." Continuum 7 (Summer
       1969): 227-41.

955 _____. "A Contemplative." Cistercian Studies 7
       (1972): no. 2, p. 153.

956 _____. "A Homily." Continuum 7 (Summer 1969):
       226.

957 _____. "Oltre l'identità." [The Cistercian] Human-
       itas 25 (1970): no. 6, pp. 601-24.

958 _____. "Qui fut Thomas Merton?" [The Cistercian]
       La vie spirituelle (Paris) (November 1969): no. 565,
       pp. 413-37.

959 _____. "The Rhinoceros." Cistercian Studies 7
       (1972): no. 2, pp. 154-55.

960 _____. "Thomas Merton as Father Louis." Con-
        densation of "The Cistercian." Catholic Digest 34
        (February 1970): 28-32.

961 _____. "The Two Cities." Cistercian Studies 7
        (1972): no. 2, p. 154.

962 Bannon, Anthony L. "Thomas Merton: A Growing
        Legend at St. Bonaventure." Magnificat (Buffalo,
        New York) (The Art Supplement) (11 March 1966):
        3-4.

963 Barnard, Roger. "Vietnam: The Paralysed Critics."
        Peace News (London) (6 October 1967): 5-6.

964 Battersby, W. J. , F.S.C. "Spiritual Reading." Review
        of Life and Holiness.   Tablet 218 (18 January 1964):
        74-75.

965 Belford, Lee A. "Thomas Merton: Saint-Scholar."
        The Witness (Dubuque, Iowa) (2 January 1969): 7-8.

966 Berrigan, Daniel, S. J.   Foreword to The Politics of the
        Gospel, by Jean Marie Paupert.   Translated by
        Gregor Roy.   New York: Holt, Rinehart and Win-
        ston, 1969, vii-xviii.

967 _____. "The Trappist Cemetery-Gethsemani Re-
        visited." A Poem. Continuum 7 (Summer 1969):
        313-18.

968 Bo, Carlo. "La poesia e la vita contemplativa di
        Thomas Merton." La fiera litteraria (Rome)
        (28 January 1951): 1, 6.

969 Bourne, Russell. "The Rain Barrel." Continuum 7
        (Summer 1969): 361-63.

970 Boyd, John D. , S. J. "Christian Imaginative Patterns
        and the Poetry of Thomas Merton." Greyfriar-
        Siena Studies in Literature 13 (1972): 3-14.

971 Bridges, Hal. American Mysticism: From William
        James to Zen.   New York: Harper and Row,
        1970, 65-72.

972 Bridget Marie, Sister. "Merton and the Metaphysicals."

Delta Epsilon Sigma Bulletin 16 (December 1971):
128-40.

973 Brock, Terry F. "Postmarked Gethsemani." Review
of Seeds of Destruction. Critic 23 (February-
March 1965): 87.

974 Browning, Mary Carmel, O. S. U. "Father Thomas
Louis Merton: (1915-) The Trappist Poet of
Contemplation," in Kentucky Authors: A History
of Kentucky Literature. Evansville, Indiana:
Keller-Crescent Co. , 1968, 214-22.

975 Bruno, Eric, O. F. M. "Letter to the Editor." Spirit
17 (March 1950): 23-25.

976 Burger, Nash K. "The Timeless Story." Review of
The Hidden Wholeness: The Visual World of
Thomas Merton, by John Howard Griffin. Boston:
Houghton Mifflin, 1970, and The Man in the Syca-
more Tree: The Good Times and Hard Life of
Thomas Merton, by Edward Rice. New York:
Doubleday and Co. , 1970. New York Times Book
Review (13 December 1970): 18-22.

977 Burke, Herbert C. "The Man of Letters." Continuum
7 (Summer 1969): 274-85.

978 Burns, Flavian, O. C. S. O. "Homélie de la messe pour
le Père M. Louis (Thomas Merton)." [Homily at
the Mass of Father M. Louis (Thomas Merton)]
Collectanea Cisterciensia 31 (1969): 7-8.

979 _____. "Homily at the Mass of Father M. Louis
(Thomas Merton)." Cistercian Studies 3 (1968):
no. 4, pp. 279-80.

980 Burton, Naomi. "I Shall Miss Thomas Merton." Cistercian Studies 4 (1969): no. 3, pp. 218-25.

981 _____. "The Path to Seven Storey Mountain." Excerpt from More Than Sentinels. New York:
Doubleday and Co. , 1964. Catholic Digest 29
(February 1965): 127-32; 29 (March 1965): 125-31;
29 (April 1965): 126-31.

982 _____. "Thomas Merton's Mountain." Excerpt

from More Than Sentinels. New York: Doubleday and Co., 1964. Sign 44 (October 1964): 46-50.

983   "Call of the Cloister." Review of Silent Life. Times Literary Supplement (London) (6 December 1957): 744.

984   Callahan, Daniel, S. J. "Unworldly Wisdom." Review of Seeds of Destruction. Commentary 39 (April 1965): 90, 92-94.

985   Cameron-Brown, Aldhelm, O. S. B. "Seeking the Rhinoceros: A Tribute to Thomas Merton." Monastic Studies 7 (September 1969): 63-73.

986   Cardenal, Ernesto. "Coplas on the Death of Merton," New Directions in Prose and Poetry, 25. Edited by James Laughlin with Peter Glassgold and Frederick R. Martin. New York: New Directions, 1972, pp. 26-39.

987   _____. "Desde la trapa." Abside (Mexico) 22 (July-September 1958): 314-24.

988   Cargas, Harry J. "Thomas Merton." A Bibliographic Essay. Catholic Library World 43 (November 1971): 131-39.

989   Casotti, Francesco. "La poesia di Thomas Merton." Aevum (Milan) 39 (May-August 1965): 370-78.

990   "Celibacy and the Ministry." Herder Correspondence 6 (September 1969): 270-84.

991   "Christian Concern." Review of Conjectures of a Guilty Bystander. Times Literary Supplement (London) (5 September 1968): 948.

992   Christopher, Michael. "Ever Changing, Ever Same." Review of Contemplative Prayer. U. S. Catholic 35 (February 1970): 47-51.

993   Clancy, William. "Karl Barth and Thomas Merton." Worldview 12 (January 1969): 11-12.

994   "Cloistered Reflections." Review of Secular Journal of Thomas Merton. Times Literary Supplement (London) (22 May 1959): 309.

995 Coffey, Warren. "The Outspoken Trappist." Review
     of Conjectures of a Guilty Bystander. Book Week
     4 (27 November 1966): 2.

996 Conner, Tarcisius, O.C.S.O. "Merton, Monastic Ex-
     change and Renewal." Monastic Exchange 1 (Sum-
     mer 1969): no. 2, article section, pp. 1-14.

997 Conover, C. Eugene. "In Defense of Solitude." Re-
     view of Disputed Questions. Christian Century 78
     (18 January 1961): 84-85.

998 Corts Grau, José. "Tomas Merton visto desde fuera
     de la orden." Cistercium 116 (1969): 315-16.

999 Davenport, Guy. "On the Eve of Conversion, a Secu-
     lar Fantasy." Review of My Argument with the
     Gestapo. Book World 3 (6 July 1969): 7.

1000 _____. "Thomas Merton RIP." National Review
     20 (31 December 1968): 1309-10.

1001 Day, Dorothy. "Thomas Merton, Trappist: 1915-
     1968." Catholic Worker 34 (December 1968): 1+.

1002 _____. "Thomas Merton, Trappist: 1915-1968."
     Catholic Mind 67 (February 1969): 30-32.

1003 Deasy, Philip. "Open Questions." Review of Life
     and Holiness. Commonweal 78 (19 April 1963):
     112-13.

1004 _____. "The Young Thomas Merton." Review of
     Secular Journal of Thomas Merton. New York
     Herald Tribune Books (9 August 1959): 11.

1005 "Death of Two Extraordinary Christians." Time 92
     (20 December 1968): 64-65.

1006 Deedy, John. "Catholic Books." Review of The
     Hidden Wholeness: The Visual World of Thomas
     Merton, by John Howard Griffin. Boston: Houghton
     Mifflin, 1970, and The Man in the Sycamore Tree:
     The Good Times and Hard Life of Thomas Merton,
     by Edward Rice. New York: Doubleday and Co.,
     1970. Critic 29 (March-April 1971): 81-82.

1007 Delgado, F. "Thomas Merton: estructura y análisis." Razón y fe 167 (January 1963): 39-48.

1008 DeLisi, Anthony. "The Prophet Is Dead." Monastic Exchange 1 (Summer 1969): no. 2, poetry section, p. 1.

1009 Dell'Isola, Frank. "Conversion and Growth of Thomas Merton." Cross and Crown 14 (March 1962): 53-61.

1010 _____. "Thomas Merton: Outlines of Growth." Catholic Book Reporter 1 (February 1961): 8-10.

1011 DeLuca, Guiseppe. "Comunicava con Dioe non fu più perchè Dio lo prese." La fiera letteraria (Rome) (15 January 1950): no. 3, p. 4.

1012 DePinto, Basil, O.S.B. "In Memoriam: Thomas Merton, 1915-1968," in The Cistercian Spirit: A Symposium in Memory of Thomas Merton. Edited by M. Basil Pennington, O.S.B. Spencer, Massachusetts: Cistercian Publications, 1969, vii-x.

1013 "Description of Cover Photos of Thomas Merton Taken by John Howard Griffin." Sign 44 (October 1964):9.

1014 Dumont, Charles, O.C.S.O. "Un contemplatif au coeur du monde: Thomas Merton." [A Contemplative at the Heart of the World: Thomas Merton] Lumen Vitae 24 (December 1969): 466-78. (French edition)

1015 _____. "A Contemplative at the Heart of the World: Thomas Merton." Lumen Vitae 24 (December 1969): 633-46.

1016 _____. "Merton's Later Life." Peace 3 (Fall-Winter 1968): 13-14.

1017 _____. "Père Louis-Thomas Merton." Collectanea Cisterciensia 31 (1969): 3-7.

1018 _____. "Prière et action dans la tradition catholique. Un témoin récent, Thomas Merton," in Recherche oecuménique: prière et action. Paris: Dessein-Tolra, 1970, 161-80.

1019   "Encuentro con un monje post-conciliar: Tomás Mer-
       ton. " La prensa literaria (Nicaragua) (28 May
       1967): 1 B, 2 B.

1020   Epple, Joques. "The Monk in the Diaspora; a reply. "
       Commonweal 80 (24 April 1964): 148-49.

1021   Evans, Illtud, O. P. "Elected Speech: Thomas Merton
       and the American Conscience. " Review of Seeds of
       Destruction. Tablet 220 (12 November 1966): 1269-
       70.

1022   _____. "Merton at Prayer. " Review of Climate of
       Monastic Prayer. Tablet 226 (15 April 1972): 351.

1023   _____. "Thomas Merton. " Tablet 223 (4 January
       1969): 22-23.

1024   _____. "Thomas Merton: 1915-1968. " Our Sunday
       Visitor (Upper Michigan Edition) (5 January 1969):
       9-10.

1025   Fabbretti, Nazareno. "Poesia e contemplazione cris-
       tiana in Thomas Merton. " Studium 49 (February
       1953): 120-23.

1026   Ferry, W. H. "The Difference He Made. " Continuum
       7 (Summer 1969): 320-22.

1027   Festa, Nicoletta. "L'Ultimo Merton. " L'Italia che
       scrive 44 (1961): 121-22.

1028   FitzGibbon, Gerald H. , S. J. "Spirituality. " Review
       of Life and Holiness. Month 31 (January 1964): 57.

1029   Flaherty, Luke. "Thomas Merton's Cables to the Ace:
       A Critical Study. " Renascence 24 (Fall 1971): 3-32.

1030   Forest, James H. "Circus of Mertons. " Review of
       The Hidden Wholeness: The Visual World of
       Thomas Merton, by John Howard Griffin. Boston:
       Houghton Mifflin, 1970, and The Man in the Syca-
       more Tree: The Good Times and Hard Life of
       Thomas Merton, by Edward Rice. New York:
       Doubleday and Co. , 1970. Commonweal 93 (22
       January 1971): 400-402.

1031 _____. "The Frozen Rainbow." Critic 28 (January-
        February 1970): 86-88.

1032 _____. "The Gift of Merton." Commonweal 89
        (10 January 1969): 463-65.

1033 _____. "Raindrops and Riddles." Review of Con-
        jectures of a Guilty Bystander. Critic 25 (April-
        May 1967): 70-72.

1034 Fowler, Albert. "Possessed by the Holy Spirit:
        Poetry of Thomas Merton and Vassar Miller."
        Approach (A Literary Quarterly) (Spring 1964):
        no. 51, pp. 33-42.

1035 Franciosa, Massimo. "Assaliro l'ollimismo?" La
        fiera letteraria (Rome) (15 January 1950): no. 3,
        p. 2.

1036 Fremantle, Anne. "Out of Time, Out of Place." Re-
        view of Mystics and Zen Masters. Reporter 37
        (21 September 1967): 50, 52.

1037 _____. "Tao for Tzu." Review of The Way of
        Chuang Tzu. Critic 25 (October-November 1966):
        108-10.

1038 Galletto, Giovanni. "Resteró mònaco fino alla mòrte."
        Famiglia cristiana (Cuneo, Italy) (4 July 1971):
        no. 27, pp. 38-42.

1039 Gavin, Rosemarie Julie, Sister. "Influences Shaping
        the Poetic Imagery of Merton." Renascence 9
        (Summer 1957): 188-97, 222.

1040 Gill, Matthias. "Evening Song: A Poem in Memory
        of Thomas Merton," in Homenaje a Merton in
        Memoriam Ludovici to Merton, the Magician.
        Honolulu: Mele, 1969? unpaged.

1041 Glimm, James York. "Exile Ends in Satire: Thomas
        Merton's Cables to the Ace." Cithara 11 (Novem-
        ber 1971): 31-40.

1042 "Goodbye, Tom Merton, Goodbye." Monastery Seasons
        (Dubuque, Iowa) (Trappist Newsletter-New Melleray
        Abbey) 10 (Spring 1969): 2.

1043   Griffin, John Howard. "In Search of Thomas Merton,"
       in Thomas Merton Studies Center, by Thomas Mer-
       ton, John Howard Griffin, and Msgr. Alfred F.
       Horrigan. Vol. 1. Santa Barbara: Unicorn Press,
       1971, 17-24.

1044   _____. "Les grand amitiés." Continuum 7 (Sum-
       mer 1969): 286-94.

1045   _____. "Merton and His Camera." Excerpt from
       A Hidden Wholeness: The Visual World of Thomas
       Merton. Boston: Houghton Mifflin, 1970. National
       Catholic Reporter 7 (20 November 1970): 6 A-7 A.

1046   Grinberg, Miguel. "El monje susurra," in Homenaje
       a Merton in Memoriam Ludovici to Merton, the
       Magician. Honolulu: Mele, 1969? unpaged.

1047   Groves, Gerald. "Fourteen Years with Thomas Mer-
       ton." Critic 21 (April-May 1963): 29-32.

1048   _____. "My Fourteen Years with Thomas Merton."
       Catholic Digest 27 (August 1963): 48-53.

1049   Guidi, Augusto. "Tutto quello che ti tocherà ti bruc-
       cerà. Thomas Merton: la sua biografia si chiude
       a Gethsemani." La fiera letteraria (Rome) (15
       January 1950): 3.

1050   Hall, Donald. "Sincerity and the Muse." Review of
       Strange Islands. Saturday Review 40 (6 July 1957):
       29.

1051   Hammer, Victor. "Four Hammer Portraits." (Cle-
       mens Von Franckenstein, Thomas Merton, Veronica
       Hammer, Martha Hauss) Good Work 28 (Summer
       1965): 78-82.

1052   Hanlon, Morgan, C. P. "The Spirituality of Thomas
       Merton." Sisters Today 44 (December 1972): 198-
       210.

1053   Hart, Patrick, O. C. S. O. "The Ecumenical Concern
       of Thomas Merton." The Lamp 70 (December
       1972): 20-23.

1054   _____. "Last Mass in the Hermitage." Continuum
       7 (Winter-Spring 1969): 213-15.

1055 _____. "Last Mass in the Hermitage." Monastic
Exchange 1 (Summer 1969): no. 2, articles section,
pp. 85-86.

1056 _____. "Last Mass in the Hermitage--A Memory
of Thomas Merton." New Book Review (October
1969): 3-4.

1057 _____. Review of A New Charter for Monasticism.
Edited and with an Introduction by John Moffitt.
Notre Dame, Indiana: University of Notre Dame
Press, 1970. Monastic Exchange 2 (Winter 1970):
no. 4, book section, pp. 10-11.

1058 _____. "Thomas Merton." The Lamp 69 (January
1971): 2.

1059 _____. "Thomas Merton's East-West Dialogue."
Monastic Exchange 2 (Winter 1970): no. 4, events
section, pp. 18-20.

1060 Harte, Barbara, and Carolyn Riley, editors. "Thomas
James Merton, 1915-1968," in 200 Contemporary
Authors. Detroit: Gale Research Company, 1969,
185-87.

1061 Haughton, Rosemary. "Bridge between Two Cultures."
Catholic World 209 (May 1969): 53-54.

1062 Hill, Joseph G. "Nuclear War and Christian Respon-
sibility." Reply to Thomas Merton's article in
Commonweal 75 (9 February 1962): 509-13.
Commonweal 76 (20 April 1962): 84.

1063 Horchler, Richard. "The Relevance of a Monk to His
Time." Review of Seeds of Destruction. Commonweal 81 (12 March 1965): 766.

1064 Horia, Vintila. "Acto sequido," in Homenaje a Merton, in Memoriam Ludovici to Merton, the Magician.
Honolulu: Mele, 1969? unpaged.

1065 Horrigan, Alfred F., Msgr. "Thomas Merton Studies
Center," in The Thomas Merton Studies Center, by
Thomas Merton, John Howard Griffin, and Msgr.
Alfred F. Horrigan. Vol. 1. Santa Barbara:
Unicorn Press, 1971, 7-11.

1066 "Housewife Joins Literati." Louisville Times (22 May 1969): 7 B.

1067 Hughes, Riley. "From Kindling to Fruit Trees." Review of Living Bread. Saturday Review 39 (17 March 1956): 22.

1068 James, Bruno S. "The Monk at Work." Review of Silence in Heaven. Tablet 208 (29 September 1956): 254-55.

1069 _____. "Thinking Out Loud." Review of Disputed Questions. Tablet 215 (8 July 1961): 659.

1070 Jessey, Cornelia. "The 'White Liberal' Myth." Way 21 (May 1965): 17-22.

1071 Johnson, Carol. "The Vision and the Poem." Review of Selected Poems. Poetry 96 (September 1960): 387-91.

1072 Justice, Donald. "Sacred and Secular." Review of Strange Islands. Poetry 91 (October 1957): 41-44.

1073 Kelly, Richard. "Thomas Merton and Poetic Vitality." Renascence 12 (Spring 1960): 139-42, 148.

1074 Kelty, Matthew, O.C.S.O. "Monastic Way of Death," in The Last Whole Earth Catalog. New York: Portola Institute/Random House, 1971, 224.

1075 _____. "Some Reminiscences of Thomas Merton." Cistercian Studies 4 (1969): no. 2, pp. 163-75.

1076 _____. "Thomas Merton, mon confrère, mon ami." [Some Reminiscences of Thomas Merton] Collectanea Cisterciensia 31 (1969): 233-42.

1077 Kennedy, X. J. "Emblems and Documents." Review of Emblems of a Season of Fury. Poetry 104 (September 1964): 378-80.

1078 Kessler, Jascha. "Keys to Ourselves." Saturday Review 53 (2 May 1970): 34-35.

1079 Kikama, Yasuwo. "Christian Arts and Spirituality." (In Japanese) Seiki (Sophia University, Japan) (September 1967): 63-69.

1080 _____. "A Dialogue between Contemplation and Religion." (In Japanese) Seiki (Sophia University, Japan) (August 1966): 37-43.

1081 _____. "Emptiness and Unity--D. T. Suzuki and Thomas Merton." (In Japanese) Koe (Diocese of Osaka, Japan) (December 1967): 35-43.

1082 _____. "The Ideas of Solitude in Thomas Merton." (In Japanese) Seiki (Sophia University, Japan) (November 1965): 74-80.

1083 _____. "In Memory of the Late Father Thomas Merton." Koe (Diocese of Osaka, Japan) (February 1969): 27-29.

1084 _____. "Thomas Merton, a Man Revolted against Himself." (In Japanese) Seiki (Sophia University, Japan) (May 1970): 43-49.

1085 _____. "Thomas Merton on Camus." (In Japanese) Seiki (Sophia University, Japan) (July 1969): 68-74.

1086 _____. "Thomas Merton's View of Poetry." (In Japanese) Seiki (Sophia University, Japan) (July 1965): 72-80.

1087 _____. "Thomas Merton's View of Peace." (In Japanese) Seiki (Sophia University, Japan) (December 1968): 52-58.

1088 Kountz, Peter. "Signpost to Beauty." Review of A Hidden Wholeness: The Visual World of Thomas Merton, by John Howard Griffin. Boston: Houghton Mifflin, 1970. Christian Century 87 (25 November 1970): 1425-26.

1089 Landess, Thomas. "Monastic Life and the Secular City." Sewanee Review 77 (Summer 1969): 530-35.

1090 Lansdell, Sarah. "In Search of Thomas Merton." Courier-Journal and Louisville Times Sunday Magazine (7 December 1969): 47-48, 50, 52, 54.

1091 LasVergnas, Raymond. "Thomas Merton." Hommes et mondes (Paris) 7 (January 1952): 148-51.

1092   Lawler, Justus George. "Balancing the Terror." Re-
        view of Breakthrough to Peace. Continuum 1
        (Spring 1963): 104-5.

1093   LeFrois, Bernard J., S.V.D. "Function of Mariology."
        American Benedictine Review 136 (April 1957): 242-
        45.

1094   Leiva, Erasmo. "For Thomas Merton--My Father
        among the Saints." Monastic Exchange 2 (Winter
        1970): no. 4, poetry section, p. 9.

1095   Lentfoehr, Mary Therese, S.D.S. "Cenobite and So-
        ciety." Review of Disputed Questions. Renascence
        14 (Winter 1961): 102-5.

1096   _____. "Cowl and Camera." Review of Silence in
        Heaven. Renascence 9 (Summer 1957): 200-205.

1097   _____. "From Harlem to Gethsemani." Review of
        Secular Journal of Thomas Merton, Prometheus:
        A Meditation, Nativity Kerygma. Renascence 12
        (Spring 1960): 149-53.

1098   _____. "The Heart of Things." Review of No Man
        Is an Island. Renascence 8 (Spring 1956): 153-57.

1099   _____. "Merton Indexed." Review of Thomas Mer-
        ton: A Bibliography, by Frank Dell'Isola. New
        York: Farrar, Straus and Cudahy, 1956. Rena-
        scence 10 (Autumn 1957): 38-41.

1100   _____. "A New Manner." Review of Strange
        Islands. Renascence 10 (Summer 1958): 214-19.

1101   _____. "No Magic." Review of Emblems of a
        Season of Fury. Renascence 17 (Fall 1964): 51-53.

1102   _____. "Out of a Cloud." America 121 (13 Decem-
        ber 1969): 585.

1103   _____. "Out of Gethsemani." Review of God Is
        My Life, Selected Poems, What Ought I to Do?
        Renascence 15 (Fall 1962): 46-50.

1104   _____. "Patristic and Titanic." Review of

Behavior of Titans and Wisdom of the Desert.
Renascence 14 (Summer 1962): 218-22.

1105 _____. "The Spiritual Writer." Continuum 7
(Summer 1969): 242-54.

1106 _____. "Thomas Merton: The Dimensions of
Solitude." American Benedictine Review 23
(September 1972): 337-52.

1107 _____. "Two Studies: The Presence of God."
Review of The Living Bread. Renascence 9
(Winter 1956): 85-89.

1108 Lieberman, Laurence. "Critic of the Month: VII. A
Confluence of Poets." Review of Cables to the
Ace and others. Poetry 114 (April 1969): 40-58.

1109 Logan, John. "Babel Theory." Review of Strange
Islands. Commonweal 66 (5 July 1957): 357-58.

1110 Lorenz, Linda. "A Modern Monk Seeks Solitude."
Tower (College of St. Mary of the Springs-
Columbus, Ohio) 28 (March 1964): 47-55.

1111 Lucchese, Romeo. "Nuove poesie tradotto." La
fiera letteraria (Rome) 17 (23 September 1962): 1.

1112 Lyons, H. P. C. "We Are Not Islands." Review of
No Man Is an Island. Month 15 (March 1956): 172-
74.

1113 McCarthy, Coleman. "Old Order Changeth: Trappists
Open Up to the World." Louisville Times (9 January 1969): A 13.

1114 _____. "Renewal Crisis Hits Trappists." National
Catholic Reporter 4 (13 December 1967): 1, 5.

1115 MacCormick, Chalmers. "The Zen Catholicism of
Thomas Merton." Journal of Ecumenical Studies 9
(Fall 1972): 802-18.

1116 McDonnell, Thomas P. "High-Water Mark." Review
of Behavior of Titans. Commonweal 74 (9 June
1961): 285-86.

1117 _____. "An Interview with Thomas Merton."
        Motive 27 (October 1967): 32-41.

1118 _____. "An Interview with Thomas Merton." U.S.
        Catholic 33 (March 1968): 28-34.

1119 _____. "On What Strange Islands?" Review of
        Strange Islands. Spirit 24 (July 1957): 85-87.

1120, _____. "Poetry of Thomas Merton." Spirit 25
        (March 1958): 23-30.

1121 _____. "Thomas Merton and the Franciscans."
        Cord 6 (January 1956): 9-13.

1122 MacEoin, Gary. "Thomas Merton: The Usefulness
        of the Useless." Ave Maria 109 (4 January 1969):
        6-7.

1123 McGreggor, Bede, O.P. "Thomas Merton on the
        Contemplative Life." New Blackfriars 53 (October
        1972): 470-76.

1124 McKenzie, John L. "Q.E.D." Critic 29 (May-June
        1971): 10, 12.

1125 McNiff, Mary Stock. "And a New World Be Borne
        from These Green Tombs." The Pilot (Boston)
        (1 March 1969): 3.

1126 Mann, Bill. "Man Picked to Write Merton's Biography
        Doesn't Look the Part." Courier-Journal (Louis-
        ville, Kentucky) (20 November 1969): 15 A.

1127 Consuelo Marie, S.B.S. "Merton or Toynbee?"
        Xavier University Studies 1: 34-38.

1128 Marty, Martin E. "Sowing Thorns in the Flesh."
        Review of Seeds of Destruction. Book Week 2
        (17 January 1965): 4.

1129 _____. "To: Thomas Merton. Re: Your Prophecy."
        National Catholic Reporter 3 (30 August 1967): 6.

1130 Mary Francis, P. C. "Poetry and the Contemplative."
        Spirit 12 (July 1955): 83-89.

1131   Mary Gilbert, S. N. J. M.   "Fusion and Fission: Two
       by Merton. " Review of New Seeds of Contempla-
       tion and Emblems of a Season of Fury.   Sewanee
       Review 72 (Autumn 1964): 715-18.

1132   Mason, H.   "Merton and Massignon. "   Muslim World
       59 (July-October 1969): 317-18.

1133   Materer, Timothy.   "Merton and Auden. "   Common-
       weal 91 (27 February 1970): 577-80.

1134   Mayhew, Alice.   "Merton against Himself. "   Common-
       weal 91 (17 October 1969): 70-74.

1135   Mayhew, Leonard F. X.   "Mystic and Poet. "   Review
       of The New Man.   Commonweal 75 (16 March 1962):
       650.

1136   Meagher, Robert E.   "Out of Soulful Silence. "   Review
       of Contemplative Prayer.   Christian Century 87
       (4 February 1970): 145.

1137   "Merton Likes Monastery but He Has Reservations. "
       Life 26 (23 May 1949): 90.

1138   "Merton Works Highlight Bellarmine Week. "   Record
       (Louisville, Kentucky) (15 November 1963): 5.

1139   "Merton's Prof to Be Ordained a Priest at 60. "   Na-
       tional Catholic Reporter 3 (26 April 1967): 1, 10.

1140   Merwin, W. S.   "Urbanity and Grace. "   Review of
       Strange Islands.   New York Times Book Review
       (26 May 1957): 28.

1141   Michelfelder, William.   "A Search beyond the Self. "
       Review of Disputed Questions.   Saturday Review 43
       (24 September 1960): 24.

1142   Moffitt, John.   "The Death of Father Louis," in A
       New Charter for Monasticism.   Edited and with
       an Introduction by John Moffitt.   Notre Dame,
       Indiana: University of Notre Dame Press, 1970,
       82-84.

1143   _____.   "New Charter for Monasticism. "   America
       120 (18 January 1969): 60-64.

1144 _____. "Thomas Merton: The Last Three Days."
Catholic World 209 (July 1969): 160-63.

1145 _____. "Thomas Merton: The Last Three Days,"
in New Theology, No. 7. Edited by Martin E.
Marty and Dean G. Peerman. New York:
Macmillan, 1970, 125-34.

1146 "Un monje peculiar." La prensa literaria (Nicaragua)
(28 May 1967): 1 B, 8 B.

1147 "Monk-Poet Merton, 53; Karl Barth, 82, Die."
National Catholic Reporter 5 (18 December 1968):
2, 9.

1148 Moody, J. N. "Meditations." Review of The Living
Bread. Commonweal 64 (6 July 1956): 354.

1149 Morrison, Richard. "Thomas Merton: The Man and
His Meaning." Laurel (Saint Bonaventure University) (Spring 1965): 14-19.

1150 Morrissey, James. "Talks with and about Thomas
Merton: Monk, Man and Myth." Courier-Journal
Sunday Magazine (Louisville, Kentucky) (23 January
1966): 15-16, 20, 25.

1151 Murray, A. Gregory, O.S.B. "Latens Deitas." Review of The Living Bread. Tablet 208 (20 October
1956): 326.

1152 Murray, Michele. "Thomas Merton, the Public Monk."
National Catholic Reporter 3 (21 December 1966): 9.

1153 Nolan, James. "Thomas Merton Center Planned at
Bellarmine." Courier-Journal (Louisville, Kentucky) (10 November 1969).

1154 Noon, W. T. "Three Traditions of Christian Spirituality." New York Times Book Review (15 March
1970): 26.

1155 Obituaries. Liturgical Arts 37 (February 1969): 52-53.

1156 _____. New York Times (11 December 1968): 1+.

1157 _____. Newsweek 72 (23 December 1968): 91.

1158 _____ . Publishers' Weekly 194 (30 December 1968):
          49.

1159 _____ . Time 92 (20 December 1968): 60.

1160 Pallis, Marco. "Thomas Merton, 1915-1968: An Ap-
          preciation of His Life and Work by One Who Knew
          Him." Studies in Comparative Religion 3 (1969):
          138-46.

1161 "Peace Council Joins (Joseph) Mulloy Draft Plea."
          Courier-Journal (Louisville, Kentucky) (22 February
          1968): 10 A.

1162 Peloquin, Charles Alexander. "To Remember."
          Liturgical Arts 37 (February 1969): 52-53.

1163 _____ . "Tribute to Thomas Merton." Providence
          Visitor (Rhode Island) (24 January 1969).

1164 Perley, M. E. "Merton Denounces Modern Ethics."
          Review of Seeds of Destruction. Louisville Times
          (Book Scene) (8 January 1965).

1165 Pillai, Joachim, O. M. I. "Remembering Thomas Mer-
          ton." Quest 4 (1969): no. 2, pp. 37-44.

1166 "Poetry: Combatting Society with Surrealism." Re-
          view of Cables to the Ace. Time 76 (24 January
          1969): 72-76.

1167 "Prayer for a Miracle." Review of Secular Journal
          of Thomas Merton. Newsweek 53 (16 February
          1959): 106.

1168 "A Priest and His Mission." Continuum 3 (Spring
          1965): 126-30.

1169 "Profile: Thomas Merton." Catholic Book Merchan-
          diser (April 1967): 12-13.

1170 Rayne, Allan. "Spirit Poets in Print." Review of
          Selected Poems. Spirit 27 (May 1960): 59-62.

1171 "Release from Despair." Review of The New Man.
          Times Literary Supplement (London) (3 August
          1962): 561.

1172   Rice, Edward. "The Pilgrimage of Thomas Merton."
       New World Outlook (March 1969): 119-23.

1173   _____. "Reflects on His Friend--Thomas Merton."
       Excerpt from Man in the Sycamore Tree: The
       Good Times and Hard Life of Thomas Merton.
       New York: Doubleday and Co., 1970. Sign 48
       (February 1969): 29-37.

1174   Riehm, Joan. "Alleluias Fill the Air at Rites for
       Monk-Poet Thomas Merton." Courier-Journal
       (Louisville, Kentucky) (18 December 1968): 13 A.

1175   _____. "Bellarmine Left Most Merton Works."
       Courier-Journal (Louisville, Kentucky) (19 April
       1969).

1176   _____. "Lover of Life Envied Promise of Death."
       Courier-Journal (Louisville, Kentucky) (15 Decem-
       ber 1968).

1177   Ross, Ilona. "Our Lady's Liveryman." The Flame
       (Little Sisters of the Assumption, London) 3
       (Autumn 1964): 15-21.

1178   Ross, Nancy Wilson. "Contemplative's Answer." Re-
       view of Mystics and Zen Masters. New York Times
       Book Review (2 July 1967): 8.

1179   Sackville-West, Edward. "Mysterium Fidei." Review
       of Living Bread. Month 17 (January 1957): 44.

1180   Saword, Anne, Sister. "Tribute to Thomas Merton."
       Cistercian Studies 3 (1968): no. 4, pp. 265-78.

1181   Schlegel, Desmond, O.S.B. "The Spiritual Life."
       Review of New Seeds of Contemplation. Tablet
       216 (15 December 1962): 1225-26.

1182   Seitz, Ron. "In Memory of Thomas Merton: Three
       Poems." U.S. Catholic and Jubilee 35 (July 1970):
       37.

1183   Shaddy, Virginia M. "Thomas Merton and No Man Is
       an Island." Catholic World 184 (October 1956): 51-
       56.

1184 "The Shaker." Replies to article by Thomas Merton,
        in Jubilee 11 (January 1964): 36-41.   Jubilee 11
        (March 1964): 5-6.

1185 Shannon, James P.   "Thomas Merton's New Mexico."
        New Mexico 49 (May-June 1971): nos. 5-6, pp. 18-
        23.

1186 Sheed, Wilfred.   "The Beat Movement, Concluded."
        Review of The Beat Generation, by Bruce Cook.
        New York: Scribner, 1971.   New York Times
        Book Review (13 February 1972): 2, 32.

1187 Shenker, Israel.   "Thomas Merton Is Dead at 53:
        Monk Wrote of Search for God."   New York Times
        (11 December 1968): 1, 42.

1188 Shuster, George N.   "Death of Merton: A 'Blessed
        Fault.' "   Record (Louisville, Kentucky) (27 March
        1969).

1189 _____.   "Merton's Death Spotlights New Wave."
        Record (Louisville, Kentucky) (31 July 1969).

1190 _____.   "Thomas Merton and the Bangkok Confer-
        ence."   True Voice (Omaha, Nebraska) (11 April
        1969): 46 A.

1191 _____.   "Was the Death of Thomas Merton a
        'Blessed Fault?' "   Catholic Messenger (Davenport,
        Iowa) (27 March 1969).

1192 Sivak, Denis.   "In Memoriam: Thomas Merton, 1915-
        1968."   Commonweal 90 (9 May 1969): 230.

1193 Speaight, Robert.   "Storming Heaven."   Review of
        Secular Journal of Thomas Merton.   Tablet 213
        (25 April 1959): 394.

1194 Stark, Philip M. , S. J.   "A Summer at Gethsemani."
        Continuum 7 (Summer 1969): 306-12.

1195 _____.   "Two Poems to a Dead Brother: Catullus
        and Thomas Merton."   Classical Bulletin 38 (April
        1962): 81-83.

1196 Steindal-Rast, David F. K.   "Recollections of Thomas

Merton's Last Days in the West." Monastic Studies
7 (1969): 1-10.

1197 Stevens, Clifford. "Thomas Merton: An Appraisal."
American Benedictine Review 18 (June 1967): 223-
26.

1198 _____. "Thomas Merton 1968: A Profile in Memoriam." American Benedictine Review 20 (March
1969): 7-20.

1199 Stuhlmueller, Carroll, C. P. "The Bible: The
Mystique of Its Literature, Traditions, and Land."
Review of Bread in the Wilderness. Bible Today
no. 59 (March 1972): 718-30.

1200 Sturm, Ralph. "Thomas Merton: Poet." American
Benedictine Review 22 (March 1971): 1-20.

1201 Sullivan, A. M. "Subliminal." Review of Cables to
the Ace. Spirit 35 (July 1968): 93.

1202 Sweeney, Francis. "The Strategy Is Love." Review
of Seeds of Destruction. New York Times Book
Review (14 February 1965): 14.

1203 Swenson, Mary. "A Poetry Chronicle." Review of
The Original Child Bomb. Poetry 102 (May 1963):
118-25.

1204 Sykes, Christopher. "The Judgement of Thomas Merton." Review of Conjectures of a Guilty Bystander.
Month 40 (October 1968): 211-12.

1205 "Thomas Merton." Time 92 (20 December 1968): 65.

1206 "Thomas Merton as Futurist." Ave Maria 109 (4 January 1969): 5.

1207 "Thomas Merton Backs Appeals of Conscientious Objector Here." Record (Louisville, Kentucky)
(22 February 1968).

1208 "Thomas Merton Center Inaugurated." Concord (Bellarmine College) 20 (19 November 1969): 1.

1209 "Thomas Merton Resigns as Novice Master." New

York Times (24 January 1965): 22.

1210 "Thomas Merton Sponsoring American Affiliate of Pax."
Pax Bulletin (London) (January 1962): no. 88, p. 6.

1211 "Thomas Merton to Be Honored by Peace Prize." Boston Globe (10 October 1963).

1212 "Thomas Merton Today." A photo essay. Jubilee 13
(March 1966): 28-33.

1213 "Thomas Merton's Early Novel." Review of My Argument with the Gestapo. Publishers' Weekly 195
(28 April 1969): 67-68.

1214 Thrapp, Dan L. "Father Merton's Continuing Search:
Reality in Religion." Courier-Journal and Louisville Times (22 December 1968): 12 A.

1215 Todd, Joyce. "For I Tell You That God Is Able of
These Stones to Raise Up Children to Abraham."
The Kentucky Alumnus 40 (Summer 1969): 10-12,
29-30.

1216 "Top of the Decade." Time 94 (26 December 1969):
41.

1217 "Trappist Author to Receive First Pax Peace Prize."
Boston Pilot (19 October 1963).

1218 Tusiani, Joseph. "Much to Praise ... Much to De-
plore." Review of Conjectures of a Guilty Bystander. Homiletic and Pastoral Review 47 (March
1967): 531.

1219 Van Doren, Mark. "Merton Unique." Michigan
Catholic (Detroit, Michigan) (2 January 1969).

1220 _____. "Thomas Merton." America 120 (4 January
1969): 21-22.

1221 Volpini, Valerio. "Nessuno giunge al cuelo da solo:
Merton apòstolo di una libertà immensa." La
fiera letteraria (Rome) (2 July 1950): no. 27, p. 6.

1222 Von Wellsheim, Anita, Sister. "Imagery in Modern
Marian Poetry." Renascence 10 (Summer 1958):
176-86.

1223 Wallace, Weldon.   "Dr. King Found a Confidant in
      Thomas Merton, Trappist."   Sun (Baltimore,
      Maryland) (6 July 1969): 26+.

1224 Walsh, M. G.   "Auden-Right Side Up."   Reply to
      article by Timothy Materer, "Merton and Auden,"
      in Commonweal 92 (27 February 1970): 577-80.
      Commonweal 92 (27 March 1970): 51, 71.

1225 Watts, Alan.   "World of the Spirit."   Review of The
      Way of Chuang Tzu.   New York Times Book Re-
      view (17 April 1966): 12.

1226 Weber, Richard, O. C. S. O.   "A Christian Monk and
      Peace."   Review of Thomas Merton on Peace.
      Catholic Worker 38 (May 1972): 6.

1227 _____.   "Merton Withdrew to Become Aware."   Re-
      view of Merton's Theology of Prayer, by John J.
      Higgins, S. J.   Cistercian Studies Series, 18.
      Spencer, Massachusetts: Cistercian Publications,
      1971.   National Catholic Reporter 8 (9 June 1972):
      11.

1228 Willis, Garry.   "A Farewell (Quite Fond) to the
      Catholic Liberals."   Critic 29 (January-February
      1971): 14-22.

1229 Wolfe, A. F.   "The Timeless Spirit and Counsel of
      the Saints."   Review of Secular Journal of Thomas
      Merton.   Saturday Review 42 (21 February 1959):
      42.

1230 Worland, Carr.   "Death of a Peacemaker."   Catholic
      Library World 40 (March 1969): 421-23.

1231 Yamasaki, Jean.   "To Merton, the Magician," in
      Homenaje a Merton in Memoriam Ludovici to
      Merton, the Magician.   Honolulu: Mele, 1969?
      unpaged.

1232 Zaehner, R. C.   "Can Mysticism Be Christian?"   New
      Blackfriars 46 (October 1964): 21-31.

1233 Zahn, Gordon C.   "Great Catholic Upheaval."   Satur-
      day Review 54 (11 September 1971): 24-27, 54-56.

1234	_____. "Original Child Monk: An Appreciation,"
	an introduction by Gordon C. Zahn to <u>Thomas Mer-</u>
	<u>ton on Peace</u>. New York: McCall Publishing Co.,
	1971, ix-xii.

1235	_____. "The Peacemaker." <u>Continuum</u> 7 (Summer
	1969): 265-73.

1236	Zanni, Pietro. "Il segno di Giona di Merton." <u>Idea</u>
	6 (14 March 1954): 4.

1237	Zeik, Michael D. "Zen Catholic." <u>Commonweal</u> 78
	(14 June 1963): 324-25.

REVIEWS OF THOMAS MERTON'S BOOKS

1238	BASIC PRINCIPLES OF MONASTIC SPIRITUALITY.
	Trappist, Kentucky: Abbey of Our Lady of
	Gethsemani, 1957. 35p.
1239	<u>Irish Ecclesiastical Record</u> 90 (September 1958):
		210.
1240	<u>Worship</u> 31 (May 1957): 369. H. Thimmesh.

1241	THE BEHAVIOR OF TITANS. New York: New Direc-
	tions, 1961. 106p.
1242	<u>Catholic World</u> 193 (August 1961): 330-31. Gervase
		Toelle, O. Carm.
1243	<u>Commonweal</u> 74 (9 June 1961): 285-86. Thomas
		P. McDonnell.
1244	<u>Critic</u> 20 (August-September 1961): 55. M. Therese
		Lentfoehr, S.D.S.
1245	<u>Dominicana</u> 46 (Summer 1961): 166
1246	<u>Jubilee</u> 9 (October 1961): 46.
1247	<u>Library Journal</u> 86 (1 May 1961): 1780. Herbert
		C. Burke
1248	<u>Renascence</u> 14 (Summer 1962): 218-22. M. Therese
		Lentfoehr, S.D.S.

1249	BREAD IN THE WILDERNESS. New York: New Di-
	rections, 1953. 146p.
1250	<u>Bible Today</u> no. 59 (March 1972): 729. Carroll
		Stuhlmueller, C.P.
1251	<u>Critic</u> 19 (February-March 1961): 61. M. Therese
		Lentfoehr, S.D.S.

1252 BREAKTHROUGH TO PEACE. Edited with an Introduction by Thomas Merton. New York: New Directions, 1962. 253p.

1253 Commonweal 79 (6 December 1963): 322. Justus
George Lawler.

1254 Continuum 1 (Spring 1963): 104-5. Justus George
Lawler.

1255 Social Action 15 (January 1964): 35-36. C. F.
Stoerker.

1256 CABLES TO THE ACE: OR, FAMILIAR LITURGIES
OF MISUNDERSTANDING. New York: New Directions, 1968. 60p.

1257 Catholic Library World 40 (September 1968): 86.

1258 Cithara 11 (November 1971): 31-40. James York
Glimm.

1259 Jubilee 15 (April 1968): 45. M. Sullivan.

1260 Library Journal 93 (1 June 1968): 2246. Elizabeth
Nelson.

1261 Poetry 114 (April 1969): 40-58. Laurence Lieberman.

1262 Publishers' Weekly 193 (19 February 1968): 88.

1263 Publishers' Weekly 195 (28 April 1969): 67-68.

1264 Renascence 24 (Fall 1971): 3-32. Luke Flaherty.

1265 Spirit 35 (July 1968): 93. A. M. Sullivan.

1266 Time 76 (24 January 1969): 72-76.

1267 Virginia Quarterly Review 44 (Summer 1968): 44.

1268 THE CLIMATE OF MONASTIC PRAYER. Foreword
by Douglas V. Steere. Cistercian Studies Series,
no. 1. Spencer, Massachusetts: Cistercian Publications, 1969. 154p.

1269 Benedictines 25 (1970): 128-34. David Kinish.

1270 Furrow (Winter 1969): 16. M. Arnall.

1271 Monastic Exchange 2 (Winter 1970): no. 4, pp. 1-2.
Stephen Leahy.

1272 New Blackfriars 51 (September 1970): 445-46.
Katherine Watson.

1273 Priest 25 (November 1969): 634. C. Dollen.

1274 Tablet 226 (15 April 1972): 351. Illtud Evans, O. P.

1275 CONJECTURES OF A GUILTY BYSTANDER. New
York: Doubleday and Co. , 1966. 328p.

1276 America 115 (10 December 1966): 781-82. Philip
M. Stark, S. J.

1277 Book Week 4 (27 November 1966): 2. Warren
Coffey.

1278   Catholic Library World 38 (May-June 1967): 611.
1279   Choice 4 (January 1968): 1256.
1280   Clergy Review 53 (October 1968): 833.   D. Nicholl.
1281   Critic 25 (April-May 1967): 70.   James H. Forest.
1282   Dominicana 52 (Spring 1967): 73.   J. Plummer.
1283   Furrow (Summer 1968): no. 5, p. 4.   D. O'Donoghue.
1284   Homiletic and Pastoral Review 67 (March 1967): 531.
             Joseph Tusiani.
1285   International Journal of Religious Education 44
             (October 1967): 17.   L. J. Gable.
1286   Jubilee 14 (March 1967): 42.   W. Claire.
1287   Library Journal 91 (15 November 1966): 5624.
             John K. Amrhein.
1288   Liguorian 55 (February 1967): 61.
1289   Liturgical Arts 35 (May 1967): 130.   Aaron W.
             Godfrey.
1290   Month 40 (October 1968): 211-12.   Christopher
             Sykes.
1291   National Catholic Reporter 3 (21 December 1966): 9.
             Michele Murray.
1292   Negro Digest 17 (December 1967): 52.   D. Llorens.
1293   New Blackfriars 49 (September 1968): 665.   Aelred
             Squire, O. P.
1294   Priest 23 (May 1967): 401-3.   John J. Eckhart.
1295   Publishers' Weekly 190 (22 August 1966): 103.
             Jessie Kitching.
1296   Publishers' Weekly 193 (8 January 1968): 69.
1297   Sign 46 (February 1967): 58.   Peter T. Rohrbach,
             O. C. D.
1298   Times Literary Supplement (London) (5 September
             1968): 948.
1299   Triumph 2 (March 1967): 34.   L. Edwards.
1300   Virginia Kirkus Service 34 (1 September 1966): 953.

1301   CONTEMPLATION IN A WORLD OF ACTION.   Intro-
             duction by Jean Leclercq, O. S. B.   New York:
             Doubleday and Co. , 1965.   384p.
1302   America 124 (8 May 1971): 490-91.   Peter J.
             Fleming.
1303   Best Sellers 31 (15 April 1971): 40-41.   Joseph
             Marie Anderson, S. S. N. D.
1304   Bloominewman (Newman Club Newsletter of the
             University of Louisville) 2 (April 1968): 1-5.
1305   Christian Century 88 (3 March 1971): 300.
1306   Cistercian Studies 7 (1972): no. 2, pp. 145-47.
             Richard Weber, O. C. S. O.
1307   Expository Times 83 (June 1972): 282.

1308   Journal of Religious Thought 28 (1971): no. 2,
          p. 149.
1309   Liturgical Arts 34 (August 1971): 113-16.   Aaron
          W. Godfrey.
1310   Monastic Exchange 3 (Summer 1971): no. 1, p. 131.
          Patrick Hart, O. C. S. O.
1311   Month 5 (Second New Series) (July 1972): 219.
          Aldhelm Cameron-Brown, O. S. B.
1312   New York Times Book Review (14 March 1971): 34-
          35.   Julius Lester.
1313   Review for Religious 30 (September 1971): 935.
          Sister P. Stork.
1314   Spiritual Life 17 (Summer 1971): 160.   Sister T.
          Benedicta.
1315   Washington Post (27 February 1971): 4 C.
          Roderick MacLeish.

1316   CONTEMPLATIVE PRAYER.   New York: Herder and
          Herder, 1969. 144p.
1317   America 121 (25 October 1969): 366-67.   Philip M.
          Stark, S. J.
1318   Christian Century 87 (4 February 1970): 145.
          Robert E. Meagher.
1319   Critic 28 (January 1970): 86-88.   James H. Forest.
1320   Encounter 31 (Summer 1970): 292.   Robert M.
          Cooper.
1321   Family Digest 25 (March 1970): 71.
1322   Library Journal 95 (15 January 1970): 163.
          Genevieve Casey.
1323   New York Times Book Review (15 March 1970): 26.
          W. T. Noon.
1324   Saint Anthony Messenger 78 (October 1970): 54.
          I. Critelli.
1325   Spiritual Life 16 (Summer 1970): 139.   A. Tittiger.
1326   Theological Studies 31 (March 1970): 207-8.
          M. Basil Pennington, O. C. S. O.
1327   U. S. Catholic 35 (February 1970): 47-51.   Michael
          Christopher.
1328   Worship 45 (August-September 1971): 445-47.
          Jane Marie Richardson, S. L.

1329   DISPUTED QUESTIONS.   New York: Farrar, Straus
          and Cudahy, 1960. 297p.
1330   America 104 (21 January 1961): 526-27.   Patricia
          Barrett, R. S. C. J.
1331   Ave Maria 93 (4 March 1961): 27.   R. J. Schoeck.
1332   Bookmark 20 (November 1960): 44.

1333   <u>Carmelus</u> 8 (1961): 269.
1334   <u>Catholic Library World</u> 32 (November 1960): 141-
          42.
1335   <u>Catholic World</u> 192 (November 1960): 115-16.   John
          J. Keating, C. S. P.
1336   <u>Catholic World</u> 203 (June 1966): 187.   Henry Peisson.
1337   <u>Christian Century</u> 78 (18 January 1961): 84-85.
          C. Eugene Conover.
1338   <u>Critic</u> 19 (December-January 1961): 30-31.   M.
          Therese Lentofehr, S. D. S.
1339   <u>Information</u> 74 (November 1960): 54.
1340   <u>Library Journal</u> 85 (1 September 1960): 2945.
          W. Charles Heiser, S. J.
1341   <u>Life of the Spirit</u> 16 (April 1962): 451.
1342   <u>Priest</u> 17 (January 1961): 72-74.   J. Joseph
          Gallagher.
1343   <u>Renascence</u> 14 (Winter 1961): 102-5.   M. Therese
          Lentfoehr, S. D. S.
1344   <u>Review for Religious</u> 21 (September 1962): 483.
1345   <u>Saturday Review</u> 43 (24 September 1960): 24.
          William Michelfelder.
1346   <u>Sign</u> 40 (January 1961): 60.   John J. Kirvan, C. S. P.
1347   <u>Spiritual Life</u> 6 (December 1960): 350.
1348   <u>Studies</u> 51 (Winter 1962): 532.
1349   <u>Tablet</u> 215 (8 July 1961): 659.   Bruno S. James.
1350   <u>Times Literary Supplement</u> (London) (16 June 1961):
          378.
1351   <u>Virginia Kirkus Service</u> 28 (15 September 1960):
          833.

1352   EMBLEMS OF A SEASON OF FURY.   A New Direc-
          tions Paperback, no. 140.   Norfolk: Connecticut:
          James Laughlin, 1963.   149p.
1353   <u>Approach</u> (Spring 1964): no. 51, pp. 33-42.   Albert
          Fowler.
1354   <u>Catholic Worker</u> 30 (May 1964): 7.   James H.
          Forest.
1355   <u>Commonweal</u> 79 (28 February 1964): 670.   Thomas
          P. McDonnell.
1356   <u>Hispania</u> 48 (September 1965): 623-24.   Pedro Juan
          Labarthe.
1357   <u>Hudson Review</u> 17 (Spring 1964): 149.   Hayden
          Carruth.
1358   <u>Poetry</u> 104 (September 1964): 378-80.   X. J. Ken-
          nedy.
1359   <u>Prairie Schooner</u> 40 (Summer 1966): 185.
1360   <u>Renascence</u> 17 (Fall 1964): 51-53.   M. Therese
          Lentfoehr, S. D. S.

1361   Review for Religious 24 (March 1965): 330.   J.
     Bowman.

1362   Sewanee Review 72 (Autumn 1964): 715-18.   Mary
     Gilbert, S. N. J. M.

1363   Southern Review 1 (Autumn 1965): 926.   R. K.
     Meiners.

1364   FAITH AND VIOLENCE: CHRISTIAN TEACHING AND
     CHRISTIAN PRACTICE.   Notre Dame, Indiana:
     University of Notre Dame Press, 1968.   291p.

1365   Ave Maria 109 (January 1969): 24-27.   W. Miller.

1366   Cistercian Studies 7 (1972): no. 2, pp. 147-48.
     Patrick Hart, O. C. S. O.

1367   Sign 48 (December 1968): 52.   Philip M. Stark, S. J.

1368   Thomist 33 (January 1969): 197-200.   Basil Cole,
     O. P.

1369   FIGURES FOR AN APOCALYPSE.   Norfolk, Connecti-
     cut: New Directions, 1947.   111p.

1370   Hudson Review 1 (1948): no. 2, p. 258.   Frederick
     Morgan.

1371   Voices (1948): no. 134, p. 60.   John Howard
     Griffin.

1372   GANDHI ON NON-VIOLENCE.   Edited with an Introduc-
     tion by Thomas Merton.   New York: New Direc-
     tions, 1965.   82p.

1373   Christian Century 82 (27 October 1965): 1326.

1374   Mountain Path 3 (April 1966): 202.   K. Swaminathan.

1375   Pacific Affairs 38 (Fall 1965-Winter 1966): 404.
     G. Woodcock.

1376   GEOGRAPHY OF LOGRAIRE.   New York: New Direc-
     tions, 1969.   153p.

1377   Saturday Review 53 (2 May 1970): 34-35.   Jascha
     Kessler.

1378   KEINER IST EINE INSEL.   [No Man Is an Island]
     Translated by Annemarie Von Puttkamer.   Zurich:
     Benziger Verlag, 1956.   247p.

1379   Stimmen der Zeit 160 (July 1957): 314.

1380   LIFE AND HOLINESS.   New York: Herder and Herder,
     1963.   162p.

1381   American Ecclesiastical Review 151 (July 1964): 71.
     Raymond F. Griese, S. J.

1382   Ave Maria 97 (30 March 1963): 28.   Gerald C.
     Hogan.

1383   Catholic Biblical Quarterly 25 (October 1963): 515-
          16. Mary Leontine, S. S. N. D.
1384   Christian Century 80 (6 March 1963): 303.
1385   Clergy Review 49 (April 1964): 262-63.
1386   Commonweal 78 (19 April 1963): 112-13.   Philip
          Deasy.
1387   Critic 21 (April-May 1963): 75-76.   Columba Cary-
          Elwes, O. S. B.
1388   Cross and Crown 15 (December 1963): 492.   Thomas
          Aquinas O'Meara, O. P.
1389   Dominicana 49 (Fall 1964): 288.
1390   Emmanuel 70 (Fall 1964): 88.   P. Hoheisel.
1391   Jubilee 11 (June 1963): 45
1392   Library Journal 88 (1 June 1963): 2255.   Andrew L.
          Bouwhuis, S. J.
1393   Liturgy 32 (October 1963): 106.   J. Crichton.
1394   Month 31 (January 1964): 57.   Gerald H. FitzGibbon,
          S. J.
1395   Pax 53 (Winter 1963): 201.   M. Small.
1396   Perspectives 8 (April 1963): 64.
1397   Princeton Seminary Bulletin 56 (May 1963): 64.
          J. R. Killinger.
1398   Religious Education 58 (November-December 1963):
          563.
1399   Review for Religious 23 (July 1964): 509.   L.
          Carlino.
1400   Sacred Heart Messenger 99 (March 1964): 51.
          D. Hurley.
1401   Spiritual Life 9 (Fall 1963): 207.   T. Kenney.
1402   Tablet 218 (18 January 1964): 74-75.   W. J.
          Battersby, F. S. C.
1403   Worship 37 (November 1963): 690.   Virginia
          Lawrence, R. C.

1404   THE LIVING BREAD.   London: Burns, Oates and
          Washbourne, 1956.   132p.
1405   America 101 (25 April 1959): 256.   Helen Dolan.
1406   Ave Maria 83 (31 March 1956): 23.   Roland Hamil-
          ton.
1407   Best Sellers 15 (15 March 1956): 386-87.   Msgr.
          Thomas J. Cawley.
1408   Blackfriars 37 (December 1956): 551.
1409   Booklist 52 (April 1956): 304.
1410   Books on Trial 14 (March 1956): 313.   M. Therese
          Lentfoehr, S. D. S.
1411   Catholic World 183 (April 1956): 72-73.   Edith
          Donovan.

1412   Chicago Sunday Tribune (4 March 1956): 2.   J. A.
         O'Brien.
1413   Clergy Review 42 (July 1957): 442.
1414   Commonweal 64 (6 July 1956): 354.   J. N. Moody.
1415   Dominicana 41 (June 1956): 152
1416   Grail 38 (May 1956): 60
1417   Library Journal 81 (15 January 1956): 191.
         Richard Breaden.
1418   Life of the Spirit 11 (December 1956): 283.
1419   Magnificat 97 (October 1956): 36.   D. Hurley.
1420   Messenger of the Sacred Heart 91 (June 1956): 76.
         J. Lynch.
1421   Month 17 (January 1957): 44.   Edward Sackville-
         West.
1422   New York Times Book Review (11 March 1956): 22.
         Richard Sullivan.
1423   Renascence 9 (Winter 1956): 85-89.   M. Therese
         Lentfoehr, S. D. S.
1424   Saturday Review 39 (17 March 1956): 22.   Riley
         Hughes.
1425   Springfield Republican (1 April 1956): 6 C.
1426   Tablet 208 (20 October 1956): 326.   A. Gregory
         Murray, O. S. B.
1427   Thought 32 (Summer 1957): 319-20.   Vincent P.
         McCorry, S. J.
1428   Today 12 (October 1956): 36-37.   Rollins Lambert.
1429   Virginia Kirkus Service 24 (1 February 1956): 86.
1430   Wisconsin Library Bulletin 52 (March 1956): 84.
1431   Worship 30 (July-August 1956): 489.   Kilian
         McDonnell.

1432 MARTHE, MARIE, ET LAZARE. Bruges: Desclée de
         Brouwer, 1956.   145p.
1433   Life of the Spirit 11 (June 1957): 575-76.   Gerard
         Meath.

1434 MONASTIC PEACE. Trappist, Kentucky: Abbey of
         Our Lady of Gethsemani, 1958.   57p.
1435   Renascence 12 (Spring 1960): 149-53.   M. Therese
         Lentfoehr, S. D. S.

1436 MY ARGUMENT WITH THE GESTAPO: A MACARONIC
         JOURNAL.   New York: Doubleday and Co. , 1969.
         259p.
1437   America 121 (16 August 1969): 102.   Philip M.
         Stark, S. J.
1438   Book World (6 July 1969): 7.   Guy Davenport.

1439   National Catholic Reporter 6 (1 October 1969): 19.
        W. Congar Beasley, Jr.
1440   New York Times (10 July 1969): 39.   J. Leonard.
1441   Saint Anthony Messenger 77 (November 1969): 58.
        T. McNally.

1442 MYSTICS AND ZEN MASTERS.   New York: Farrar,
        Straus and Giroux, 1967.   303p.
1443   America 117 (22 July 1967): 93-94.   Philip M.
        Stark, S. J.
1444   America 118 (24 February 1968): 266.   Thomas P.
        McDonnell.
1445   Choice 4 (November 1967): 1004.
1446   Christian Century 84 (10 May 1967): 627.
1447   Library Journal 92 (15 April 1967): 1628.   Donald
        J. Pearce.
1448   Liturgical Arts 36 (November 1967):   27-28.
        Aaron W. Godfrey.
1449   Liturgical Arts 38 (November 1969): 31-32.
        Aaron W. Godfrey.
1450   New York Times Book Review (2 July 1967): 8.
        Nancy Wilson Ross.
1451   New York Times Book Review (24 December 1967):
        15.   Nash K. Burger.
1452   Newsletter-Review 2 (Autumn 1967): 40-41.   D. H.
        Salman.
1453   Publishers' Weekly 191 (17 April 1967): 58
1454   Reporter 37 (21 September 1967): 50, 52.   Anne
        Fremantle.
1455   Thought 43 (Spring 1968): 139-140.   Helene Magaret.
1456   Virginia Kirkus Service 35 (15 March 1967): 391.

1457 NATIVITY KERYGMA.   Trappist, Kentucky: Abbey of
        Our Lady of Gethsemani, 1958.   16p.
1458   Renascence 12 (Spring 1960): 149-53.   M. Therese
        Lentfoehr, S. D. S.

1459 THE NEW MAN.   New York: Farrar, Straus and
        Cudahy, 1961.   248p.
1460   American Ecclesiastical Review 148 (January 1963):
        65-66.   Claude C. H. Williamson.
1461   Ave Maria 95 (3 February 1962): 26.   Bernard
        Hrico.
1462   Best Sellers 21 (15 February 1962):454.   Bernard Hrico.
1463   Booklist 58 (15 March 1962): 464.
1464   Catholic Messenger 80 (8 February 1962): 11.
        E. Pfister.

1465   Catholic World 195 (April 1962): 44.   Cornelius B.
        Outcault.
1466   Commonweal 75 (16 March 1962): 650.   Leonard F.
        X. Mayhew.
1467   Critic 20 (March 1962): 72.   John L. McKenzie,
        S. J.
1468   Cross and Crown 15 (June 1963): 232-33.   Lambert
        Trutter, O. P.
1469   Cross Currents 12 (Winter 62): 104-5.   William
        Birmingham.
1470   Dominicana 47 (Summer 1962): 223.
1471   Jubilee 9 (March 1962): 52.
1472   Library Journal 87 (1 January 1962): 104.
1473   New York Herald Tribune Books (11 February 1962):
        14.
1474   Pax 52 (Summer 1962): 88.
1475   Review for Religious 21 (September 1962): 483.
1476   Sponsa Regis 33 (August 1962): 364
1477   Times Literary Supplement (London) (3 August
        1962): 561.
1478   Virginia Kirkus Service 29 (15 November 1961):
        1033.
1479   Worship 36 (October 1962): 604-5.   Kathryn Sulli-
        van, R. S. C. J.

1480 NEW SEEDS OF CONTEMPLATION.   New York: New
        Directions, 1961.   297p.
1481   Ave Maria 95 (3 March 1962): 27-28.   Mary
        Vianney, S. S. J.
1482   Clergy Monthly 28 (May 1964): 195.   C. Cherian.
1483   Life of the Spirit 18 (July 1963): 36.
1484   Month 31 (January 1964): 57-58.   Gerald H.
        FitzGibbon, S. J.
1485   Sewanee Review 72 (Autumn 1964): 715-18.   Mary
        Gilbert, S. N. J. M.
1486   Studies 52 (Fall 1963): 334.   M. Sweetman.
1487   Tablet 216 (15 December 1962): 1225-26.   Desmond
        Schlegel, O. S. B.

1488 NO MAN IS AN ISLAND.   New York: Harcourt, Brace,
        and Co. , 1953.   264p.
1489   Blackfriars 38 (February 1957): 84-85.   Aelred
        Squire, O. P.
1490   Clergy Review 41 (September 1956): 575.
1491   Downside Review 74 (Summer 1956): 281.   P. Jebb.
1492   Irish Ecclesiastical Record 85 (May 1956): 381.
1493   Life of the Spirit 10 (March 1956): 414.   R. Velarde.

1494   Month 15 (March 1956): 172. H. P. C. Lyons.
1495   Renascence 8 (Spring 1956): 153. M. Therese
          Lentfoehr, S. D. S.
1496   Studies 45 (Autumn 1956): 368. H. Kelly.
1497   Torch 40 (June-July 1956): 5-7. Herbert E.
          Moulton.

1498 LE NOUVEL HOMME. [The New Man] Translated by
          Marie Tadié. Paris: Éditions du Seuil, 1969.
          192p.
1499   Nouvelle revue theologique 93 (October 1971): 889.
          J. Delcuve, S. J.

1500 OPENING THE BIBLE. Collegeville, Minnesota:
          Liturgical Press, 1970. 84p.
1501   Cistercian Studies 7 (1972): no. 2, p. 148. Patrick
          Hart, O. C. S. O.
1502   Monastic Exchange 3 (Summer 1971): no. 2, p. 120.
          Patrick Hart, O. C. S. O.
1503   Sisters Today 43 (March 1972): 449. Sister M.
          Wenstrup.
1504   Worship 46 (January 1972): 56-57. Richard Weber,
          O. C. S. O.

1505 ORIGINAL CHILD BOMB: POINTS FOR MEDITATION
          TO BE SCRATCHED ON THE WALLS OF A CAVE.
          Abstract Drawings by Emil Antonucci. New York:
          New Directions, 1962.
1506   Ave Maria 95 (26 May 1962): 26. Robert G.
          Strobridge.
1507   Booklist 58 (1 June 1962): 677.
1508   Library Journal 87 (1 June 1962): 2151. Gerald D.
          McDonald.
1509   Poetry 102 (May 1963): 118-25. May Swenson.

1510 A PRAYER OF CASSIODORUS. From the Treatise
          'De Anima.' Preface and Translation by Thomas
          Merton. Worcester, England: Stanbrook Abbey
          Press, 1967. 15p.
1511   Cistercian Studies 2 (1967): no. 2, pp. 187-88.
          Patrick Hart, O. C. S. O.

1512 PROMETHEUS: A MEDITATION. Lexington, Ken-
          tucky: Margaret I. King Library Press, University
          of Kentucky, 1958. 10p.
1513   Renascence 12 (Spring 1960): 149-53. M. Therese
          Lentfoehr, S. D. S.

1514   RAIDS ON THE UNSPEAKABLE. New York: New Di-
       rections, 1966. 182p.
1515   Choice 3 (January 1967): 1007.
1516   Christian Century 83 (10 August 1966): 990.
1517   Critic 25 (April-May 1967): 70-72. James H. Forest.
1518   Library Journal 91 (August 1966): 3738. W.
       Charles Heiser, S. J.
1519   National Catholic Reporter 3 (21 December 1966): 9.
       Michele Murray.
1520   Publishers' Weekly 189 (20 June 1966): 79.
       Barbara A. Bannon.

1521   REDEEMING THE TIME. London: Burns and Oates,
       1966. 187p.
1522   Month 36 (December 1966): 343. Quentin de la
       Bedoyere.

1523   REFLEXIONS D'UN SPECTATEUR COUPABLE. [Con-
       jectures of a Guilty Bystander] Translated by
       Marie Tadié. Paris: Editions Albin Michel, 1970.
       397p.
1524   Foi et vie 70 (1971): no. 1, p. 100.

1525   LA REVOLUTION NOIRE: LETTRE A UN BLANC
       LIBERAL SUIVIE DE LA LEGENDE DE TUCKER
       CALIBAN. [The Black Revolution] Translated by
       Marie Tadié. Tournai: Casterman, 1964. 128p.
1526   Etudes 321 (October 1964): 457. A. Lauras.
1527   Nouvelle revue theologique 86 (December 1964):
       1237. P. Swartenbroeckx, S. J.

1528   DIE SCHWARZE REVOLUTION. [The Black Revolu-
       tion] Translated by Hans Schmidthus. Freiburg
       im Breisgau: Herder Freiburg, 1965. 125p.
1529   World Justice 10 (March 1969): 374. L. Lauwers.

1530   SEASONS OF CELEBRATION. New York: Farrar,
       Straus and Giroux, 1964. 248p.
1531   Best Sellers 25 (1 January 1966): 386. M.
       Gregory, O. P.
1532   Catholic World 202 (February 1966): 311-12.
       Michael Glazier.
1533   Christian Century 82 (8 December 1965): 1515.
1534   Critic 24 (February-March 1966): 74-75. R. Hovda.
1535   Library Journal 91 (1 January 1966): 115. W.
       Charles Heiser, S. J.
1536   Sign 45 (January 1966): 69. John Kirvan, C. S. P.

1537   Sisters Today 37 (June 1966): 363.   T. Maeder.
1538   Virginia Kirkus Service 34 (1 February 1966): 123.
          J. F. Bernard.

1539   SECULAR JOURNAL OF THOMAS MERTON.   New
          York: Farrar, Straus and Cudahy, 1959.   270p.
1540   American Ecclesiastical Review 141 (August 1959):
          141-42.   John J. King, O. M. I.
1541   Ave Maria 89 (6 June 1959): 27.   Thomas H.
          Donohue.
1542   Blackfriars 40 (June 1959): 284-85.   Geoffrey Webb.
1543   Booklist 55 (15 February 1959): 313.
1544   Chicago Sunday Tribune (1 February 1959): 2.
          J. A. O'Brien.
1545   Christian Century 76 (21 October 1959): 1215.
          Paul Elmen.
1546   Commonweal 69 (27 February 1959): 574.   Philip
          Deasy.
1547   Critic 17 (February-March 1959): 23-24.   M.
          Therese Lentfoehr, S. D. S.
1548   Cross and Crown 13 (June 1961): 245-46.   M.
          Therese Lentfoehr, S. D. S.
1549   Extension 53 (April 1959): 26.
1550   Information 73 (March 1959): 55.
1551   Library Journal 84 (1 February 1959): 521.   Her-
          bert Cahoon.
1552   Magnificat 102 (March 1959): 37.   D. Hurley.
1553   Month 23 (January 1960): 58-59.
1554   New York Herald Tribune Books (9 August 1959): 11.
          Philip Deasy.
1555   Newsweek 53 (16 February 1959): 106.
1556   Priest 15 (October 1959): 860-62.   Vincent M.
          Eaton, S. S.
1557   Renascence 12 (Spring 1960): 149-53.   M. Therese
          Lentfoehr, S. D. S.
1558   San Francisco Chronicle (1 March 1959): 17.
1559   Saturday Review 42 (21 February 1959): 42.   A. F.
          Wolfe.
1560   Sign 38 (April 1959): 62-63.   Sister Mary Genevieve.
1561   Tablet 213 (25 April 1959): 394.   Robert Speaight.
1562   Times Literary Supplement (London) (22 May 1959):
          309.
1563   Virginia Kirkus Service 27 (15 January 1959): 49.

1564   SEEDS OF DESTRUCTION.   New York: Farrar, Straus
          and Giroux, 1964.   328p.
1565   America 112 (16 January 1965): 83-84.   Thomas F.
          Greene.

1566   Ave Maria 101 (17 April 1965): 26.   Angela Am-
         brose.
1567   Best Sellers 24 (15 January 1965): 405.   E. A.
         Dooley.
1568   Book Week 2 (17 January 1965): 4.   Martin E.
         Marty.
1569   Catholic Library World 36 (March 1965): 469.
1570   Choice 2 (June 1965): 238.
1571   Commentary 39 (April 1965): 90+.   Daniel J.
         Callahan.
1572   Commonweal 81 (12 March 1965): 766.   Richard
         Horchler.
1573   Critic 23 (February-March 1965): 87.   Terry F.
         Brock.
1574   Extension 59 (February 1965): 49.   J. Keenan.
1575   Library Journal 89 (1 June 1964): 2350.   John M.
         Christ.
1576   Louisville Times (8 January 1965): Book Scene.
         M. E. Perley.
1577   New York Review of Books 4 (11 February 1965): 6.
         Laura Carper.
1578   New York Times Book Review (14 February 1965):
         14.   Francis Sweeney.
1579   Publishers' Weekly 191 (30 January 1967): 114.
         Leonore Fleischer.
1580   Review and Expositor 64 (Summer 1967): 402-3.
         H. H. Barrette.
1581   Saturday Review 48 (6 February 1965): 39.   J. M.
         Pratt.
1582   Sign 44 (March 1965): 69-70.   Sonya Quitslund.
1583   Tablet 220 (12 November 1966): 1269-70.   Illtud
         Evans, O. P.
1584   Time 85 (5 February 1965): 116.
1585   U. S. Catholic 30 (February 1965): 65.   J. Wells.

1586 SELECTED POEMS.   With an Introduction by Mark Van
         Doren.   New York: New Directions, 1967.   140p.
1587   Critic 18 (April-May 1960): 28-29.   Thomas P.
         McDonnell.
1588   Poetry 96 (September 1960): 387-91.   Carol Johnson.
1589   Renascence 15 (Fall 1962): 46-50.   M. Therese
         Lentfoehr, S. D. S.
1590   Spirit 27 (May 1960): 59-62.   Allan Rayne.
1591   Voices (May-August 1960): no. 172, pp. 39-42.
         Lewis Turco.

1592 THE SIGN OF JONAS.   New York: Harcourt, Brace,

and Co. , 1953. 362p.

1593 Liguorian 44 (August 1956): 510.

1594 SILENCE IN HEAVEN: A BOOK OF THE MONASTIC
      LIFE. With 90 Photographs and Many Texts from
      Religious Writings (Selected and Arranged by the
      Monks of La Pierre-qui-Vire). Translated by
      Phyllis Cummins. New York: Studio Publications
      in association with Thomas Y. Crowell, 1956. 68p.
1595 America 96 (12 January 1957): 428.
1596 Blackfriars 38 (August 1957): 351.
1597 Books on Trial 15 (December 1956): 212. J.
      Meredith Tatton.
1598 Clergy Review 42 (July 1957): 437. Anne Fremantle.
1599 Commonweal 65 (7 December 1956): 257.
1600 Commonweal 65 (22 February 1957): 540. Anne
      Fremantle.
1601 Dominicana 42 (March 1957): 48.
1602 Downside Review 75 (April 1957): 179.
1603 Month 17 (January 1957): 48.
1604 New York Times Book Review (18 November 1956):
      56. Nash K. Burger.
1605 Renascence 9 (Summer 1957): 200. M. Therese
      Lentfoehr, S. D. S.
1606 Saturday Review 40 (9 March 1957): 41. Siegfried
      Mandel.
1607 Tablet 208 (29 September 1956): 254. Bruno S.
      James.

1608 THE SILENT LIFE. New York: Farrar, Straus and
      Cudahy, 1957. 178p.
1609 America 96 (23 February 1957): 587. Vincent de
      Paul Hayes.
1610 Ave Maria 85 (26 January 1957): 23-24. R. L.
      Langlois.
1611 Best Sellers 16 (15 January 1957): 355-56. Thomas
      A. Wassmer, S. J.
1612 Booklist 53 (15 January 1957): 237.
1613 Bookmark 15 (January 1957): 85.
1614 Books on Trial 15 (January-February 1957): 275-76.
      Roger Mercurio, C. P.
1615 Catholic World 184 (February 1957): 396-97.
      Frank Dell'Isola.
1616 Chicago Sunday Tribune (6 January 1957): 8. J. A.
      O'Brien.
1617 Clergy Review 44 (January 1959): 59.
1618 Cross and Crown 12 (December 1960): 491-92.
      Patrick M. J. Clancy, O. P.

1619   Irish Ecclesiastical Record 90 (September 1958):
        210-11.
1620   Library Journal 81 (1 December 1956): 2842.
        W. Charles Heiser, S. J.
1621   Life of the Spirit 12 (December 1957): 287. H.
        Farme.
1622   Magnificat 98 (April 1957): 34. D. Hurley.
1623   Messenger of the Sacred Heart 92 (August 1957):
        54. D. Hurley.
1624   New York Herald Tribune Books (13 January 1957):
        13.
1625   Saturday Review 40 (18 May 1957): 39.   John
        LaFarge.
1626   Sign 36 (March 1957): 65-66.   Richard C. Crowley.
1627   Studies 47 (Winter 1958): 473.   M. Sweetman.
1628   Times Literary Supplement (London) (6 December
        1957): 744.
1629   Virginia Kirkus Service 24 (1 December 1956): 883.

1630 SPIRITUAL DIRECTION AND MEDITATION.   College-
        ville, Minnesota: Liturgical Press, 1960.   99p.
1631   Ave Maria 93 (20 May 1961): 27.   Willard F.
        Jabusch.
1632   Cross and Crown 13 (March 1961): 110-12.   M.
        Therese Lentfoehr, S. D. S.
1633   Dominicana 46 (Summer 1961): 166.
1634   Furrow 12 (February 1961): 137.   L. Ryan.
1635   Priest 17 (September 1961): 780.   Raymond Gribbin.
1636   Renascence 15 (Fall 1962): 46.
1637   Review for Religious 21 (May 1962): 279.

1638 STRANGE ISLANDS: POEMS.   New York: New Direc-
        tions, 1957.   102p.
1639   America 97 (13 July 1957): 408.   Edwin Morgan.
1640   Books on Trial 15 (June-July 1957): 468.   A. Vader.
1641   Commonweal 66 (5 July 1957): 357-58.   John Logan.
1642   Dominicana 42 (December 1957): 368.
1643   Library Journal 82 (1 May 1957): 1248.   Gerald D.
        McDonald.
1644   Life of the Spirit 12 (April 1958): 476.   Geoffrey
        Webb.
1645   New York Times Book Review (26 May 1957): 28.
        W. S. Merwin.
1646   Poetry 91 (October 1957): 41-44.   Donald Justice.
1647   Prairie Schooner 31 (Fall 1957): 171-81.   Joseph
        Warren Beach.
1648   Renascence 10 (Summer 1958): 214-19. M. Therese
        Lentfoehr, S. D. S.

1649   Saturday Review 40 (6 July 1957): 29.   Donald Hall.
1650   Spirit 24 (July 1957): 85.   Thomas P. McDonnell.
1651   Sponsa Regis 28 (July 1957): 307.
1652   Voices (January-April 1958): no. 165, pp. 35-37.
        John T. Napier.

1653   THE TEARS OF THE BLIND LIONS.   New York: New
        Directions, 1949.   32p.
1654   Hopkins Review 3 (1949): no. 2, p. 54.   Manly
        Johnson.

1655   THOMAS MERTON ON PEACE.   Edited with an Intro-
        duction by Gordon C. Zahn.   New York: McCall
        Publishing Co. , 1971.   269p.
1656   America 125 (21 August 1971): 102-3.   Peter T.
        Rohrbach, O. C. D.
1657   American Ecclesiastical Review 165 (November
        1971): 208-9.   John J. Higgins, S. J.
1658   Catholic Worker 38 (May 1972): 6.   Richard Weber,
        O. C. S. O.
1659   Cistercian Studies 7 (1972): no. 2, p. 152.   Patrick
        Hart, O. C. S. O.
1660   Critic 29 (May-June 1971): 85-86.   John Deedy.
1661   Library Journal 96 (1 June 1971): 1993.   Joseph A.
        Boissé.
1662   Sign 51 (November 1971): 48.   Thomas Heath, O. P.

1663   A THOMAS MERTON READER.   New York: Harcourt,
        Brace and World, 1962.   553p.
1664   Catholic Worker 30 (April 1964): 5.   James H.
        Forest.
1665   Commonweal 77 (22 February 1963): 575.   Francis
        J. Lally.
1666   Critic 21 (December 1962-January 1963): 82.
1667   Dominicana 48 (Spring 1963): 70.
1668   Library Journal 87 (15 October 1962): 3676-77.
        Lloyd W. Griffin.
1669   New York Times Book Review (2 December 1962):
        6, 44.   David Dempsey.
1670   Ramparts 2 (May 1963): 96.   Helen B. English.
1671   Review for Religious 22 (November 1963): 703.
        J. Lotze.
1672   Sign 42 (March 1963): 70.

1673   THOUGHTS IN SOLITUDE.   New York: Farrar, Straus
        and Cudahy, 1958.   124p.
1674   Apostolic Perspectives 3 (September 1958): 32.
        B. Murchland.

1675   Ave Maria 88 (19 July 1958): 27.   John Mahoney.
1676   Best Sellers 18 (15 August 1958): 188.   Henry J.
            Erhart, S. J.
1677   Booklist 54 (1 June 1958): 548-49.
1678   Bookmark 17 (May 1958): 195.
1679   Catholic Worker 24 (June 1958): 1+.   R. Steed.
1680   Catholic World 187 (July 1958): 319-20.   Ashley
            Pettis.
1681   Critic 16 (June-July 1958): 46.   M. Therese Lent-
            foehr, S. D. S.
1682   Cross and Crown 13 (December 1961): 475.   Hilary
            Freeman, O. P.
1683   Dominicana 43 (Fall 1958): 333.
1684   Furrow 13 (April 1962): 242.
1685   Irish Ecclesiastical Record 92 (July 1959): 64-65.
1686   Jubilee 6 (July 1958): 38.   Peter Walsh.
1687   Magnificat 101 (June 1958): 37.   D. Hurley.
1688   Manchester Guardian (7 November 1958): 5.
1689   Messenger of the Sacred Heart 93 (October 1958):
            43.   J. Nash.
1690   Month 21 (March 1959): 194-95.
1691   Priest 14 (August 1958): 694-95.   F. J. Mueller.
1692   Sign 38 (August 1958): 62-63.   Paula Bowes.
1693   Virginia Kirkus Service 26 (15 May 1958): 373.

1694   LES TITANS.   [Selections from The Behavior of Titans
            and Raids on the Unspeakable]   Translated by Marie
            Tadié.   Paris: Editions du Seuil, 1971.   123p.
1695   Nouvelle revue theologique 93 (October 1971): 889.
            L. Denis.

1696   THE TRUE SOLITUDE: SELECTIONS FROM THE
            WRITINGS OF THOMAS MERTON.   Selected by
            Dean Wally.   Kansas City: Hallmark Éditions,
            1969.   61p.
1697   Cistercian Studies 7 (1972): no. 2, pp. 148-49.
            Patrick Hart, O. C. S. O.

1698   VIE ET SAINTETE.   [Life and Holiness]   Translated
            by Marie Tadié.   Paris: Editions du Seuil, 1966.
            154p.
1699   Verbo caro 21 (1967): no. 82, pp. 107-8.

1700   THE WAY OF CHUANG TZU.   Free Renderings of
            Selections from the Works of Chuang Tzu, Taken
            from Various Translations.   New York: New Di-
            rections, 1965.   159p.

1701   Booklist 62 (1 January 1966): 421.
1702   Choice 3 (April 1966): 127.
1703   Critic 25 (October-November 1966): 108-10.   Anne
        Fremantle.
1704   Expository Times 82 (September 1971): 355-56.
1705   New York Times (12 June 1966): section 4, p. 7.
1706   New York Times Book Review (17 April 1966): 12,
        14.   Alan Watts.
1707   Prairie Schooner 40 (Fall 1966): 28.   P. Callahan.
1708   Renascence 18 (Spring 1966): 163-66.   M. Therese
        Lentfoehr, S. D. S.
1709   Virginia Kirkus Service 33 (15 September 1965):
        1016.

1710 WHAT OUGHT I TO DO?   SAYINGS FROM THE
      DESERT FATHERS OF THE FOURTH CENTURY
      (Verba Seniorum).   Translated by Thomas Merton.
      Lexington, Kentucky: Stamperia del Santuccio,
      1959.   35p.
1711   Renascence 15 (Fall 1962): 46-50.   M. Therese
        Lentfoehr, S. D. S.

1712 THE WISDOM OF THE DESERT: SAYINGS FROM THE
      DESERT FATHERS OF THE FOURTH CENTURY
      (Verba Seniorum).   Translated by Thomas Merton.
      New York: New Directions, 1960.   81p.
1713   Catholic World 193 (August 1961): 330-31.   Gervase
        Toelle, O. Carm.
1714   Commonweal 74 (9 June 1961): 285-86.   Thomas P.
        McDonnell.
1715   Critic 20 (August-September 1961): 55.   M. Therese
        Lentfoehr, S. D. S.
1716   Doctrine and Life 13 (September 1963): 492.
        D. Mould.
1717   Dominicana 46 (Summer 1961): 166.
1718   Jubilee 9 (October 1961): 46.
1719   Library Journal 86 (1 May 1961): 1780-81.
        Charles G. Gros.
1720   Life of the Spirit 16 (October 1961): 157.
1721   Month 26 (July 1961): 61-62.
1722   Renascence 14 (Summer 1962): 218.   M. Therese
        Lentfoehr, S. D. S.
1723   Sign 41 (November 1961): 72.

1724 ZEN AND THE BIRDS OF APPETITE.   New York:
      New Directions, 1968.   141p.
1725   Choice 6 (May 1969): 382.

1726   Library Journal 93 (15 October 1968): 3791.
         Donald J. Pearce.
1727   New York Times Book Review (30 March 1969): 46.
         Francis Sweeney.
1728   Publishers' Weekly 194 (9 September 1968): 59.
1729   Virginia Kirkus Service 36 (15 August 1968): 960.

REVIEWS OF BOOKS ABOUT THOMAS MERTON

1730   BAKER, James T. Thomas Merton, Social Critic: A
         Study. Lexington, Kentucky: University Press of
         Kentucky, 1971. 173p.
1731   American Ecclesiastical Review 166 (April 1972):
         282-83. John J. Higgins, S. J.
1732   Booklist 68 (15 January 1972): 401.
1733   Cistercian Studies 7 (1972): no. 2, p. 152. Patrick
         Hart, O. C. S. O.
1734   Courier-Journal and Louisville Times (7 May 1972):
         5 F. John Filiatreau.
1735   Critic 30 (December 1971-January 1972): 87-88.
         John Deedy.
1736   Library Journal 96 (1 September 1971): 2656.
         Genevieve Casey.
1737   Review for Religious 31 (July 1972): 676. T. Lay.

1738   GRIFFIN, John Howard. A Hidden Wholeness: The
         Visual World of Thomas Merton. Photographs by
         Thomas Merton and John Howard Griffin. Text by
         John Howard Griffin. Boston: Houghton Mifflin
         Co. , 1970. 147p.
1739   America 124 (20 February 1971): 181-82. Thomas
         P. McDonnell.
1740   Best Sellers 30 (15 November 1970): 358.
1741   Catholic Worker 36 (October-November 1970).
         Sister Donald Corcoran.
1742   Choice 8 (May 1971): 369.
1743   Christian Century 87 (25 November 1970): 1425-26.
         Peter Kountz.
1744   Cistercian Studies 7 (1972): no. 2, pp. 150-51.
         Patrick Hart, O. C. S. O.
1745   Commonweal 92 (22 January 1971): 400-403. James
         H. Forest
1746   Courier-Journal and Louisville Times (4 October

1970): 5.   P. Shirley Williams.
1747   Critic 29 (February-March 1971): 81.   John Deedy.
1748   Last Whole Earth Catalog. New York: Portola
        Institute/Random House, 1971. 423. Stewart
        Brand.
1749   Frontier 14 (August 1971): 189-90. Richard Weber,
        O. C. S. O.
1750   Library Journal 96 (1 January 1971): 69. Genevieve
        Casey.
1751   Liturgical Arts 34 (August 1971): 113-16. Aaron
        W. Godfrey.
1752   National Catholic Reporter 7 (19 February 1971): 11.
        Michele Murray.
1753   New York Times Book Review (13 December 1970):
        18, 20, 22. Nash K. Burger.
1754   Saint Anthony Messenger 78 (April 1971): K.
        Katafiasz.
1755   Sisters Today 42 (January 1971): 282.   H. Witzman.
1756   Southwest Review 56 (Winter 1971): 7.   Robert
        Bonazzi.

1757 HIGGINS, John J. , S. J.   Merton's Theology of Prayer.
        Cistercian Studies Series, 18.   Spencer, Massachu-
        setts: Cistercian Publications, 1971. 160p.
1758   America 128 (10 March 1973): 224-25.   Patrick
        Hart, O. C. S. O.
1759   Cistercian Studies 7 (1972): no. 2, pp. 149-50.
        Patrick Hart, O. C. S. O.
1760   National Catholic Reporter 8 (9 June 1972): 11.
        Richard Weber, O. C. S. O.
1761   Review for Religious 31 (July 1972): 681.   T. Lay.
1762   Sign 52 (March 1973): 45-47. Gertrude Wilkinson,
        O. SS. R.
1763   Tablet 226 (15 April 1972): 351. Illtud Evans, O. P.

1764 NOUWEN, Henri J. M.   Pray to Live--Thomas Merton:
        A Contemplative Critic. [Bidden om het leven]
        Notre Dame, Indiana: Fides Publishers, 1972.
        157p.
1765   America 128 (10 March 1973): 224-25.   Patrick
        Hart, O. C. S. O.

1766 PENNINGTON, M. Basil, O. C. S. O. (editor) The Cis-
        tercian Spirit: A Symposium in Memory of Thomas
        Merton. Cistercian Studies Series, 3.   Spencer,
        Massachusetts: Cistercian Publications, 1970.
        284p.

1767   Theological Studies 31 (December 1970): 769-70.
          William F. Hogan, C. S. C.

1768   RICE, Edward. Man in the Sycamore Tree: The Good
          Times and Hard Life of Thomas Merton. New York:
          Doubleday and Co., 1970. 144p.
1769   Best Sellers 30 (15 January 1971): 445. Sister
          Gregory Duffy.
1770   Cistercian Studies 7 (1972): no. 2, pp. 155-61.
          John Eudes Bamberger, O. C. S. O.
1771   Commonweal 93 (22 January 1971): 400-402. James
          H. Forest.
1772   Courier-Journal and Louisville Times (31 January
          1971): 5. John Filiatreau.
1773   Critic 29 (February-March 1971): 81. John Deedy.
1774   Homiletic and Pastoral Review 71 (April 1971): 77-
          79. Regis Appel.
1775   Library Journal 96 (1 March 1971): 828. Genevieve
          Casey.
1776   Liturgical Arts 34 (August 1971): 113-16. Aaron
          W. Godfrey.
1777   Monastic Exchange 2 (Winter 1970): no. 4, pp. 7-
          10. Tarcisius Connor, O. C. S. O.
1778   National Catholic Reporter 7 (19 February 1971): 11.
          Michele Murray.
1779   New York Times Book Review (13 December 1970):
          18, 20, 22. Nash K. Burger.
1780   Saint Anthony Messenger 78 (April 1971): 55. K.
          Katafiasz.
1781   Sign 50 (February 1971): 52. R. Shaw.
1782   Sisters Today 42 (February 1971): 336. Mary
          Stock McNiff.
1783   Time 96 (7 December 1970): 59. Mayo Mohs.
1784   Washington Post (27 February 1971): 4 C. Roderick
          MacLeish.

          SELECTED THESES AND DISSERTATIONS

1785   Baker, James Thomas. "Thomas Merton: The
          Spiritual and Social Philosophy of Union." Doctoral
          dissertation, Florida State University, 1968.

1786   Campbell, Susan Margaret. "The Poetry of Thomas

Merton: A Study in Theory, Influences and Form."
Doctoral dissertation, Stanford University, 1954.

1787   Cotty, Marion William, Sister. "Christian Wisdom and
Merton's Poetry." Master's thesis, Boston College,
1966.

1788   Dufresne, Oliver J. "Thomas Merton: A Man for
Our Times." Master's thesis, Catholic University
of Louvain, 1971.

1789   Flaherty, Luke. "Mystery and Unity as Anagogical
Vision in Thomas Merton's Cables to the Ace: A
Critical Explication." Master's thesis, University
of Louisville, 1969.

1790   Gavin, Rosemarie Julie, Sister. "An Analysis of
Imagery in Selected Poems of Thomas Merton."
Master's thesis, Catholic University of America,
1951.

1791   Hergott, Alvin W. "Thomas Merton and the Image of
Man." Master's thesis, University of Saskatchewan,
1971.

1792   Higgins, John J., S.J. "The Theology of Prayer in
the Spirituality of Thomas Merton." Doctoral dissertation, Catholic University of America, 1971.

1793   Kelly, Frederic Joseph, S.J. "The Social Dimension
of Religious Man in the Writings of Thomas Merton." Doctoral dissertation, Catholic University
of America, 1972.

1794   McInery, Dennis Quentin. "Thomas Merton and Society:
A Study of the Man and His Thought against the
Background of Contemporary American Culture."
Doctoral dissertation, University of Minnesota, 1969.

1795   Voigt, Robert J. "Thomas Merton: A Different
Drummer." Master's thesis, Saint Cloud State
College, 1971.

1796   Whalen, James M. "Merton on Non-Violence." Jersey
City State, n. d.

FOREIGN LANGUAGE BOOKS
ABOUT THOMAS MERTON

1797   Belmonte, Leopoldo.   Thomas Merton ... y envolvia
       en humo su cara y sus palabras.   Barcelona:
       Ediciones Domingo Savio, 1964.   28p.

1798   Casotti, Francesco.   "Thomas Merton," in Saggi e
       ricerche.   Milan: Societa editrice vita e pensiero,
       1962.   83p.

1799   Nouwen, Henri J. M.   Bidden om het leven.   Het
       contemplatief engagement van Thomas Merton.
       [Pray to Live--Thomas Merton: A Contemplative
       Critic] Bilthoven: Amboboeken, 1970.   139p.

FILMS

1800   Thomas Merton Documentary Film of the Bangkok Con-
       ference.   (Motion Picture) Nederlandse Televisie
       Stichting (Roman-Catholic Section), December 9-10,
       1968.

1801   Thomas Merton Documentary Film of the Bangkok Con-
       ference.   (Motion Picture) Radiotelevisione Italiana,
       December 9-10, 1968.

"A la reconquête du paradis"
749
A Moretti, Emanuel 822
"Abbey of Our Lady of Geth-
semani" see "Interlude:
..."
Abbott, Elisabeth 136
Abdelnour, M. Madeline,
S. C. N. 937
Abele, Carl 938
"Abnegation and Holiness" 36-38
"Absurdity in Sacred Decora-
tion" 22-24, 879
"Action and Non-Action" 113
"Active Life" 113
"Acto sequido" (Horia) 1064
Adam de Perseigne 325, 757
Adaption of the Monastic Life 1
"Adult Christians" 36-38
"Advent" 89
"Advent: Hope or Delusion?"
85
"The Advent Mystery" 202
"Advice to a Young Prophet"
26, 203
"Advising the Prince" 113
"Aegeus in Prison" (Cortes)
697
Aelred of Rievaulx 153
African Genesis (Ardrey) 356,
388, 389
"After the Night Office-Geth-
semani Abbey" 89, 106
"Agàpe" 41, 42
Agliano, Maria Teresa Galleani
D' 817, 818
Agnes, Saint 89, 103, 104,
106, 644, 650
Aguas de Siloe 854
"Air" (Cortes) 698

Aixala see Vallverdu Aixala,
Josep
"Albada-Harlem" 880
"Albert Camus and the Church"
119, 204
Albert Camus' 'The Plague':
Introduction and Commen-
tary 2
Alberic, Saint 89
Alberti, Rafael 473, 680
Aldea, José Verde y 909
Alexandre, Marianne 162
Alexandria 126
All the Collected Short Poems,
1956-1964 (Zukofsky) 453, 591
"All the Way Down" 82
Allchin, A. M. 939-940
"Alleluias Fill the Air at Rites
for Monk-Poet, Thomas
Merton" (Riehm) 1174
Alone with God (Leclercq) 172
"Ambiguities of the Secular" see
"Is the World a Problem?..."
Ambrose, Angela 1566
American Mysticism (Bridges)
971
Amrhein, John K. 1287
"An Analysis of Imagery in
Selected Poems of Thomas
Merton" (Gavin) 1790
Anastacio, Timoteo Amoroso,
O. S. B. 855, 860, 863
"The Anatomy of a Cliché"
see "Red or Dead:..."
"The Anatomy of Melancholy"
103, 104
"And a Few More Cargo Songs" 31
"And a New World Be Borne
from These Green Tombs"
(McNiff) 1125

"And So Goodbye to Cities" 26
"And the Children of Birming-
ham" 26, 592
Anderson, Joseph Marie,
S. S. N. D. 1303
Andrade, Carlos Drummond de
106, 681
Andrews, Edward Deming 88,
152
Andrews, Faith 152
Andrews, James F. 941
"Anger" (Vallejo) 731
Anglican Devotion (Stranks)
205
"Anglicanisme" 206
"The Annunication" 103, 104,
106
Anselm, Saint 333, 476, 478,
493, 565
"The Answer of Minerva:
Pacifism and Resistance in
Simone Weil" 28, 105
"Answers on Art and Freedom"
80, 207
An Anthology of Contemporary
American Poetry see A
Controversy of Poets:...
An Anthology of Modern Rus-
sian Religious Thought
(Schmemann) see Ultimate
Questions:...
"An Anti-Poem: Plessy vs.
Ferguson: Theme and Varia-
tions" 208, 641
Antoninus, Brother, O. P. 242
Antonucci, Emil 70, 1505
"Apertura e vita claustrale"
808
"Aphorisms for a Contempla-
tive" (Carmody) 357
Apocalypse of the New World
791
Apokalypse der neuen Welt 791
"Apologies" 113
"Apologies to an Unbeliever"
28, 351; see also "How It
Is:..."
Appel, Regis 1774
"April" 89
Arasteh, A. Reza 320
Ardrey, Robert 356, 388, 389
Arendt, Hannah 215
"An Argument--of the Passion

of Christ" 106, 593
"Ariadne" 89
"Ariadne at Labyrinth" 89
Arias, Maximino 221
Arnall, M. 1270
Arrayo, J. Alvarez 564
"Art and Morality" 120
"Art and Spirituality" 106
"Art and Worship" 209
L'Art irlandais (Henry) 210
"The Art of William Congdon"
121
"El arte sacro y la vida es-
piritual" 881
"As a Man Is, So He Prays
..." 106
"As Man to Man" 211, 754
Ascensão para a verdade 855
The Ascent to Truth 764, 855
"The Ascetic Doctrine of Saint
John of the Cross" see
"Light in Darkness:..."
"Asceticism and Sacrifice" 106
Ascetismo e monachesimo pre-
benedittino (Turbessi) 212
"Ash Wednesday" 85, 89, 106,
213
Asian Journal 3
"Asian Letter" 761
"Asian Letter I" 214
"Aspects of the Spiritual Life"
107, 108
"Assaliro l'ollimismo?" (Fran-
ciosa) 1035
"At School in England" 106
"At the Gates of Aerea" (Char)
694
"At This Precise Moment of
History" 31
Atarashii hito 177, 838
Atkins, Anselm 942
"Atlas and the Fat Man" 6,
80, 106
"Atlas Watches Every Evening"
80, 122; see also "Mar-
tin's Predicament:..."
"Atonement" 41, 42
L'Attende dans le silence: Le
Père Marie-Joseph Cassant,
O. C. S. O. (Chenevière) 173
"Aubade-Harlem" 89, 106,
880, 888
"Aubade: Lake Erie" 89, 106

"Aubade--The City" 89
Auden, Wystan Hugh 593, 614,
    1133, 1224
"Auden--Right Side Up"
    (Walsh) 1224
Augustine, Saint 81, 88, 553
Auschwitz 405
"Auschwitz: A Family Camp"
    105, 215
Authors Take Sides on Vietnam:
    Two Questions on the War
    in Vietnam Answered by the
    Authors of Several Nations
    193
"The Autobiography of a Crow
    Indian" see "War and
    Vision:..."
"Autumn" (Maritain) 475, 721,
    727
"Autumn Floods" 113
Averroes 664
The Awakening of a New Con-
    sciousness in Zen (Suzuki)
    216

"Babel Theory" (Logan) 1109
Baciu, Stefan 943, 944
Bagguley, John 193
Bail, Jay 945
Baird, M. Julien, Sister 946
Bakardios, Antonius 807
Baker, Augustine 54-56
Baker, James T. 928, 947-
    951, 1730, 1785
A Balanced Life of Prayer
    904, 913
"Balancing the Terror" (Law-
    ler) 1092
Baldwin, James 88
Ball, John 952
Balthasar, Hans Urs von 582,
    793
Bamberger, John Eudes,
    O.C.S.O. 953-961, 1770
Bangkok 164, 1190, 1800,
    1801
Bannon, Anthony L. 962
Bannon, Barbara A. 1520
" 'Baptism in the Forest':
    Wisdom and Initiation in
    William Faulkner" 123, 217
Barbieri, Antonio 826

Barnard, Roger 963
Barnes, Joseph 527
"The Baroness" 106
"A Baroque Gravure" 594,
    595
Barrett, Patricia, R.S.C.J.
    1330
Barrette, H. H. 1580
Barsotti, Divo 258
Barth, Karl 993, 1147
Barthes, Roland 583
"Barth's Dream" 18, 19, 218
"Barth's Dream and Other Con-
    jectures" 219
Basic Principles of Monastic
    Spirituality 4, 5, 805, 845,
    1238-1240
Basil, Saint 76
Battersby, W. J., F.S.C.
    964, 1402
"Be My Defender" 82
Beach, Joseph Warren 1647
Beasley, W. Congar, Jr. 1439
"Beast" see "Landscape:..."
Beat Generation (Cook) 1186
"Beat Movement, Concluded"
    (Sheed) 1186
Behavior of Titans 6, 1104,
    1116, 1241-1248
Belford, Lee A. 965
Belgian translations 737-739
Bellarmine College Library
    127
"Bellarmine Left Most Merton
    Works" (Riehm) 1175
Belmonte, Leopoldo 1797
Belziaux, Pierre 210
Benedict, Saint 13, 95-98
Benedict XII 13
Benedicta, T., Sister 1314
"The Benedictines" 95-98
The Benedictines: A Digest
    for Moderns (Knowles) 220
"The Benedictines of Galicia"
    221
Bengolea, Maria Raquel 882,
    892
Bernard, J. F. 1538
Bernard, Saint 22-24, 85,
    106, 136
Bernard de Clairvaux 189
Bernard of Clairvaux 136
Bernardini, Franco 829, 833,
    834

Bernardo de Claraval 856
"Bernardo prope par, Thomas
     noster" (Bamberger) 953
Berrigan, Daniel, S. J. 966,
     967
Berrigan, Philip, S. S. J. 151
Beschouwend gebed 744
Bettencourt, Estêvao, O. S. B.
     867
"Betting on the Whole Human
     Species" see "Teilhard's
     Gamble:..."
"Beyond Identity" see "The
     Cistercian"
"Beyond the Sacred: A Letter
     to the Editor" 222
Bhagavad Gita 190
The Bhagavad Gita As It Is
     190
Bhaktivendanta, Swami, A. C.
     190
"The Bible--The Mystique of
     Its Literature, Traditions,
     and Land" (Stuhlmueller)
     1199
Bidden om het leven. Het con-
     templatief engagement van
     Thomas Merton (Nouwen)
     933, 1799
"The Biography" 89
"Birdcage Walk" 89, 103, 104
Birmingham, William 1469
"Birth of the Sun" (Cuadra)
     708, 713
"Bisschop Robinson zonder
     Mythe: Het Debate over
     'Eerlijk voor God' " 792
The Black Revolution: Letters
     to a White Liberal 7, 88,
     176, 223-226, 378, 780, 799,
     800, 830, 909-911
"Black Stone on Top of a White
     Stone" (Vallejo) 732
Blake, William 106, 227, 679,
     946
"Blake and the New Theology"
     227
"Blake, Hopkins, and Thomas
     Merton" (Baird) 946
Blecker, P. M., O. S. B. 415
Blessed Are the Meek: The
     Roots of Christian Nonvio-
     lence 8, 105, 228, 402, 758

"A 'Blessed Fault' " see
     "Death of Merton:..."
"Blessed Virgin Mary Com-
     pared to a Window" 596
Bo, Carlo 968
"A Body of Broken Bones" 63,
     64, 106
Bogaard, Cyprianus van den
     746
Boissé, Joseph A. 1661
"The Bombarded City" 106
Bonaventure, Saint 86, 87
Bonazzi, Robert 1756
A Book of Shaker Furniture
     see Religion in Wood:...
A Book of the Monastic Life
     see Silence in Heaven:...
Boom!!! Poemo de Lucovico
     Silva 184
Boosman, J. 737
Borel, Jacques 784
"Boris Pasternak and the Peo-
     ple with Watch Chains" 229
Bourgoint, Jacques 291
Bourne, Russell 969
Bouwhuis, Andrew L. 1392
Bowes, Paula 1692
Bowman, J. 1361
Boyd, John D., S. J. 970
"Bramachari" 106
Brault, Jacques 694
Bread in the Wilderness 170,
     745, 824, 867, 904, 922,
     1199, 1249-1251
The Bread Is Rising 671
"The Bread of God" 41, 42
Breaden, Richard 1417
Breakthrough to Peace 9, 105,
     149, 168, 458, 1092, 1252-
     1255
"The Breath of Nature" 113
"Bridge between Two Cultures"
     (Haughton) 1061
Bridges, Hal 971
Bridget Marie, Sister 972
A Brief Account of Zazen
     (Wienpaha) see The Matter
     of Zen:...
Brink, J. K. van den 747
Brock, Terry F. 973, 1573
Brōd I odemarken 922
Brood in de woestijn 745
"Brothers and Aggiornamento"
     230

Browning, Mary Carmel,
O. S. U.   599, 661, 677, 974
Bruno, Eric, O. F. M.   975
Bruno, Saint 494
Buddhism 302, 391
"Buddhism and the Modern
World" 54-56, 231
"Buddhist Monasticism and
Meditation" see "Two
Letters of the Late Thomas
Merton:..."
Buffevent see François de
Sainte Marie, Father
Buhler, Charlotte 267
"Building Community on God's
Love" 232
Burden, Shirley 39, 150
Burger, Nash K.   976, 1451,
1604, 1753, 1779
"Buried with Ceremony in the
Teutoburg Forest" see
"Two British Airmen:..."
Burke, Herbert C.   977, 1247
Burnett, Whit 191
"The Burning of Papers, the
Human Conscience and the
Peace Movement" 233
Burns, Flavian, O. C. S. O.
978, 979
Burton, Naomi 3, 980-982;
see also Stone, Naomi
Burton
"A Buyer's Market for Love?"
234

Cables to the Ace: Or, Fa-
miliar Liturgies of Mis-
understanding 10, 597, 809,
1029, 1041, 1108, 1166,
1201, 1256-1267, 1789
Cablogrammi e profezie 809
Cahoon, Herbert 1551
"Cairo 1326" 31
Caliban, Tucker 88, 176, 428,
780, 1525
"Calicut" 31
"Call of the Cloister" 983
Callahan, Daniel, S. J. 984,
1571
Callahan, P. 1707
"Called out of Darkness" 36-
38, 60-62, 235

"Calypso's Island" 89
"The Camaldolese" 95-98
"Cambridge" 106
Cameron-Brown, Aldhelm,
O. S. B. 985, 1311
Campbell, Susan Margaret
1786
Camus, Albert 2, 119, 204,
236, 538, 547, 1085
Camus: Journals of the Plague
Years" 236
"Can Mysticism Be Christian?"
(Zaehner) 1232
"Can We Choose Peace" 81,
88, 237
"Can We Survive Nihilism?"
238, 848
"Cana" 89, 106
"The Candlemas Procession"
89, 598
"Canon Law" 239
"Canto Bilinque" see "Letters
to Che:..."
"The Captives--A Psalm" 89,
106
Cardenal, Ernesto 138, 157,
183, 552, 682-686, 877,
880, 888, 908, 986, 987
Cargas, Harry J. 988
"Cargo Catechism" 31
"Cargo Songs" 31
Carlino, L. 1399
"Carmelite Deserts" 22-24
"Carmelite Origins" 22-24
Carmody, J. , S. J. 357
"Carol" 89, 599
"A Carol" 600
Carper, Laura 1577
Carrera Andrade, Jorge 106,
687-692
Carruth, Hayden 598, 611,
665, 1357
"Carta a Pablo Antonia Cuadra
con respecto a los gigantes"
882
"Carta a Pablo Antonio Cuadra
sobre los gigantes" 883
"Carta a un poeta sobre Vallejo"
240
"The Carthusians" 95-98
Cary-Elwes, Columba, O. S. B.
1387
"The Case for a Renewal of

Eremitism in the Monastic
State" 20
"The Case for Eremitism" 20
Casey, Genevieve 1322, 1736,
1750, 1775
Casotti, Francesco 989, 1798
Cassant, Marie-Joseph,
O. C. S. O. 173
Cassian 76
Cassian and the Fathers 11
Cassiodorus, Senator, Flavius
Magnus Aurelius 693
"A Catch of Anti Letters" 241
"The Catholic and Creativity:
Theology of Creativity" 242
"Catholic Books" (Deedy) 1006
Catholic Critics 170
Catholic Encyclopedia for
School and Home 125, 128,
146, 192
A Catholic Prayer Book 163
"Catullus and Thomas Merton"
see "Two Poems to a Dead
Brother:..."
Cawley, Thomas J., Msgr.
1407
"Ce Xochitl: The Sign of
Flowers" 31
"Celebrating Giacometti" 694
"Celibacy and the Ministry"
990
"The Cell" 20, 243
"Cenobite and Society" (Lent-
foehr) 1095
"Cenobite Life" 95-98
"Centinela del fuego" 884
"Ceremony for Edward Dahl-
berg" 601
Ceylonese translations 740,
741
Chagall" (Maritain) 475, 722,
727
Chaigne, Hervé 759
Chakravarty, Amiya 3
"Challenge of Responsibility"
244
"Chant to Be Used in Proces-
sion Around a Site with
Furnaces" 26, 106, 602,
603
Char, René 694
"Charity" 36-38
Chautard, Jean Baptiste,

O. C. S. O. 156, 695
Les chemins de la joie 750
Chenevière, Marie-Etienne,
O. C. S. O. 173
Cherian, C. 1482
Chiang Ping-Lun 742
"Chilam Balam" 31
"Children in the Market Place"
106
"Children of the Resurrection"
4, 5
Chinese translations 742
Chow, Napoleon 884
"Les chrétiens et guerre
atomique" 751
Les chrétientés celtiques
(Loyer) 245
Christ, John M. 1575
"Christ in the Demented Inn"
(Ball) 952
Christ in the Desert 12
Christ in the Wilderness: The
Wilderness Theme in the
Second Gospel and Its Basis
in the Biblical Tradition
(Mauser) 580
"Christ, the Way" 36-38, 246
"Christian Action in World
Crisis" 105, 247
"Christian Arts and Spirituality"
(Kikama) 1079
"The Christian as Peacemaker"
81, 88, 248
Christian Commitment: Essays
in Pastoral Theology (Rah-
ner) 249
"Christian Concern" 991
"Christian Culture Needs
Oriental Wisdom" 106, 250
"Christian Duties and Perspec-
tives" see "Peace:..."
"Christian Ethics and Nuclear
War" 105, 251
Christian Faith and Zen Exper-
ience 841
"Christian Freedom and Monas-
tic Formation" 252
"Christian Humanism" 253
"Christian Humanism in the
Nuclear Era" 81
"Christian Ideals" 36-38
"Christian Imaginative Patterns
and the Poetry of Thomas

Merton" (Boyd) 970
"The Christian in the Diaspora"
   88
"The Christian in Time of
   Change" 254
"The Christian in World Cri-
   sis" 81, 88, 105, 852
"A Christian Looks at Zen"
   118, 124
"The Christian Message in a
   Changing World" 255
"A Christian Monk and Peace"
   (Weber) 1226
"Christian Morality and Nuclear
   War" 256
"Christian Perfection" 125
Christian Roots of Nonviolence
   [sic] see Blessed Are the
   Meek:...
"The Christian Sacrifice" 41,
   42
"Christian Self-Denial" 85
"Christian Solitude" 20
"Christian Solitude: Notes on
   an Experiment" 257
Christian Teaching and Chris-
   tian Practice see Faith
   and Violence:...
"Christian Wisdom and Mer-
   ton's Poetry" (Cotty) 1787
"Christianisme et question
   raciale aux Etats-Unis" 752
Christianisme Russe (Barsotti)
   258
"Christianity and Defense in the
   Nuclear Age" 105
"Christianity and Mass Move-
   ments" 259
"Christianity and Race in the
   United States" 752
"Christianity and Totalitarian-
   ism" 22-24
"Christmas Night" 106
The Christmas Sermons of
   Blessed Guerric of Igny
   158
Christopher, Michael 992,
   1327
"Christ's Love for Us" 41,
   42
Chuang Tzu 113, 114, 748,
   790, 874, 1037, 1225, 1700
"Chuang Tzu's Funeral" 113

"Church and Bishop" 260
"Church and Bishop in Saint
   Ignatius of Antioch" 85
"The Church and the 'Godless
   World' " 81, 862
"The Church in World Crisis"
   261
"The Church Sanctifies Her
   Members" 36-38
Cimnaghi, M. R. 836
"Cinco poemas" 885
Cinthio, Erik 923
"Circus of Mertons" (Forest)
   1030
"The Cistercian" (Bamberger)
   954, 960
The Cistercian Order from the
   Death of St. Benedict to the
   Reform of Benedict XII
   (1153-1335) 13
The Cistercian Spirit: A Sym-
   posium in Memory of
   Thomas Merton 934, 1012,
   1766, 1767
"The Cistercians" 95-98
"Cistercians and Study" 262
"The City" see "Aubade:..."
"The City's Spring" 25
"Civil Rights of the Monk in
   Roman and Canon Law: The
   Monk as 'Servus' " 415
Claire, W. 1286
Clancy, Patrick M. J., O.P.
   1618
Clancy, William 993
"Classic Chinese Thought" 54-
   56
Clemens, Senator, Titus
   Flavius 126, 696
Clement of Alexandria: Selec-
   tions from the 'Protreptikos'
   126, 696
"A Clever Strategem; Or, How
   to Handle Mystics" 31
Il clima della preghiera monas-
   tica 810
"Le climat de la prière monas-
   tique" 753
"The Climate of Mercy" 264
The Climate of Monastic
   Prayer 14-16, 265, 744,
   753, 789, 810, 906, 1022,
   1268-1274; see also Con-
   templative Prayer

"Cloistered Reflections" 994
"The Cloud" (Maritain) 475,
    727
"Cocoa Tree" (Carrera
    Andrade) 687, 691
Coffey, Warren 995, 1277
Cogul, Fort I. 312
"Cold War and Theology" 106
Cole, Basil, O. P. 1368
Colla, Rienzo 820
The Collected Works of
    Ramana Maharsi 266
A Collection of Contemplatives
    see Come, South Wind:...
Colom, Guillem 899
Colombas, G. M. 343
"Columbia" 106
"Combatting Society with
    Surrealism" see "Poetry:
    ..."
"Come Dance in Baronies" 694
Come, South Wind: A Collec-
    tion of Contemplatives 143,
    144, 147, 196
"Come to the Marriage Feast"
    41, 42
Come to the Mountain: New
    Ways and Living Traditions
    in the Monastic Life 17
"Comment on Charlotte Buhler,
    Tom Stonier, Walter A.
    Weisskopf" 267
"Comments on Dr. Prince's
    and Dr. Savage's Paper on
    Mystical States and Regres-
    sion" 268
Commission histoire de l'ordre
    de Citeaux 189
"Communication or Commu-
    nion?" see "Symbolism:
    ..."
"Communion and Its Effects"
    41, 42
"Community" 269
"Community: A Monastic Wit-
    ness" (Shaw) 269
"Community of Pardon" 85
"Community, Politics, and
    Contemplation" 270
"La comparsa oriente" 25
"Comunicava con Dioe non
    fu più perchè Dio lo
    prese" (DeLuca) 1011

"Concentration" 101, 102
"The Concept of Acedia" 271
"Concerning the Collection in
    the Bellarmine College Li-
    brary--A Statement, Novem-
    ber 10, 1963" 127
"Il concilio e la vita dei
    religiosi" 811
"A Conference on Prayer,
    Calcutta, October 27, 1968"
    272
The Confessions of Nat Turner
    (Styron) 577
Confessions of the Man of the
    Twentieth Century 806
"A Confluence of Poets" see
    "Critic of the Month:
    VII. ..."
"Confucius and the Madman"
    113
Congdon, William 121, 581
"A Congo" 25
Conjectures of a Guilty By-
    stander 18, 19, 273, 738,
    778, 806, 813, 871, 886,
    887, 991, 995, 1033, 1204,
    1218, 1275-1300, 1523
Conjeturas de un espectador
    culpable 886, 887
Conner, Tarcisius, O. C. S. O.
    996, 1777
Conover, C. Eugene 997,
    1337
"The Conquest of France:
    Speech and Testimonials,
    1941" 52, 274
"Conquistador, Tourist, and
    Indian" 106, 275
Consuelo Marie, S. B. S. 1127
Het contemplatief engagement
    van Thomas Merton see
    Bidden om het leven:...
"Un contemplatif au coeur du
    monde: Thomas Merton"
    (Dumont) 1014
"Contemplation" 128
"Contemplation and Dialogue"
    54-56
"Contemplation and Ecumenism"
    276
Contemplation in a World of
    Action 20, 277, 1301-1315
"A Contemplative" (Bamberger)
    955

"The Contemplative and the
  Atheist" 20, 278
"A Contemplative at the Heart
  of the World: Thomas
  Merton" (Dumont) 1015
A Contemplative Critic (Nou-
  wen) see Pray to Live--
  Thomas Merton:...
"Contemplative Life" 20
"The Contemplative Life in the
  Modern World" 28, 279
Contemplative Prayer 21, 992,
  1136, 1316-1328; see also
  Climate of Monastic Prayer
"Contemplatives and the Crisis
  of Faith" 280
"Contemplative's Answer"
  (Ross) 1178
"Il contemplativo e l'àteo" 812
Contemporary Philosophical
  Explorations see The
  Critique of War:...
A Controversy of Poets: An
  Anthology of Contemporary
  American Poetry 595, 604,
  610, 642, 651, 655, 670
"Convergence of the Many"
  694
Conversatio Morum 27, 281,
  316
"Conversion and Growth of
  Thomas Merton" (Dell'Isola)
  1009
Cook, Bruce 1186
Cooper, Robert M. 1320
"Coplas on the Death of Mer-
  ton" (Cardenal) 986
Corcoran, Donald, Sister 1741
Cornell, Thomas C. 119, 161
Coronel Urtecho, José 914
"Correspondence: Note on
  Joyce's Ulysses" 282
Cortes, Alfonso 26, 697-707
Cortese, Don 35
Corts Grau, José 998
Cotty, Marion William, Sister
  1787
"The Council and Monasticism"
  129
"The Council and Religious
  Life" 283, 811
"Count from Sun to Tree..."
  (Abele) 938

"Cowl and Camera" (Lentfoehr)
  1096
"Cracking the Safe" 113
"Creative Silence" 284
Crichton, J. 1393
Cristofolini, M. E. 342
The Criterion Book of Modern
  American Verse 593, 614
Critelli, I. 1324
"Critic of the Month: VII. A
  Confluence of Poets"
  (Lieberman) 1108
"A Critical Observer of the
  Archetypal Myth" see
  "Mircea Eliade:..."
The Critique of War: Contem-
  porary Philosophical Explor-
  ations 197
"Cross Fighters--Notes on a
  Race War" 285
Crowley, Richard C. 1626
"Crucifixion en Harlem" 888
"Crusoe" 89, 106
Cuadra, Pablo Antonio 376,
  708-718, 882, 883
"Cuando en el alma del sereno
  discípulo" 889
"Cuba" 86, 87
"Cuba Project: Letter to the
  Editor" 286
Cuestiones discutidas 891
"The Cultural Cold War: Com-
  ments" 287
Cummins, Phyllis 92-94, 148,
  1594
Cuneo, Paul 134
"Cup with a Jaguar for the
  Drinking of Health" (Cuadra)
  709, 713
Cuttat, Jacques-Albert 520
"Cutting Up an Ox" 113
Cyprian, Saint 318
"Czas i liturgia" 847
Czechoslavakian translations
  743
"Czy przetrwamy nihilism?"
  848

"D. T. Suzuki: el hombre y
  su obra" 892
"D. T. Suzuki: The Man and
  His Work" 118, 288

Dahlberg, Edward 601
"Dance of Death" 289
Daniel-Rops, Henri 136
"Danish Non-Violent Resistance
    to Hitler" 105
Dario, Ruben 649
Da Schio, L. 819
Davenport, Guy 999, 1000,
    1438
Davidson, William, M. D. 242
Day, Dorothy 88, 545, 1001,
    1002
"Day of a Stranger" 112, 290,
    398
"Day Six O'Hare Telephone"
    31
"Day unto Day" 106
De Anima 74, 693, 1510
Deasy, Philip 1003, 1004,
    1386, 1546, 1554
"Death" 130
"The Death of a Holy Terror:
    The Strange Story of Frère
    Pascal" 291
"Death of a Peacemaker"
    (Worland) 1230
"The Death of Father Louis"
    (Moffitt) 1142
"The Death of God and the End
    of History" 28, 292
"The Death of God, I: The
    Death of God and the End
    of History" 292
"Death of Merton: A 'Blessed
    Fault' " (Shuster) 1188
"Death of Two Extraordinary
    Christians" 1005
"Het Debate over 'Eerlijk voor
    God' " see "Bisschop Robin-
    son zonder Mythe:..."
DeBezieux, Ch. Roux 258
Deedy, John 1006, 1660,
    1735, 1747, 1773
DeGasztold, Carmen Bernos
    776
DeKay, George 159
De la Bedoyere, Quentin 1522
Delcuve, J., S.J. 1499
Delgado, F. 1007
"Delhi" 31
DeLisi, Anthony 1008
Dell'Isola, Frank 929, 1009,
    1010, 1099, 1615

Delp, Alfred 154, 392
DeLuca, Guiseppe 1011
Dempsey, David 1669
"Demythologizing Bishop Robin-
    son: The 'Honest to God'
    Debate" 293, 792
Den heliga tystnaden 923
Denis, L. 1695
DePinto, Basil, O.S.B. 1012
"Description of Cover Photos
    of Thomas Merton Taken by
    John Howard Griffin" 1013
"Desde la trapa" (Cardenal)
    987
"The Desert Source" see
    "Life and Prayer:..."
"Despairing Man Draws a Ser-
    pent" (Cuadra) 710
"Detachment" 63, 64
"Devout Meditation in Memory
    of Adolf Eichmann" 80,
    105, 131, 294, 295, 399
D'Helfta, Gertrude, Saint 496
"Dialog with Mister Clapcott"
    31
"Dialogue About the Hidden
    God" (Nicolas of Cusa) 720
"Dialogue and Renewal" 20
"Dialogue and Renewal in the
    Contemplative Life" 296
"A Dialogue between Contem-
    plation and Religion"
    (Kikama) 1080
Diario di un testimòne colpevole
    813
Diario secolare 814
Diario secular 857
Diarios (Jovellanos) 299
"The Diary of Nishida Kitaro"
    (Knauth) see "Life Is
    Tragic:..."
The Diaspora 81, 88, 417,
    418, 763, 1020
Dickey, Terrell 39
Diekmann, Godfrey, O.S.B.
    88
"Dieu n'est pas un problème"
    754
"The Difference He Made"
    (Ferry) 1026
A Different Drummer (Kelly)
    426
A Different Drummer (Voigt)

see Thomas Merton:...
A Digest for Moderns
The Benedictines:...
"The Dimensions of Solitude"
(Lentfoehr) see "Thomas
Merton:..."
Direção espiritual e meditacão
858
Direction spirituelle et médita-
tion 755
Direzione spirituale e medita-
zione 815
"Dirge for a Town in France"
89
"Dirge for the City of Miami"
25
"Dirge for the Proud World"
106
"Dirge for the World Joyce
Died in" 25
Disch, Robert 199
"The Discovery of God" 112
Disputed Questions 22-24,
422, 777, 829, 870, 890,
891, 997, 1069, 1095, 1141,
1329-1351
Dissertations 1785, 1786,
1792-1794
"Distractions" 63, 64
"Distractions in Prayer" 132
"Dr. King Found a Confidant
in Thomas Merton, Trap-
pist" (Wallace) 1223
La doctrine spirituelle de
Théophane le Reclus: le
coeur et l'esprit (Spidlik)
297
Doherty, Catherine de Hueck
88
Dolan, Helen 1405
Dollen, C. 1273
"Dom Vitalis te Gethsemani"
298
"Don Gaspar Melchor de Jove-
llanos" 299
Donohue, Thomas H. 1541
Donnelly, Sally 391
Donovan, Edith 1411
Dooley, E. A. 1567
Dorn, Edward 512
"Doubt and Asceticism" 106
Dougherty, Jude 129
"Drake in the Southern Sea"

(Cardenal) 682-684
"Dramas of the Evening" 10
"The Drawings of Thomas
Merton--A Note by the Ar-
tist" 300
"A Dream at Arles on the
Night of the Mistral" 26
"Dream of the Rood" 301
"Dream of the Rood and
Anglo-Saxon Monasticism"
(Fleming) 301
Dru, Alexander 582
"Dry Places" 89, 106
"Du Bouddhisme au Catholic-
isme" 302
Du-Bos, Juliette Charles 762
Duffy, Gregory, Sister 1769
Dufresne, Oliver J. 1788
Duhamel, Pierre Albert 169
"Duke Hwan and the Wheel-
wright" 113
Dumont, Charles, O. C. S. O.
325, 757, 1014-1018
Dumoulin, Heinrich, S. J. 534
Dunaway, Philip 159, 195
Dunne, Finley P., Jr. 135,
165
"Duns Scotus" 89, 604
Duran, Herminia Grau de 901
Dutch Catholic Television 1800
Dutch translations 744-748
"Dylan Thomas" 106
"Dzules" 31

"Early Blizzard" 10, 605
"The Early Legend" 80, 133
"Early Mass" 103, 104
Early Poems/1940-42 25
The Earth Is the Lord's:
Poems of the Spirit 668
"Earthquake" 82
"East" 31
East-West Dialogue 165, 520,
1059
"East with Ibn Battuta" 31
"East with Malinowski:
Tupuseleia" 31
Easter Sermons (Guerric of
Igny) 341
"Easter: The New Life" 85,
134, 303, 773, 869
Eaton, Vincent M., S. S. 1556

"Ecclesiastical Baroque"   304
Eckhart, John J.   1294
The Ecological Conscience:
   Values for Survival   199
"The Ecumenical Concern of
   Thomas Merton" (Hart)
   1053
"Ecumenism and Monastic Re-
   newal"   305
"Ecumenism and Renewal"   20
Edwards, L.   1299
Eichmann, Adolf   131, 294,
   295, 311, 399
"Eight Freedom Songs"   82,
   759, 905
Eight Sacred Poems   see
   Reflections on Love:...
Elected Silence   924
"Elected Speech: Thomas
   Merton and the American
   Conscience" (Evans)   1021
"Elegy for a Trappist"   306
"An Elegy for Ernest Heming-
   way"   26, 106, 606
"An Elegy for Five Old Ladies"
   26, 89, 607, 885
"Elegy for James Thurber"
   26, 608, 609
"Elegy for the Monastery Barn"
   89, 103, 104, 106, 610, 611
Eliade, Mircea   404
"Elias: Variations on a Theme"
   103, 104, 106, 307
Eliot, T. S.   106
Ellul, Jacques   535
Elmen, Paul   1545
Emblemi di un'età di violenza
   816
"Emblems and Documents"
   (Kennedy)   1077
Emblems of a Season of Fury
   26, 682, 685, 686-690, 692,
   697-699, 701, 702, 704-712,
   714-718, 721-726, 728, 731-
   734, 793, 1077, 1101, 1131,
   1352-1363
"Emptiness and Unity" (Kikama)
   1081
"The Empty Boat"   113
"Encuentro con un monje post-
   conciliar: Tómas Merton"
   1019
"The Endless Inscription"

   see   "Prologue:..."
"An Enemy of the State"   28,
   105, 308
English, Helen, B.   1670
"The English Mystics"   54-56,
   309, 310
English Spirituality (Thornton)
   206
Enomija-Lasalle, H. M. , S. J.
   590
"Epitaph for a Public Servant:
   In Memoriam, Adolf Eich-
   mann"   311
Epple, Joques   1020
Eranos Yearbook   216, 555
"Eremitism"   312
"Eremitism in Mallorca"   313
"L'Eremitisme a la catalunya
   nova" (Cogul)   312
Erhart, Henry J. , S. J.   1676
Espiñeira, Maria   893
Essays in Pastoral Theology
   (Rahner)   see   Christian
   Commitment:...
Essays in the American Catho-
   lic Tradition   169
"Estais Muertos" (Vallejo)   733
"Ethics and War: A Footnote"
   314
"Etienne Gilson"   106
"The Eucharist and the Church"
   41, 42
"Eurydice" (Maritain)   475, 727
Evans, Fallon   166
Evans, Harold   155
Evans, Illtud, O. P.   1021-1024,
   1274, 1583, 1763
Evans, Melvin   195
"Evening"   89, 106
"Evening of the Visitation"   612
"Evening Prayer"   82
"Evening Song: A Poem in
   Memory of Thomas Merton"
   (Gill)   1040
"Evening: Zero Weather"   89,
   106
"Events and Pseudo Events"
   28, 315
"Ever Changing, Ever Same"
   (Christopher)   992
"Everything That Is, Is Holy"
   63, 64, 106
Examination of Conscience and

'Conversatio Morum' 27
316
Exile Ends in Glory 893, 904
"Exile Ends in Satire: Thomas
    Merton's Cables to the Ace"
    (Glimm) 1041
El exilio y la gloria 893
"The Existence of God" 36-
    38
Exomologēseis tou anthrōpou
    eikostou aiōnos 806
"Exploits of a Machine Age"
    103, 104
"Extemporaneous Remarks"
    135
"Extracts from a Monastic
    Notebook" see "Few
    Questions and Fewer An-
    swers:..."
"The Extremists, Black and
    White: The Mystique of
    Violence" 317
"Eye Is a Dog Howling in the
    Distance" (Cuadra) 711,
    713

Fabbretti, Nazareno 1025
"The Face: Tertullian and
    St. Cyprian on Virgins"
    318
"Faces of Girls Looking at
    Themselves in the River"
    (Cuadra) 713
"Faction du Muet" (Char) 694
"Faith" 63, 64
Faith and Violence 28, 105,
    756, 817, 818, 1364-1368
"Faith in God" 36-38
"The Fall" 26, 613
"False Mysticism" 106
Familiar Liturgies of Misunder-
    standings see Cables to
    the Ace:...
"A Family Camp" see
    "Auschwitz:..."
"A Farewell (Quite Fond) to
    the Catholic Liberals"
    (Wills) 1228
Farme, H. 1621
"The Fasting of the Heart"
    113
Fateful Moments That

Revealed Men and Made
    History see Turning
    Point:...
"Father Merton's Continuing
    Search: Reality in Religion"
    (Thrapp) 1214
"Father Moore, Dan Walsh,
    Jacques Maritain" 106
"Father Thomas Louis Merton:
    (1915-) The Trappist Poet
    of Contemplation" (Browning)
    974
Faulkner, William 123, 217,
    518
Faulkner: A Collection of
    Critical Essays 518
"Faulkner and His Critics"
    see "The Sounds Are
    Furious"
Fede e violenza 817
Fede, resistènza, protesta
    818
Fénelon, François de Salignac
    de la Mothe- 187, 188
Fénelon Letters 187
Ferry, W. H. 1026
Festa, Nicoletta 1027
"Few Questions and Fewer
    Answers" 319
"The Fiery Arrow" 22-24
"The Fight for Peace" 106
"Fighters" 694
"The Fighting Cock" 113
"Figures for an Apocalypse"
    614, 793, 1369-1371
Filiatreau, John 1734, 1772
"Filii et haeredes Dei" 4, 5
Films 1800, 1801
"Final Integration in the Adult
    Personality" (Arasteh) 320
"Final Integration: Toward a
    'Monastic Therapy' " 20,
    321
"Fire Watch--July 4, 1952"
    884
First, Wesley 160
"First Lesson about Man" 615,
    616
FitzGibbon, Gerald H., S. J.
    1028, 1394, 1484
"The Five Enemies" 113
Flaherty, Luke 1029, 1789
"Flannery O'Connor: A Prose

Elegy" 80, 322
Fleischer, Leonore 1579
Fleming, J. 301
Fleming, Peter J. 1302
"Flesh and Spirit" 36-38
"Flight from Benevolence" 113
"Flight from the Shadow" 113
"The Flight into Egypt" 89, 106
"The Flight of Lin Hui" 113
"Flower of the Fruit" (Cortes) 699, 700
Foi et violence 756
"A Footnote from Ulysses" see "Peace and Revolution:..."
For a Renewal of Eremitism in the Monastic State 29, 323
"For I Tell You That God Is Able of These Stones to Raise up Children to Abraham" (Todd) 1215
"For My Brother: Reported Missing in Action, 1943" 89, 106
"For Robert Lax" see "Proverbs"
"For the Feast of Saint Agnes" see "Prelude:..."
"For the Spanish Poet Miguel Hernandez" 617
For the Union Dead (Lowell) 324
"For Thomas Merton--My Father among the Saints" (Leiva) 1094
Forest, James H. 119, 161, 543, 1030-1033, 1281, 1319, 1354, 1517, 1664, 1745, 1771
Foreword to Bernard of Clairvaux (Daniel-Rops) 136
Foreword to Notes on the Lord's Prayer (Maritain) 137
Foreword to The Psalms of Struggle and Liberation (Cardenal) 138
Foreword to Vietnam: Lotus in a Sea of Fire (Nhat-Hanh) 139
"The Fork in the Road" 18, 19

"La formation monastique selon Adam de Perseigne" 325, 757
"Found Macaronic Antipoem" 52, 618
"The Foundation of Gethsemani Abbey" 106
"Four Freedom Songs" 140
"Four Hammer Portraits" 1051
"Fourteen Years with Thomas Merton" (Groves) 1047
Fowler, Albert 1034, 1353
"A Fragment" 25
Franciosa, Massimo 1035
Francis, Dale 163
Francis, Saint 495
"Franciscan Eremitism" 20, 326
Franciscans 1121
François de Sainte Marie, Father 155
"Free Speech" 60-62
"Freedom" 106
"Freedom as Experience" 89, 106
"Freedom Songs" 140
"Freedom under Obedience" 63, 64
Freeman, Hilary, O.P. 1682
Fremantle, Anne 1036, 1037, 1454, 1598, 1600, 1703
French translations 176, 749-790
"Friends and Comrades" 106
Frimage, George J. 667
"From Faith to Wisdom" 63, 64
"From Harlem to Gethsemani" (Lentfoehr) 1097
"From Kindling to Fruit Trees" (Hughes) 1067
"From Non-Violence to Black Power" 28, 105
"From Pilgrimage to Crusade" 54-56, 327
From Primitives to Zen: A Thematic Sourcebook of the History of Religions (Eliade) 404
"From the Abbey of Gethsemani" 328
"From the Second Chapter of

a Verse History of the World"
25
Fromm, Erich 198
"The Frozen Rainbow" (Forest)
1031
"Function of Mariology"
(LeFrois) 1093
"The Function of Monastic Re-
view" 329
"Fundamentals" 101, 102
"Fusion and Fission: Two by
Merton" (Sister Mary
Gilbert) 1131

Gable, L. J. 1285
Galicia 221, 330, 409
"Galician Nuns" 330
Gallagher, J. Joseph 1342
Galletto, Giovanni 1038
Gallois, Geneviève, Sister
776
"Gandhi and the One-Eyed
Giants" 141, 331, 819
Gandhi e a não-violência 859
"Gandhi e il ciclope" 819
Gandhi on Non-Violence 30,
141, 332, 859, 1372-1375
Garcia Lorca, Federico 89,
885
A Garland for Dylan Thomas
667
Gaspar Melchor de Jovellanos,
Don 299
Gavin, Rosemarie Julie, Sister
1039, 1790
Gebete (Anslem) 333
"Gelassenheit" 10
Gendai no seijin towa 839
"The General Dance" 63, 64,
106, 334
"The Gentle Revolutionary" 335
The Geography of Lograire 31,
52, 809, 1376, 1377
German translations 791-805
Gertrude, Saint 496
Gethsemani 39, 43, 47, 86,
87, 89, 106, 150, 298, 328,
437, 685
"Gethsemani, Abbey of" 142
Gethsemani: A Life of Praise
32
Gethsemani (chronique de nos

Abbayes: Annual Report-
Gethsemani, written in
French) 336
"Gethsemani Abbey" see
"After the Night Office:..."
"Gethsemani Revisited" (Ber-
rigan) see "The Trappist
Cemetery:..."
"Ghost Dance" 31
"The Gift of Merton" (Forest)
1032
"The Gift of Understanding"
63, 64
"Los gigantes" 894
Gill, Matthias 1040
Gilson, Etienne 106
Ginsberg, Robert 197
Gisi, Marta 793
Gita yaduma 740
Giustiniani, Paul, Blessed 22-
24, 172
"The Glass of His Humanity"
143
"Glass Orchard" (Maritain)
475, 727
Glassgold, Peter 986
Glazier, Michael 1532
Glimm, James York 1041,
1258
"Gloss on the Sin of Ixion" 26,
619
"The Glove" (Maritain) 475,
727
"God and the World" 81
"God as Unknown Soldier" see
"Violence and the Death of
God:..."
God Is My Life: The Story of
Our Lady of Gethsemani
(Burden) 150, 1103
"God Speaks His Name in the
Center of Our Soul" 144
Godfrey, Aaron W. 1289,
1309, 1448, 1449, 1751,
1776
"Godless Christianity?" 28,
81, 337
Golden Age of Zen (Wu) 124
"Good Fortune" 113
"The Good News of the Nativity:
A Monastic Reading of the
Christmas Gospels" 338
"The Good Samaritan" 85, 106

The Good Times and Hard
    Life of Thomas Merton
    (Rice) see The Man in
    the Sycamore Tree:...
"Goodbye, Tom Merton, Good-
    bye" 1042
Goss-Mayr, Hildegard see
    "To Jean"
Goss-Mayr, Jean see "To
    Jean"
"Grace and the Sacraments"
    36-38
"Grace's House" 26, 793
Graham, Aelred 589
"Les grand amitiés" (Griffin)
    1044
"The Grandmontines" 339
Grau see Corts Grau, José
Grazias Haus: Gedichte 793
"Great and Small" 113
"Great Catholic Upheaval"
    (Zahn) 1233
"Great Knowledge" 113
"Great Prayer" (Cortes) 701
Great Stories and Experiences
    of Spiritual Crisis, Inspira-
    tion, and the Joy of Life by
    Forty Famous Contempor-
    aries see Spirit of Man:...
Greek translations 806, 807
"The Greek Woman" 89
Green, Julian 551
Greene, Thomas F. 1565
Gregoire, R., O.S.B. 565
Gregory, Horace 650
Gregory, M., O.P. 1531
Gribbin, Raymond 1635
Griese, Raymond F., S.J.
    1381
Griffin, John Howard 127,
    930, 931, 976, 1006, 1013,
    1030, 1043-1045, 1065,
    1088, 1371, 1738-1756
Griffin, Lloyd W. 1668
Grinberg, Miguel 1046
Gros, Charles G. 1719
"The Grove and Beyond" 106
Groves, Gerald 1047, 1048
"Growth in Christ" 36-38,
    340
Guerric of Igny, Blessed 158
"Guerric of Igny's Easter
    Sermons" 341

Guevara, Ernesto "Che" 162
Guidi, Augusto 1049
Guigo the Carthusian 99, 145,
    342, 719
"The Guilty Bystander" 6
"The Guns of Fort Knox" 89,
    103, 104, 620

"Hagia Sophia" 26, 33, 621
Hall, Donald 1050, 1649
Hallier, Amédée 153
The Hallmark Book of Poetry
    see Poetry for Pleasure:...
Hamai, Shinzo, Hon. 88
Hamilton, Roland 1406
Hammer, Veronica 1051
Hammer, Victor 1051
"A Handbook for Hermits" 343
Hanlon, Morgan, C.P. 1052
"Hare's Message (Hottentot)"
    31
"Harlem" see "Aubade:..."
"The Harmonies of Excess"
    10, 622
Hart, Patrick, O.C.S.O. 3,
    345, 1053-1059, 1310, 1366,
    1501, 1502, 1511, 1659,
    1697, 1733, 1758, 1759,
    1765
Harte, Barbara 1060
Harvest, 1960 134
Hastings, Cecily 249
Hasumi, Toshimitsu 585, 586
Hat giống chiem niệm 925
"A Hat Salesman and a Capable
    Ruler" 113
Haughton, Rosemary 554,
    1061
Hauscherr, Irenee, S.J. 346
Hauss, Martha 1051
Hayes, Vincent de Paul 1609
"He Who Is Not with Me Is
    against Me" 63, 64
Heaney, Columban 153
"The Heart of Things" (Lent-
    foehr) 1098
Heath, Thomas, O.P. 1662
"The Heavenly City" 89, 106
Heibling, Leo, O.S.B. 333
Heilig in Christus 794
"Der heilige Johannes vom
    Krenz" 795

Heiser, W. Charles, S. J.
1340, 1518, 1535, 1620
"Hell as Hatred" 63, 64, 106
Hemingway, Ernest 606
Henry, Françoise 210
"Herakleitos: A Study" 6
"Herakleitos the Obscure" 6,
106, 344
Hergott, Alvin W. 1791
"The Heritage of Celtic Monas-
ticism" (Hart) 345
"Hermit Life" 95-98, 146
Hernandes, Miguel 617
Herr, Dan 134
Heschasme et prière (Hausherr)
346
"Hesychasm" 346
"Heureux les doux-les racines
de la non-violence chré-
tienne" 758
A Hidden Wholeness: The
Visual World of Thomas
Merton (Griffin) 930, 976,
1006, 1030, 1045, 1088,
1738-1756
Higgins, John J. , S. J. 932,
1227, 1657, 1731, 1757-
1763, 1792
"High-Water Mark" (McDonnell)
1116
Hill, Joseph G. 1062
"Historical Consciousness"
347
Hitler, Adolf 105
Hogan, Gerald C. 1382
Hogan, William F. , C. S. C.
1767
Hoheisel, P. 1390
"Holiness and Humanism" 36-
38
"The Holiness of Created
Things" 147
"Holy Camp" 348
"Holy Child's Song" 623
El hombre nuevo 895
Los hombres no son islas
896
"Homélie de la messe pour le
Père M. Louis (Thomas
Merton)" (Burns) 978
Homem algum e uma ilha 860
O homem novo 861
Homenaje a Merton, In

Memoriam Ludovici to Mer-
ton the Magician 615, 652,
656, 784, 938, 1040, 1046,
1064, 1231
"A Homily" (Bamberger) 956
"Homily at the Mass of Father
M. Louis (Thomas Merton)"
(Burns) 979
"A Homily on Light and the
Virgin Mary" 85, 349
"Honest to God" 28
Honest to God (Robinson) 350
"The 'Honest to God' Debate"
see "Demythologizing Bis-
hop Robinson:..."
Honest to God: Letter to a
Radical Anglican 34
"Hope or Delusion?" see
"Advent:..."
Hopkins, Gerard Manley 946
Hora sedmi stupňů 743
Horchler, Richard 1063, 1572
Horia, Vintila 1064
Horrigan, Alfred F. , Msgr.
127, 1043, 1065
Hoste, A. , O. S. B. 360
"The Hot Summer of Sixty-
Seven" 28
Hourlier, Jacques 496
"The House of Caiphas" 89
"Housewife Joins Literati"
1066
Hovda, R. 1534
"How Deep Is Tao!" 113
"How It Is: Apologies to an
Unbeliever" 28, 351
"How to Enter a Big City"
103, 104
"How to Handle Mystics" see
"The Clever Strategem:..."
"How to Meditate" 101, 102
"How to Profit by Direction"
101, 102
Hrico, Bernard 1462
Hughes, Riley 1067, 1424
"Huit chants de liberté" 759
"Human Faiths" 36-38
"The Humanity of Christ in
Monastic Prayer" 352
"Humility against Despair"
63, 64
Hurley, D. 1400, 1419, 1552,
1622, 1623, 1687

Hyeondaeineui sinang saenghwal
  181, 846
Hymn of Not Much Praise for
  New York City" 25
"Hymn to Commerce" 25
"Hymns of Lograire" 31

"I Have Called You" 82
"I Have Called You My Friends"
  41, 42
"I Have Chosen You" 353
I Salmi 820
"I Shall Miss Thomas Merton"
  (Burton) 980
I Sing of a Maiden: The Mary
  Book of Verse 596, 612
Ibn Abbad 80
Ibn Battuta 31
"Ideas and Reality" 36-38
Ideas and Words in Revolution
  see Prophetic Voices:...
"The Ideas of Solitude in
  Thomas Merton" 1082
"The Identity Crisis" 20
"If Even There Was a Country"
  106
"If You Seek a Heavenly Light"
  624
Ignatius of Antioch, Saint 85
A igreja e o mundo sem Deus
  862
Ikemoto, Takashi 841
"Image and Likeness" 60-62
"An Image in the Making:
  Thomas Merton's Early
  Interpreters" (Baker) 947
"Imagery in Modern Marian
  Poetry" (Von Wellsheim)
  1222
The Impact of Vatican II 129
"An Imperfect Ideal" 36-38
"The Importance of Being
  Toothless" 113
"In a New World" 106
"In Acceptance of the Pax
  Medal, 1963" 105
"In Defense of Solitude"
  (Conover) 997
"In Laboribus Multis" 95-98
"In Many Labors" 95-98
"In Memoriam" 22-24
"In Memoriam: Thomas

Merton, 1915-1968" (DePinto)
  1012
"In Memoriam: Thomas Mer-
  ton (1915-1968)" (Sivack)
  1192
"In Memory of the Late Father
  Thomas Merton" (Kikama)
  1083
"In Memory of the Spanish
  Poet Federico Garcia
  Lorca" 89, 885
"In Memory of Thomas Mer-
  ton: Three Poems" (Seitz)
  1182
In My Disc of Gold (Congdon)
  121
"In My End Is My Beginning"
  113
In Search of a Yogi (Rutledge)
  174
"In Search of Thomas Merton"
  (Griffin) 1043
"In Search of Thomas Merton"
  (Lansdell) 1090
"In Silence" 103, 104
"In Silencio" 85, 92-94, 148,
  801, 923
In Solitary Witness: The Life
  and Death of Franz Jager-
  statter 308
"In Tabernaculo Altissimi" 95-
  98
"In the Face of Death" 106
"In the Highest Tabernacle"
  95-98
"In the Monastic Community"
  106
"In the Rain and the Sun" 89,
  106
"In the Shows of the Round Ox"
  see "Song:..."
"In Truth" 95-98
In Tune with the World: A
  Theory of Festivity (Pieper)
  354
"In Unitate" 95-98
"In Unity" 95-98
"In Veritate" 95-98
Incursiónes en lo indecible
  897
"Influences Shaping the Poetic
  Imagery of Merton" (Gavin)
  1039

"The Inner Law" 113
"Integrity" 63, 64
"Interlude: Abbey of Our Lady
  of Gethsemani" 86, 87
"An Interview with Thomas
  Merton" (McDonnell) 1117,
  1118
"Introducing a Book" 355
Introduction to Breakthrough
  to Peace 149
Introduction to God Is My Life:
  The Story of Our Lady of
  Gethsemani (Burden) 150
Introduction to No More
  Strangers (Berrigan) 151
Introduction to Religion in
  Wood: A Book of Shaker
  Furniture (Andrews) 152
Introduction to The Monastic
  Theology of Aelred of
  Rievaulx: An Experimental
  Theology (Hallier) 153
Introduction to The Prison
  Meditations of Father Alfred
  Delp 154
Introduction to The Simple
  Steps to God (Father Fran-
  çois de Sainte Marie) 155
Introduction to The Soul of the
  Apostolate (Chautard) 156
Introduction to To Live Is to
  Love (Cardenal) 157
Introductory Essay in The
  Christmas Sermons of
  Blessed Guerric of Igny
  158
"Inward Destitution" 63, 64
"Iphigenie" see "Semiotic
  Poem:..."
"Is Buddhism Life-Denying?"
  118
"Is Direction Necessary?" 101,
  102
"Is Man a Gorilla with a Gun?"
  28, 356
"Is the Contemplative Life an
  Evasion?" 357
"Is the Contemplative Life
  Finished?" 20, 358
"Is the World a Problem?
  Ambiguities of the Secular"
  20, 359
"Isaac de l'Étoile" 360

"Isaac of Stella: An Introduc-
  tion to Selections from His
  Sermons" 361
"Isfahan" 31
"Ishi: A Meditation" 105, 362,
  363
Ishi, Last of His Tribe (Kroe-
  ber) 362, 363
"It Was a Moment of Crisis
  ... a Moment of Searching
  ... a Moment of Joy" 159
Italian Television 1801
Italian translations 808-837
"Itinerary to Christ" 364
"Its Spiritual Character" 22-
  24

J. F. Powers 166
Jabusch, Willard F. 1631
Jagerstatter, Franz 308
"Jaguar Myth" (Cuadra) 712
"The Jaguar Myth and Other
  Poems" (Cuadra) 713
James, Bruno S. 1068, 1069,
  1349, 1607
James, William 971
"Japanese Tea Ceremony" 365
Japanese translations 177-180,
  355, 387, 838-845
Jebb, P. 1491
Jeong-Jin Kim see Kim,
  Jeong-Jin
Jessey, Cornelia 1070
"The Jesuits in China" 54-56,
  366
"The Jesus Prayer" see "Life
  and Prayer:..."
John of the Cross, Saint 22-
  24, 106, 795
John the Baptist, Saint 106
"John the Volcano" 31
Johnson, Carol 1071, 1588
Johnson, Manly 1654
Johnston, William, S. J. 584
"Jorge Carrera Andrade" 106
Journal d'un laïc 760
"Journal of Thomas Merton"
  367
"Journey in Christ" see "Life
  and Prayer:..."
"Journey Through the Wilder-
  ness" 63, 64

"The Joy of Fishes" 113
Joyce, James 25, 282, 431
"The Judgement of Thomas
    Merton" (Sykes) 1204
Justice, Donald 1072, 1646

Kabir 446
Kacmarcik, Frank 772
O kainourgios anthropōs   807
Kallad till tystand 924
"Kane Relief Expedition" 31
Kansō no tane 178, 840
Kapita, Helen 806
Kapleau, Philip 587
"Karl Barth and Thomas Mer-
    ton" (Clancy) 993
Karpowich, Lorraine 328
Karrer, Otto 368
Katafiasz, K. 1754, 1780
Keating, John J., C.S.P. 1335
Keenan, J. 1574
Keeper of the Flocks (Pessoa)
    729
Keiner ist eine Insel 1378,
    1379
Kelley, William M. 426
Kelly, Frederic Joseph, S.J.
    1793
Kelly, H. 1496
Kelly, Richard 1073
Kelly, Robert 595, 604, 610,
    642, 651, 655, 670
Kelty, Matthew, O.C.S.O.
    1074-1076
Kende, Eugen 794
"Keng Sang Chu" 113
"Keng's Disciple" 113
Kennedy, X. J. 1077, 1358
Kenney, T. 1401
Kentucky Authors: A History
    of Kentucky Literature
    (Browning) 599, 661, 677,
    974
Kerouac, Jack see "Two
    Poems Dedicated to Thomas
    Merton"
Kessler, Jascha 1078, 1377
"Keys to Ourselves" (Kessler)
    1078
Khong ai la mot hon da'o
    182, 926
Kikama, Yasuwo 177, 178,

180, 838, 840, 842, 1079-
    1087
Killinger, J. R. 1397
Kim, Jeong-Jin 181
King, John J., O.M.I. 1540
King, Martin Luther 1223
The Kingdom of God Today
    368
"The Kingly Man" 113
Kinish, David 1269
Kirisuto kyō to zen taiken 841
Kirvan, John J., C.S.P. 1346,
    1536
Kishi, Augustin Hideshi 519
Kitaro, Nishida 380, 530
Kitching, Jessie 1295
Kiuchi, Fujisaburo 845
Knauth, Lothar 380
Knowles, David, O.S.B. 220
Kobayashi, Mezuo 839
Kodoku no naka no shisaku
    180, 842
Korean translations 181, 846
Kountz, Peter 1088, 1743
Kroeber, Theodora K. B.
    362, 363
Kucera, Dom 484
Kudo, Tadishi 179
Kuoni, Alfred 791, 803, 804

Labarthe, Pedro Juan 1356
"Lactantius" 369
"The Ladder of Divine Ascent"
    370
"The Ladies of Tlatilco" 31
LaFarge, John 1625
"Lake" (Maritain) 475, 723,
    727
"Lake Erie" see "Aubade:..."
Lakey, George 233
Lally, Francis J. 1665
Lambert, Rollins 1428
"Lament of a Maiden for the
    Warrior's Death" (Cuadra)
    713, 714
Landess, Thomas 1089
"The Landfall" 89, 106
"Landscape" 89, 103, 104,
    106
"Landscape: Beast" 89, 106
Landscape, Prophet and Wild
    Dog 35, 89

Lansdell, Sarah 1090
"Lao Tzu's Wake" 113
Larsen, Magda 802
"Last Mass in the Hermitage"
    (Hart) 1054-1056
Last of the Fathers 856
"The Last Three Days"
    (Moffitt) see "Thomas
    Merton:..."
Last Whole Earth Catalog
    1074, 1748
LasVergnas, Raymond 1091
"Latens Deitas" (Murray) 1151
"Latin America and Spain in
    the Poetic World of Thomas
    Merton" (Baciu) 943
Laughlin, James 3, 122, 131,
    133, 186, 194, 200, 598,
    611, 627, 636, 638, 641,
    657, 665, 666, 672, 674,
    682, 683, 685-692, 697-
    699, 701, 702, 704-718,
    721-726, 728, 731-734, 986
"Laughter in the Dark" 106
Lauras, A. 1526
Lauwers, L. 1529
Lawler, Justus George 1092,
    1253, 1254
Lawrence, Virginia, R. C.
    1403
Lax, Robert 52, 88, 241, 675
Lay, T. 1737, 1761
Leahy, Stephen 1271
"Learn to Be Alone" 63, 64
"Learning to Live" 160
Leary, Paris 594, 595, 604,
    610, 642, 651, 655, 670
"Leaving Things Alone" 113
Lebendige stille 796
Leclercq, Jean, O. S. B. 20,
    172, 1301
Ledoux, F. 790
Lee Ying 26
LeFrois, Bernard J., S. V. D.
    1093
"Legacy of Herakleitos" 6
"The Legacy of Machiavelli"
    81, 88
"The Legend of Tucker
    Caliban" 88
Leighton, Clare 668
Leiva, Erasmo 1094
"Lent" 25

"Lent in a Year of War" 89,
    106
Lentfoehr, M. Therese, S. D. S.
    596, 612, 1095-1107, 1244,
    1248, 1251, 1338, 1343,
    1360, 1410, 1423, 1435,
    1458, 1495, 1513, 1547,
    1548, 1557, 1589, 1605,
    1632, 1648, 1681, 1708,
    1711, 1715, 1722
Leonard, J. 1440
Lester, Julius 1312
"Let the Poor Man Speak"
    371, 372
"Letter from Father Thomas
    Merton" 373
"Letter from Thomas Merton--
    February, 1962" 161
A Letter of Guigo see The
    Solitary Life:...
"A Letter on 'Disinterested
    Love' " 88
"Letter to a Bishop--August
    1968" 374
"Letter to a Papal Volunteer"
    375
"Letter to a Poet about Vallejo"
    240
Letter to a Radical Anglican
    see Honest to God:...
"Letter to an Innocent By-
    stander" 6, 80
"A Letter to Dylan Thomas"
    see "Sports without Blood:
    ..."
"A Letter to Pablo Antonio
    Cuadra concerning Giants"
    26, 376, 882, 883, 894
"Letter to Surkov" 106
"Letter to the Editor" 377
"Letter to the Editor" (Bruno)
    975
"Letters in a Time of Crisis"
    88
Letters of Love and Counsel
    (Fénelon) 188
"The Letters of Saint Bernard"
    106
"Letters to a White Liberal"
    88, 223-226, 378; see also
    "The Black Revolution:..."
"Letters to Che: Canto
    Bilinque" 162

Lettre à un blanc libéral suivie
   de la légende de Tucker
   Caliban see La révolution
   noire:...
"Lettre d'asie" 761
Levend brood 737
"A Liberator, a Reconciler"
   (Allchin) 939
Na liberdade da solidão 863
Lieberman, Laurence 1108,
   1261
"Life and Celebration" 927
"Life and Community" 927
"Life and Contemplation" 927
The Life and Death of Franz
   Jagerstatter see In Soli-
   tary Witness:...
"Life and God's Love" 927
Life and Holiness 36-38, 181,
   746, 787, 794, 806, 834,
   839, 846, 875, 916, 919,
   1003, 1028, 1380-1403
"Life and Prayer: The Desert
   Source" 927
"Life and Prayer: The Jesus
   Prayer" 927
"Life and Prayer: Journey in
   Christ" 927
"Life and Prophecy" 927
"Life and Solitude" 927
"Life and the Holy Spirit" 927
"Life and Truth" 927
"Life and Work" 927
Life at Gethsemani 39
"A Life Free from Care" 379
"Life in Christ" 60-64
"Life in the Spirit" 36-38
"Life Is Tragic: The Diary of
   Nishida Kitaro" (Knauth)
   380
"The Life of Faith" 36-38,
   381
A Life of Praise see Geth-
   semani:...
"A Life of Prayer" 163
"The Life That Unifies" 382
"Light in Darkness: The
   Ascetic Doctrine of Saint
   John of the Cross" 22-24
Lima, Paulo Alceu Amoroso
   88, 857, 864, 868, 872,
   874, 875
"Lion" 625

"The Literary Catalyst" (Baciu)
   944
Littledale, A. V. 582
Liturgical Feasts and Seasons
   40
"Liturgical Renewal: The Open
   Approach" 85, 383
"Liturgy and Spiritual Per-
   sonalism" 85, 384
Living Bread 41, 42, 737,
   771, 797, 825, 868, 1067,
   1107, 1148, 1151, 1179,
   1404-1431
Llorens, D. 1292
Logan, J. 1109, 1641
Lograire 31
Lopez Sanz, Jaime 900
Lorca see Garcia Lorca,
   Federico
"The Lord Is Good" 82
Lorenz, Linda 1110
Loretto and Gethsemani 43
"The Lost Pearl" 113
Lotus in a Sea of Fire (Nhat-
   Hanh) see Vietnam:...
Lotze, J. 1671
"Love" 106
"Love and Maturity" 385
"Love and Obedience" 38
"Love and Person" 386
"Love and Solitude" 180, 387
"Love and Tao" 54-56
"Love Can Be Kept Only by
   Being Given Away" 106
"Love in Meditation" 106
"Love of Solitude" 107, 108
"Love of the Sultan" 31
"Love Winter When the Plant
   Says Nothing" 26, 626
"Lover of Life Envied Promise
   of Death" (Riehm) 1176
Lowell, Robert 106, 324
Loyer, Olivier 245
Lucas, Leroy 512
Lucchese, Romeo 809, 816,
   828, 1111
Lynch, J. 1420
Lyons, H. P. C. 1112, 1494

"Macarius and the Pony" 26
"Macarius the Younger" 26
A Macaronic Journal see

My Argument with the
    Gestapo:...
McCabe, Elizabeth 172
McCaffery, Hugh 153
McCarthy, Coleman 1113,
    1114
MacCormick, Chalmers 1115
McCorry, Vincent P. , S. J.
    1427
McDonald, Gerald D. 1508,
    1643
McDonnell, Kilian 1431
McDonnell, Thomas P. 1116-
    1121, 1243, 1355, 1444,
    1587, 1650, 1714, 1739
MacEoin, Gary 1122
McEwen, John 187, 188
McGreggor, Bede, O. P. 1123
McGregor, Robert, Brother
    318, 369
Machiavelli 81, 88
"The Machine Gun in the Fall-
    out Shelter" 105
McInerny, Dennis Quentin
    1794
McKenzie, John L. , S. J.
    1124, 1467
MacLeish, Roderick 1315,
    1784
McNally, T. 1441
McNiff, Mary Stock 1125,
    1782
McPherson, M. W. , O. S. B.
    479
Madeleva, M. , Sister 88
"The Madman Runs to the East"
    18, 19
Maeder, T. 1537
Magaret, Helene 1455
"Magnetic North" 106
Mahabharata 190
Maharsi, Ramana 266
Mahoney, John 1675
The Making of a Crow
    Warrior (Nabokov) see
    Two Leggings:...
Malachy, Saint 89, 106,
    651
Malcolm X 28, 394
Malinowski 31
Mallorca Eremitica 313
Man and Transformation
    216, 555

"A Man from Ecuador beneath
    the Eiffel Tower" (Carrera
    Andrade) 688, 691
The Man in the Sycamore Tree:
    The Good Times and Hard
    Life of Thomas Merton
    (Rice) 935, 976, 1006,
    1030, 1173, 1768-1784
"The Man in the Wind" 89
"Man Is a Gorilla with a Gun:
    Reflections on a Best Seller"
    105, 388, 389
"Man Is Born in Tao" 113
"The Man of Letters" (Burke)
    977
"The Man of Tao" 113
"Man Picked to Write Merton's
    Biography Doesn't Look
    the Part" (Mann) 1126
"Man the Master" 627
"The Man with One Foot and
    the Marsh Pheasant" 113
Manaure, Mateo 900
Mandel, Siegfried 1606
"Manifestation of Conscience
    and Direction" 101, 102
Mann, Bill 1126
Mansions of the Spirit 123,
    217
"Un manual de ermitanos"
    (Colombas) 343
Maragall, Angeles 909
Marcel, Gabriel 391
"Marcel and Buddha: A Meta-
    physics of Enlightenment"
    (Donnelly) 391
Marcks, Gerhard 109, 110
Maria Valverde, José 886,
    895, 897, 912, 915
Marinoff, Irene 796, 797
Maritain, Jacques 88, 106
Maritain, Raissa 137, 475
"Mark Van Doren" 106
Marta, Marie e Lázaro 864
Marthe, Marie, et Lazare 44,
    762, 864, 1432
Martin, Frederick R. 986
Martinez, G. 330, 409
Martinez Alinari, Juana 891
Martinez Alinari, Maria
    Josephina 890, 903, 907
"Martin's Predicament, or
    Atlas Watches Every

Evening" 80, 122
Marty, Martin E.   427, 485,
    566, 1128, 1129, 1145,
    1568
"A Martyr for Peace and
    Unity" 105
"Martyr to the Nazis" 392
The Mary Book of Verse see
    I Sing of a Maiden:...
Mary Francis, P. C.   1130
Mary Genevieve, Sister 1560
Mary Gilbert, S. N. J. M.   1131,
    1362, 1485
Mary Leontine, S. S. N. D.
    1383
Mary Vianney, S. S. J.   1461,
    1481
"Marxism and Monastic Per-
    spectives" 164
Marzolla, Franco Bernardini
    821, 831, 837
Mason, H.   1132
Massignon, Louis 1132
Mateo Gomez, Isabel 299
Materer, Timothy 1133, 1224
Material for Retreat Confer-
    ences 45
"Matins" see "The Trappist
    Abbey:..."
"A Matter of Choice" see
    "Monastic Attitudes:..."
The Matter of Zen: A Brief
    Account of Zazen (Wienpaha)
    393
Mauser, Ulrich 580
Maximus, Saint 105
"May, 1962" 106
Mayhew, Alice 1134
Mayhew, Leonard F. X.   1135,
    1466
Maze, Thibaud 753
Mê kuan shêng huo t'an pi 742
Meagher, Robert E.   1136,
    1318
"The Meaning and Purpose of
    Spiritual Direction" 101,
    102
"The Meaning of Malcolm X"
    28, 394
"The Meaning of Satyagraha"
    395
"Means and Ends" 113
Meath, Gerard 1433

"Mecca" 31
"Meditatio Pauperis in Soli-
    tudine" 106
"Meditation" 396
"Meditation: Action and Union"
    101, 102, 397
"Meditation before an Ancient
    Poem" 713
"Meditation in Scripture" 101,
    102
"Meditation in the Woods" 398
"A Meditation on Adolf Eich-
    mann" 399
"A Meditation on Ways to
    Unity" see "The Poorer
    Means:..."
"Le 'meditationes' del Beato
    Guigo Certosino" 342
"Meditations" (Moody) 1148
Meier, Fritz 555
Meilwes, Margret 805
Meiners, R. K.   1363
Meisō no shushi 843
Melchers, Erna 801
Mello, Carmen de 877
"Memories of the Ancient
    World" 681
Mendes, Oscar 854
Meneses Ocón, Gonsalo 896
Meng Tzu 167, 452
"Mensaje a los poetas" 898
"Mental Prayer" 63, 64
The Mentor Book of Religious
    Verse 650
"Mentors and Doctrines" 106
Mercurio, Roger, C. P.   1614
Merton, Owen 514
Merton, Robert K.   535
"Merton against Himself"
    (Mayhew) 1134
"Merton and Auden" (Materer)
    1133
"Merton and His Camera"
    (Griffin) 1045
"Merton and Massignon"
    (Mason) 1132
"Merton and the Metaphysicals"
    (Sister Bridget Marie) 972
"Merton at Prayer" (Evans)
    1022
"Merton Denounces Modern
    Ethics" (Perley) 1164
"Merton Indexed" (Lentfoehr)
    1099

"Merton Likes Monastery But
He Has Reservations" 1137
"Merton, Monastic Exchange,
and Renewal" (Conner) 996
"Merton on Non-Violence"
(Whalen) 1796
"Merton or Toynbee?" (Sister
Consuela Marie) 1127
"Merton: Regain the Old
Monastic Charism: Letter
to the Editor" 400
The Merton Tapes 927
"Merton Unique" (Van Doren)
1219
"Merton View of Monasticism:
Seeking God Through Total
Love Is Goal" 401
"Merton Withdrew to Become
Aware" (Weber) 1227
"Merton Works Highlight
Bellarmine Week" 1138
"Merton's Death Spotlights
New Wave" (Shuster) 1189
"Merton's Later Life" (Du-
mont) 1016
"Merton's Prof to Be Ordained
a Priest at 60" 1139
Merton's Theology of Prayer
(Higgins) 932, 1227, 1757-
1763
"Merton's View on Nonviolence"
402
Merwin, W. S. 1140, 1646
"Message aus amis de Gandhi,
January 31, 1965" 105
"Message of Contemplatives to
the Modern World" 812
"Message to Poets" 80, 898
"Message to Poets from
Thomas Merton" 403
"The Messenger" 89
"A Messenger from the Hori-
zon" 26, 628
"A Metaphysics of Enlighten-
ment" (Donnelly) see "Mar-
cel and Buddha:..."
"Metamorphosis" 113
Meyer, Louis, O.S.B. 239
"Miami You Are About to Be
Surprised" 31
Michelfelder, William 1141,
1345
Miller, Vassar 1034

Miller, W. 1365
Miller, William Robert 435
"Mircea Eliade: A Critical
Observer of the Archetypal
Myth" 404
"Mirror's Mission" (Carrera
Andrade) 689, 691
"Mississippi y Auschwitz" 405
Mistici e maèstri zen 821
Der mit dir lebt: Betrachtungen
ueber die Eucharistie 797
"Mnich i mysliwi" 849
"A Modern Monk Seeks Soli-
tude" (Lorenz) 1110
"Modern War: Letter to the
Editor" 406
Modlimy sie slowami Psalmou
850
Moffitt, John 164, 1057, 1142-
1145
Mohs, Mayo 1783
"Le moine dans la Diaspora"
763
"The Moment of Truth" 629
"Monachesimo del futuro:
quale?" 407
"Monachisme bouddhique: Le
Zen" 408
"Monasterior y monjes en los
Diarios de Jovellanos" 299
"Los monasterios de Benedic-
tinos de Galicia" (Arias)
221
"Los monasterios de monjas
en Galicia" (Martinez) 409
"Monasterium Carcer" (Penco)
410, 471
"The Monastery" 106
"Monastery at Midnight" 411
Monastery of Christ in the
Desert 12
"Monastic Attitudes: A Matter
of Choice" 412
"Monastic Experience and the
East-West Dialogue" 165
"Monastic Formation According
to Adam Perseigne" 325,
757
A Monastic Introduction to
Sacred Scripture 46
"Monastic Life and the Secular
City" (Landess) 1089
Monastic Life at Gethsemani
47

Monastic Orientation 48
Monastic Peace 49, 95-98,
    772, 907, 1434, 1435
"A Monastic Reading of the
    Christmas Gospels" see
    "The Good News of the
    Nativity:..."
"Monastic Renewal" 20
"Monastic Renewal Revisted:
    Resourcement Aggiorna-
    mento" (Peifer) 484
The Monastic Theology of
    Aelred of Rievaulx: An
    Experimental Theology
    (Hallier) 153
"Monastic Thought in the Rus-
    sian Diaspora" 81, 88
"Monastic Vocation and Modern
    Thought" 413, 921
Monastic Vocation and the
    Background of Modern
    Secular Thought 50
Monastic Vows 51
"Monastic Way of Death"
    (Kelty) 1074
"A Monastic Witness" (Shaw)
    see "Community:..."
Der monastische Gedanke
    (Parpert) 472
"Un monje peculiar" 1146
"El monje susurra. A Poem
    in Memory of Thomas Mer-
    ton" (Grinberg) 1046
"Monk and Apostle" see "St.
    Bernard:..."
"The Monk and Sacred Art"
    414
"The Monk and the World"
    95-98
"The Monk as a Slave" 415
"Monk as Marginal Man" 416
"The Monk as 'Servus' "
    (Blecker) see "Civil
    Rights of the Monk in
    Roman and Canon Law:..."
"The Monk at Work" (James)
    1068
"The Monk in a Changing
    World" 4, 5
"The Monk in the Diaspora"
    81, 88, 417, 418, 763,
    1020
"Monk, Man, and Myth"

(Morrissey) see "Talks
    with and about Thomas Mer-
    ton:..."
"Monk-Poet Merton, 53; Karl
    Barth, 82, Die" 1147
"The Monk Today" 20, 419
"Monk Wrote of Search for
    God" (Shenker) see "Thomas
    Merton Is Dead at 53:..."
"Monkey Mountain" 113
"Monks and Hunters" 849
Monks, Nuns, and Monasteries
    (Sitwell) 348
Monks Pond 52
La montée vers la lumière
    764
Moody, J. N. 1148, 1414
Moore, Father 106
"Moral Confusion" 106
"The Moral Theology of the
    Devil" 63, 64, 106
Morales, Armando 908
More, Gertrude, Dame 27,
    54-56
More Than Sentinels (Burton)
    981, 982
Morgan, Edwin 1639
Morgan, Frederick 1370
Morris, João 862
Morrison, Richard 1149
Morrissey, James 1150
Morstin-Gorska, Maria 851
"Morte D'Urban: Two Cele-
    bration" 166, 420
"Mosaic: St. Praxed" (Mari-
    tain) 475, 724, 727
"The Moslems' Angel of Death:
    Algeria 1961" 26, 630
Motion Pictures 1800, 1801
Moubaroc, Y. 258
Mould, D. 1716
Moulton, Herbert E. 1497
"Mount Athos" 22-24, 421,
    422
"A Mountain of Monks" 422
"The Movie Career of Robert
    Lax" see "Western Fellow
    Student Salute with Calypso
    Anthem:..."
"Much to Praise ... Much to
    Deplore" (Tusiani) 1218
Mueller, F. J. 1691
Muir, Edwin 558

Mulka, Robert Karl Ludwig
   215
Mulloy, Joseph 1161
La muntanya dels set cercles
   899
Murchland, B. 1674
Murray, A. Gregory, O.S.B.
   1151, 1426
Murray, Michele 1152, 1291,
   1519, 1752, 1778
My Argument with the Gestapo:
   A Macaronic Journal 53,
   999, 1213, 1436-1441
"My Fourteen Years with
   Thomas Merton" (Groves)
   1048
"My Lord God" 631
"My Soul Remembered God"
   106
"Mysterium Fidei" (Sackville-
   West) 1179
"Mystery and Unity as Anagog-
   ical Vision in Thomas Mer-
   ton's Cables to the Ace: A
   Critical Explication"
   (Flaherty) 1789
"The Mystery of Christ" 63,
   64
"Mystic and Poet" (Mayhew)
   1135
Mystics and Zen Masters 54-
   56, 423, 1036, 1178, 1442-
   1456
"Mystique et zen" 765
"The Mystique of Violence"
   see "The Extremists,
   Black and White:..."

Nabokov, Peter 572, 573
Nabokov, Vladimir 106
Nagasawa, Junji 843
"Nahoa Urn, for a Woman"
   (Cuadra) 713
Nakata, Yuji 841
"Name of the Lord" 57, 85,
   424, 766
Nanae no yama 179, 844
Napier, John T. 1652
Nash, J. 1689
Nash, Roderick 578, 579
Nasr, Seyyed Hossein 546
Nativity Kerygma 58, 59,

   106, 425, 1097, 1457, 1458
"Nature and Art in William
   Blake: An Essay in Inter-
   pretation" 679
Naumann, Bernd 215
Nazis 392
"The Need for a New Educa-
   tion" 20
"The Need to Win" 113
"The Negro Revolt" 426
"Negro Violence and White
   Non-Violence" 427
"Neither Caliban nor Uncle
   Tom" 428
Nelson, Elizabeth 1260
Nessun uomo è un'isola 822
"Nessuno giunge al cuelo da
   solo: Merton apòstolo di
   una libertà immensa"
   (Volpini) 1221
New Catholic Encyclopedia
   120, 142
A New Charter for Monasti-
   cism 164, 1057, 1143
"A New Christian Conscience"
   429
"The New Commandment" 41,
   42
"New Consciousness" 118
New Directions in Prose and
   Poetry, 17 186, 200, 683,
   691, 713
New Directions in Prose and
   Poetry, 18 122, 131, 133
New Directions in Prose and
   Poetry, 19 627, 636, 638,
   657, 666, 672, 674
New Directions in Prose and
   Poetry, 20 194
New Directions in Prose and
   Poetry, 21 641
New Directions in Prose and
   Poetry, 25 986
A New Directions Reader 598,
   611, 665
"The New Law" 36-38
The New Man 60-62, 177,
   430, 767, 807, 833, 838,
   861, 895, 1135, 1171, 1459-
   1479
"A New Manner" (Lentfoehr)
   1100
New Seeds of Contemplation

63, 64, 768, 802, 823, 866,
903, 1131, 1181, 1480-1487
"The New Society" 106
"New Testament Faith" 36-38
New Ways and Living Traditions
in the Monastic Life see
Come to the Mountain:...
"New Year, 1962" 88
"New York and St. Bonaven-
ture" 86, 87
"News from the School at
Chartres" 26
"News of the Joyce Industry"
431
"Newscast" 10
Nhat-Hanh, Thich 139
"Nhat Hanh Is My Brother"
28, 105, 432, 433
Nicholl, D. 1280
Nicolas of Cusa 720
"Night-Flowering Cactus" 26,
632
"Night of Destiny" 633
"The Night of the Senses"
63, 64
"Night Spirit and the Dawn
Air" 18, 19, 367, 434
"The Night Train" 89, 106
Nikt nie jest samotna wyspa
851
Niña boma original 900
Ningun no es una illa 901
Nirvâna 118, 790
"Nishida: A Zen Philosopher"
118
"No Magic" (Lentfoehr) 1101
"No Man Is an Island" 106
No Man Is an Island 105, 182,
747, 806, 822, 851, 860,
896, 901, 926, 1098, 1112,
1183, 1488-1497
No More Strangers (Berrigan)
151
"Nocturne" 103, 104
Noite sem estrelas 865
Nolan, James 1153
"Le nom du seigneur" 766
Non-Violence: A Christian
Interpretation (Miller)
435
Non-Violence and the Christian
Conscience (Régamey) 175

"Non-Violence and the Christian
Conscience" 28
"Nonviolence Does Not, Cannot
Mean Passivity" 436
Non-Violence in Peace and
War (Gandhi) 30, 141
"Non-Violence: True and
False" 30
Noon, W. T. 1154, 1323
"North" 31, 52
"Not to Be Numb" see "To
Sons:..."
"Notas sobre arte sagrado y
profano" 902
"Note for Ave Maria" 105
"Note on Civil Disobedience
and Nonviolent Revolution"
105
"Note on Joyce's Ulysses"
see "Correspondence:..."
"Note on the New Church at
Gethsemani" 437
"A Note: Two Faces of
Prometheus" 6, 106
"Notes by the Artist for an
Exhibit of His Drawings"
65
"Notes for a New Liturgy" 31,
634
"Notes for a Statement on Aid
to Civilian War Victims in
Vietnam" 105
"Notes of a Parachute Jumper"
(Carrera Andrade) 690,
691
"Notes on a Race War" see
"Cross Fighters:..."
"Notes on an Experiment" see
"Christian Solitude:..."
"Notes on Christian Existen-
tialism" see "The Other
Side of Despair:..."
"Notes on Contemplation" 438
Notes on Genesis 66
"Notes on Love" 439
"Notes on Prayer and Action"
440
"Notes on Sacred and Profane
Art" 441, 902
Notes on Sacred Art 67
"Notes on Spiritual Direction"
442

"Notes on the Future of
Monasticism" 20, 443
Notes on the Lord's Prayer
(Maritain) 137
Le nouvel homme 767, 1498,
1499
Nouvelles semences de con-
templation 768
Nouwen, Henri J. M. 933,
1764, 1765, 1799
Novak, Michael 503
Novas sementes de contem-
placão 866
"Nuclear War and Christian
Responsibility" 444, 1062
Nuevas semillas de contempla-
ción 903
La nuit privée d'étoiles 769
"Nuove poesie tradotto"
(Lucchese) 1111
Nuovi semi di contemplazione
823
"The Nusayris" 31

"O Sweet Irrational Worship"
26
"Oakham" 106
Obituaries 1155-1159
Obras completas 904
O'Brien, J. A. 1412, 1544,
1616
Ocampo, Victoria 88
"Ocho cantos de liberatad"
905
Ockenden, Rosaleen 368
O'Connor, Flannery 80, 322,
556
O'Donoghue, D. 1283
"Odpowiedzialnosć wystawiana
na próbe" 852
Oeuvres spirituelles (D'Helfta)
496
"Of the Passion of Christ"
see "An Argument-..."
O'Gorman, Ned 130, 185
"The Ohio River--Louisville"
89, 885
"Old Order Changeth--Trappists
Open up to the World"
(McCarthy) 1113
"Oltre l'identità" (Bamberger)
957

O'Meara, Thomas Aquinas,
O. P. 1388
"On Aid to Civilian Victims in
Vietnam" 445
"On Praying for Peace" 106
"On the Anniversary of My
Baptism" 89
"On the Eve of Conversion, a
Secular Fantasy" (Davenport)
999
"On the Future of Monasticism"
see "Two Letters of the
Late Thomas Merton:..."
"On What Strange Islands?"
(McDonnell) 1119
One Hundred Poems of Kabir
446
Onorat, Franco 830
"The Open Approach" see
"Liturgical Renewal:..."
"An Open Letter to the Ameri-
can Hierarchy" see
"Schema XIII:..."
"Open Questions" (Deasy) 1003
Opening the Bible 68, 69, 447,
1500-1504
"Openness and Cloister" 20,
448, 449, 770, 808
Oplettende toeschouwer 738
La oración en la vida religiosa
906
Origen 81, 88
"Origen" 635, 636
Original Child Bomb: Points
for Meditation to Be
Scratched on the Walls of
a Cave 70, 900, 1203,
1505-1509
"Original Child Monk: An Ap-
preciation" (Zahn) 1234
"Original Sin, a Memorial An-
them for Father's Day" 10
"The Originators" 637
"Orthodoxy and the World" 450
Osborne, Arthur 266
"The Other Side of Despair"
54-56
"The Other Side of Despair:
Notes on Christian Existen-
tialism" 451
"Our Journey to God" 41, 42
"Our Lady of Cobre" 106
"Our Lady of Sorrows" 106

"Our Lady of the Museums"
  106
"Our Lady of the Valley"
  see "St. Bonaventure..."
"Our Lady's Liveryman" (Ross)
  1177
Our Monastic Observances   71
"Our Response" 41, 42
"Out of a Cloud" (Lentfoehr)
  1102
"Out of Gethsemani" (Lent-
  foehr) 1103
"Out of Soulful Silence"
  (Meagher) 1136
"Out of Time, Out of Place"
  (Fremantle) 1036
Outcault, Cornelius 1465
"Outlines of Growth" (Dell'Isola)
  see "Thomas Merton:..."
"The Outspoken Trappist"
  (Coffey) 995
"Ouverture et cloture"   770
Overpeinzingen van een
  christen 746
"An Overwhelming Atrocity"
  see "The Vietnam War:..."
"Ovid" 52
"Owl and Phoenix" 113
"The Ox Mountain Parable of
  Meng Tzu" 167, 452

Pacem in Terris 81, 88
Pachomius, Saint 76
"Pacifism and Resistance in
  Simone Weil" 28, 105;
  see also "The Answer of
  Minerva:..."
"Pages from a Monastic Note-
  book" see "Truth and
  Crisis:..."
"Pain Is an Eagle Clinging to
  Your Name" (Cuadra) 26,
  713, 715
Le pain vivant 771
La paix monastique 772
Palestine 77
Pallis, Marco 790, 1160
Il pane del deserto 824
Il pane vivo 825
Panichas, George A.   123,
  217
O pão no deserto   867

O pão vivo   868
Papabasileios, Johannos Th.
  807
"Pâques, une vie nouvelle"
  773
"Paradise Bugged" 453
"The Paradise Ear" see
  "Zukofsky:..."
"The Paralysed Critics" (Bar-
  nard) see "Vietnam:..."
Parpert, F. 472
Pascal, Frère 291
"Páscoa: uma vitória" 869
"Passage" 106
"Passivity and the Abuse of
  Power" 105, 454
Pasternak, Boris 22-24, 229,
  455, 826
Pasternak 826
"The Pasternak Affair" 22-24
"The Pasternak Affair in Per-
  spective" 455
"The Path to Seven Storey
  Mountain" (Burton) 981
"Patristic and Titanic" (Lent-
  foehr) 1104
Pauchard, Marianne 922
Paul, Saint 89
Paupert, Jean Marie 966
Paustovsky, Konstantin 527
Pax Peace Prize 1211, 1217
"Peace: A Religious Respon-
  sibility" 105, 168
"Peace and Protest" 28, 456
"Peace and Revolution: A
  Footnote from Ulysses"
  105, 457
"Peace: Christian Duties and
  Perspectives" 105
"Peace Council Joins (Joseph)
  Mulloy Draft Plea" 1161
Peace in the Post-Christian
  Era 72
"Peace, the Wasp" (Vallejo)
  734
"The Peacemaker" (Zahn) 1235
Pearce, Donald J. 1447, 1726
Peerman, Dean G. 1145
Peifer, Claude, O.S.B. 484
Peisson, Henry 1336
Peloquin, Charles Alexander
  82, 140, 1162, 1163
Penco, Gregorio 410, 471

Penido, Basilo, O. S. B.   858,
    866, 876
Pennington, M. Basil,
    O. S. C. O.   934, 1012, 1326,
    1766
A Penny a Copy: Readings
    from the 'Catholic Worker,'
    119, 161
Pensamientos de la soledad y
    la paz monástica   907
"Pensamientos de Merton:
    conjeturas de un espectador
    culpable"   887
Pensieri nella solitudine   827
"The People with Watch-Chains"
    22-24
"Père Louis-Thomas Merton"
    (Dumont)   1017
"Le père spirituel dans la
    tradition du desert"   774
"Perfect Joy"   113
"The Peril"   89
"Peril of Nuclear Hell Spurs
    Peace Seekers"   458
Perley, M. E.   1164, 1576
Perrin, Father   111
"Perry Street, New York"   86,
    87
Persia   77
Pessoa, Fernando   729, 730
Peter Damian, Saint   497
Petrie, John   585, 586
Pettis, Ashley   1680
Pfister, E.   1464
"The Philosophers"   25
"Philosophy of Solitude"   22-
    24
"Picture of a Black Child with
    a White Doll"   638
"Picture of a Negro Child with
    a White Doll"   639
"A Picture of Lee Ying"   26
Pieper, Josef   354
La Pierre-qui-Vire   92-94,
    148, 1594
"The Pilgrimage of Thomas
    Merton" (Rice)   1172
Pillai, Joachim, O. M. I.   1165
"Pillars" (Maritain)   26, 475,
    725, 727
Pio XII, Pontifex Maximus,
    Postridie Kalendas Martias,
    1876-1956   171

Piponnier, Françoise   749
"The Pivot"   113
"La place de l'obeissance dans
    le renouveau monastique"
    775
"Place Names"   31
"The Place of Obedience"   20
"The Place of Obedience in
    Monastic Renewal"   459,
    775
The Plague (Camus)   2, 236
"The Planet over Eastern
    Parkway"   10, 640
"The Plaster Saint"   36-38
"Pleasant Hill"   54-56
"Plessy vs. Ferguson: Theme
    and Variation"   see   "An
    Anti-Poem:..."
Plotz, Helen   668
Plummer, J.   1282
Poborska, Krystyna   853
"Poem"   25
Poemas   908
Poemo de Ludovico Silva   see
    Boom ! ! !...
Poems of the Spirit   see   The
    Earth Is the Lord's:...
"La poesia di Thomas Merton"
    (Casotti)   989
"Poesia e contemplazione cris-
    tiana in Thomas Merton"
    (Fabbretti)   1025
"La poesia e la vita contem-
    plativa di Thomas Merton"
    (Bo)   968
Poesias (Cardenal)   877
Poesie   828
"Poetry and Contemplation"
    169
"Poetry and Contemplation: A
    Reappraisal"   89, 106, 460
"The Poetry and Criticism of
    Edwin Muir"   see   "The
    True Legendary Sound:..."
"Poetry and the Contemplative"
    (Sister Mary Francis)   1130
"Poetry and the Contemplative
    Life"   904, 913
"A Poetry Chronicle" (Swenson)
    1203
"Poetry: Combatting Society
    with Surrealism"   1166
Poetry for Pleasure: The

Hallmark Book of Poetry
673
"Poetry of Thomas Merton"
(McDonnell) 1120
"The Poetry of Thomas Mer-
ton: A Study in Theory,
Influences, and Form"
(Campbell) 1786
"Poetry of Thomas Merton
and Vassar Miller"
(Fowler) see "Possessed
by the Holy Spirit:..."
"Poetry, Symbolism, and
Typology" 106, 170
"Le point vierge in Thomas
Merton" (Abdelnour) 937
Points for Meditation to Be
Scratched on the Walls of
a Cave see Original
Child Bomb:...
Polish translations 847-853
"The Political Scope of Non-
Violence" 30
The Politics of the Gospel
(Paupert) 966
The Poorer Means: A Medi-
tation on Ways to Unity
73, 461, 462
"Pope of the Virgin Mary"
171, 463
Portmann, Paul F. 802
Portuguese translations 854-
878
"Possessed by the Holy Spirit:
Poetry of Thomas Merton
and Vassar Miller" (Fowler)
1034
"Postface" 118
"Postmarked Gethsemani"
(Brock) 973
Pouchet, Robert 476
"Poverty of an Anti-Hero" see
"The Stranger:..."
"The Power and Meaning of
Love" 22-24
Powers, J. F. 166
Pozo, Mariano del 913
"Practical Problems" 36-38
"A Practical Program for
Monks" 89, 106, 642, 643
Pratt, J. M. 1581
Praxed, Saint 475, 724, 727
"Pray for Your Own

Discovery" 63, 64
Pray to Live--Thomas Merton:
A Contemplative Critic
(Nouwen) 933, 1764, 1765,
1799
"Prayer and Conscience" 464
"Prayer and the Subconscious"
106
"Prayer as Worship and Ex-
perience" see Climate of
Monastic Prayer and Con-
templative Prayer
"Prayer for a Miracle" 1167
"Prayer for Guidance (in Art)"
465
"Prayer for Peace" 105, 106,
466
A Prayer from the Treatise
'De Anima' 74, 693, 1510,
1511
Prayer of Cassiodorus 74,
693, 1510, 1511
"Prayer, Personalism, and the
Spirit" 467
"Prayer to Saint Anatole" 10
"Prayer, Tradition, and Ex-
perience" 468
Praying the Psalms 75, 740,
741, 776, 820, 850
Pre-Benedictine Monachism.
Series I: Rufinus, Cassian,
St. Pachomius, St. Basil,
etc. 76
Pre-Benedictine Monachism.
Series II: Syria, Persia,
Palestine 77
Preface to Alone with God
(Leclercq) 172
Preface to L'Attende dans le
silence: Le Père Marie-
Joseph Cassant, O. C. S. O.
(Chenevière) 173
Preface to In Search of a Yogi
(Rutledge) 174
Preface to Non-Violence and
the Christian Conscience
(Régamey) 175
Preface to the French Edition
of The Black Revolution
176
Preface to the Japanese Edition
of The New Man 177
Preface to the Japanese Edition

of Seeds of Contemplation
178
Preface to the Japanese Edition
of Seven Storey Mountain
179
Preface to the Japanese Edition
of Thoughts in Solitude 180
Preface to the Korean Edition
of Life and Holiness 181
Preface to the Vietnamese Edi-
tion of No Man Is an Island
105, 182
"Preghiera al Sacro Cruore"
469
"A Prelude: For the Feast of
St. Agnes" 106, 644
Présence à Dieu et a soi-
même (Father François de
Sainte Marie) 155
"The Presence of God" (Lent-
foehr) see "Two Studies:..."
"Presuppositions to Meditation"
470
"Prière et action dans la tra-
dition catholique. Un témoin
récent, Thomas Merton"
(Dumont) 1018
"A Priest and His Mission"
1168
"The Priest in Union with Mary
Immaculate" see "Two
Meditations for Our Mem-
bers:..."
"Primitive Benedictines (La
Pierre-qui-Vire)" 95-98
"The Primitive Carmelite
Ideal" 22-24
Prince, Raymond H. 268
"Principles of Non-Violence"
30
Prioij H. Graf, Reguliere
Kanunnikessen van de 739
Prions les psaumes 776
"Prison" 471
The Prison Meditations of Father
Alfred Delp 28, 154, 392
"Prisoner" (Maritain) 475,
726, 727
"Prisoner's Base" 106
"The Problem of Unbelief"
106
Problèmi dello spirito 829
"Problems and Prospects" 20

"Profile: Thomas Merton"
1169
Prologo dos Vida en el amor
(Cardenal) 183
Prologo para Boom!!! Poemo
de Ludovico Silva 184
"Prologue" 80
"Prologue: The Endless In-
scription" 31
"Promethean Theology" 60-62
Prometheus: A Meditation 6,
78, 80, 106, 1097, 1512,
1513
"The Proper Atmosphere of
Prayer" 101, 102
"The Prophet Is Dead" (DeLisi)
1008
"The Prophetic Spirit" 22-24
Prophetic Voices: Ideas and
Words in Revolution 130,
185
"Proposed Canon on Monastic
Life" (Meyer) 239
"The Prospects of Nostrada-
mus" 10
"The Protest of Vitalism" 81
"Protestant Monasticism" 54-
56, 472
Protreptikos 126, 696
"Proverbs (For Robert Lax)"
52
"A Psalm" 89, 106, 645
"The Psalms Are Our Prayer"
79
Psalms of Struggle and Libera-
tion (Cardenal) 138
"The Pure Heart" 63, 64
"Pure Love" 63, 64
"Puritas Cordis" 95-98
"Purity" 185
"Purity of Heart" 95-98
"The Purity of Non-Violence"
30

"Q. E. D. " (McKenzie) 1124
"Queens Tunnel" 31
"Quem Quaeritus?" 4, 5
Questions disputées 777
Questões abertas 870
"Qui fut Thomas Merton?"
(Bamberger) 958
"The Quickening of St. John

the Baptist" 106
Quitslund, Sonya 1582

Racine, Jean Baptiste 52
"Rafael Alberti and His Angels"
    473
Raggendrof, Joseph 534
Rahner, Karl 249
"Rahner's Diaspora" 81, 88
Raids on the Unspeakable 80,
    399, 786, 897, 1514-1520,
    1694, 1695
"Rain and the Rhinoceros" 80,
    474
"Rain and Vision" 646
"The Rain Barrell" (Bourne)
    969
"Raindrops and Riddles"
    (Forest) 1033
"Raissa Maritain's Poems"
    475, 727
Rampini, Gino 813, 832
Ransom, John Crowe 106
"The Ranters and Their Pleads"
    31
Ravier, A., S.J. 494
Rayne, Allan 1170, 1590
"The Reader" 89, 106, 885
"Readings from Ibn Abbad" 80
Readings from the 'Catholic
    Worker' see A Penny a
    Copy:...
"The Real Presence" 41, 42
"Realism in the Spiritual Life"
    36-38
"Reality in Religion" (Thrapp)
    see "Father Merton's Con-
    tinuing Search:..."
"Recipe" (Maritain) 475, 727
"Recollection" 101, 102
"Recollections of Thomas Mer-
    ton's Last Days in the West"
    (Steindal-Rast) 1196
"The Recovery of Paradise"
    106, 186, 749
La rectitudo chez saint Anselme:
    un itinéraire augustinien de
    l'âme à Dieu (Pouchet) 476
"Red or Dead: The Anatomy
    of a Cliché" 83, 477
Redeeming the Time 81, 1521,
    1522

"Reflections on a Best Seller"
    see "Man Is a Gorilla with
    a Gun:..."
Reflections on Love: Eight
    Sacred Poems 82
"Reflections on Merton's Notes"
    (Atkins) 942
"Reflections on Some Recent
    Studies of St. Anslem" 478
"Reflections on the Character
    and Genius of Fénelon" 187,
    188
"Reflections on the Moral Cli-
    mate of the 1960's" see
    "Christian in World Crisis:
    ..."
"Reflects on His Friend--
    Thomas Merton" (Rice) 1173
Réflexions d'un spectateur
    coupable 778, 1523, 1524
Reflexoes de um espectador
    culpado 871
"Reform and Apostolate" 22-
    24
Régamey, Raymond 175
"The Regret" 89
Reinhardt, Kurt 157, 552
"Release from Despair" 1171
"The Relevance of a Monk to
    His Time" (Horchler) 1063
"The Relevancy of RB" 479
"Relevancy of the Rule Today"
    (McPherson) 479
Religion and Race in the United
    States" 28, 480
"Religion and the Bomb" 481
Religion in Wood: A Book of
    Shaker Furniture (Andrews)
    152
"A Religious Responsibility"
    see "Peace:..."
"Remembering Thomas Merton"
    (Pillai) 1165
"A Renaissance Hermit: Blessed
    Paul Giustiniani" 22-24
"Renewal and Discipline" 20
"Renewal and Discipline in the
    Monastic Life" 482
"Renewal Crisis Hits Trappists"
    (McCarthy) 1114
"Renewal in Monastic Education"
    483, 779
"Renouveau de la formation

monastique" 779
"Renunciation" 63, 64
"The Reply of Pacem in Ter-
    ris" 81, 88
"Reply to Dom Kucera" 484
"Reply to Martin E. Marty"
    485
"Resourcement and Aggiorna-
    mento" (Peifer) see
    "Monastic Renewal Re-
    visited:..."
"A Responsory, 1948" 89, 106
"Restero mònaco fino alla
    mòrte" (Galletto) 1038
"The Restoration of the Pic-
    tures" (Maritain) 475, 727,
    728
Retour Amont 694
"Retreat, November 1964:
    Spiritual Roots of Protest"
    105
Return Upstream [Retour
    Amont] 694
La revolución negra 909-911
La révolution noire: lettre à
    un blanc libéral suivie de la
    legénde de Tucker Caliban
    176, 780, 1525-1527
"The Rhinoceros" (Bamberger)
    959
Rice, Edward 935, 976, 1006,
    1030, 1172, 1173, 1768-
    1784
Richards, I. A. 167
Richardson, Jane Marie, S. L.
    1328
Riehm, Joan 1174-1176
Rievaulx 153
Riley, Carolyn 1060
"Rilke's Epitaph" 647
"Rites for the Extrusion of a
    Leper" 486, 487
La rivoluzione negra 830
"The Road Ahead" 81
"Roar of Red Woodracer Eats
    Field" 31
Robbins, Ruth 362, 363
"Robert Lowell" 106
Robinson, J. A. T. 293, 350
Rodocanachi, Lucia P. 814
Rohrbach, Peter T., O.C.D.
    1297, 1656
Roman Nocturnes (Alberti)
    680

"The Root of War" 83, 106,
    488, 489, 751, 798
"The Root of War" and "Red
    or Dead" 83
"The Root of War Is Fear"
    63, 64
Roots of Christian Nonviolence
    see Blessed Are the Meek:
    ...
Rootzén, Kajsa 922
Rose of Lima, Sister 158
Rospigliosi, Elena Lante 815,
    823
Ross, Ilona 1177
Ross, Nancy Wilson 1178,
    1450
"A Round and a Hope for
    Smithgirls" 648
Roy, Gregor 966
"Ruben Dario" 649
Rufinus 76
"Russian Mystics" 54-56
Rutledge, Denys 174
Ryan, L. 1634

Sackville-West, Edward 1179,
    1421
"The Sacrament of Advent in
    the Spirituality of St. Ber-
    nard" 85
"Sacramental Contemplation"
    41, 42
"Sacramental Illumination" 60,
    61
Sacraments and Orthodoxy
    (Schmemann) 450
"Sacred and Secular" (Justice)
    1072
"Sacred Art and the Spiritual
    Life" 22-24, 490, 881
"The Sacred City" 491, 492
"Sacred Heart" 25
"Sacred Land" 106
"The Sacrificial Swine" 113
La sagesse du désert: apoph-
    tegmes des pères du désert
    du IVe siecle 781
"Sagesse et vacuité: dialogue
    entre Daizetz T. Suzuki et
    le R. P. Thomas Merton"
    782
"St. Agnes: A Responsory"
    89, 650

St. Alberic" 89
"St. Anselm and His Argu-
    ment" 493
"St. Antonin" 106
"Saint Augustine as Psycho-
    therapist" (Versfeld) 553
"St. Benedict" 95-98
Saint Bernard et Ses Fils 136
"Saint Bernard, moine et
    apôtre" 189
"St. Bernard: Monk and
    Apostle" 22-24
"St. Bonaventure, Harlem,
    and Our Lady of the
    Valley" 86, 87
"St. Bruno" 494
Saint Bruno, le premier des
    ermites de Chartreuse
    (Ravier) 494
"St. Francis and Peace" 495
"St. Gertrude" 496
"Saint Jason" 89
"St. John of the Cross" 106,
    795
"St. Malachy" 89, 106, 651
"Saint Maximus the Confessor
    on Nonviolence" 105
"St. Paul" 89
"St. Peter Damian and the
    Medieval Monk" 497
"Saint Praxed's" (Maritain)
    see "Mosaic:..."
"Saint-Scholar" (Belford) see
    "Thomas Merton:..."
Salet, G. , S. J. 360
"La Salette" 89
Salman, D. H. 1452
Salstrom, Paul 233
"Salve Regina" 84
Sananes, Mary-Lu 900
"Sanctity in Christ" 36-38
Sangita pustakam 741
Santos, Ceferino, S. J. 905
Satyagraha 395
Savage, C. S. 268
Saword, Anne, Sister 1180
Sayings from the Desert
    Fathers 115-117, 735,
    736, 1710, 1711
"Schema XIII: An Open
    Letter to the American
    Hierarchy" 498-500
Schmemann, Alexander 450

Schlegel, Desmond, O.S.B.
    1181, 1487
Schmidthus, Hans 799, 1528
Schmitt, Albert 496
Schoeck, R. J. 1331
Die schwarze Revolution 798,
    1528, 1529
"Die schwarze Revolution in
    Amerika" 799
Schweigen im Himmel 800
"A Search beyond the Self"
    (Michelfelder) 1141
Seasons of Celebration 85,
    785, 832, 873, 915, 1530-
    1538
"The Second Adam" 60-62
"Second Coming" 501
"Le secret" 652, 653
"Secret of the Burning Stars"
    (Cuadra) 713, 716
Secular Journal of Thomas
    Merton 86, 87, 502, 760,
    804, 814, 857, 994, 1004,
    1097, 1167, 1193, 1230,
    1539-1563
"Secular Saint" 503
"Secular Signs" 654
Seeds of Contemplation 63,
    64, 106, 143, 144, 147,
    178, 196, 237, 742, 840,
    843, 904, 925
Seeds of Destruction 88, 783,
    806, 831, 872, 912, 973,
    984, 1021, 1063, 1128, 1164,
    1202, 1564-1585
"Seeking God" 504
"Seeking God through Total
    Love Is Goal" see "Mer-
    ton View of Monasticism:..."
"Seeking Our Redeemer" 505
"Seeking the Rhinoceros: A
    Tribute to Thomas Merton"
    (Cameron-Brown) 985
"Il segno di Giona di Merton"
    (Zanni) 1236
Seitz, Ron 1182
Selected Poems 89, 793, 828,
    1071, 1103, 1170, 1586-
    1591
"Selections from 'Gethsemani,
    Kentucky' " (Cardenal) 685
Selections from the 'Protrep-
    tikos' (Clement of

Alexandria) 126, 696
Selections from the Writings of
    Thomas Merton see The
    True Solitude:...
Selections on Prayer 90
"Self-Denial and the Christian"
    904, 913
"Self-Knowledge in Gertrude
    More and Augustine Baker"
    54-56
"The Self of Modern Man and
    New Christian Consciousness"
    506
Semences de destruction 783
Sementes de destruicão 872
Semi di distruzione 831
Semillas de destrucción 912
"Semiotic Poem from Racine's
    'Iphigenie' " 52
La senda de la contemplación
    913
"Seneca" 655-658
"Seneque" 784
"Senescente Mundo" 89, 106
"Sensation Time at Home" see
    "A Song:..."
"Sense and Sensibility" see
    "Zen:..."
"Sense of Indigence" 101, 102
"Sentences" 63, 64
"Sentences on Hope" 106
"O sentido de nossa doacão"
    507
"Septentrion" 694
Seraphim von Sarow (Zander)
    508
Sermons (Isaac de l'Etoile)
    360
Sertorius, Lili 793
Seul avec Dieu (Leclercq) 172
"Seven Archaic Images" 26,
    659
"Seven Poems from Retour
    Amont" 694
"Seven Qualities of the Sacred"
    509, 914
Seven Storey Mountain 179,
    355, 743, 769, 806, 844,
    865, 899, 904, 981
Seward, Desmond 339
"Sewende" 31
Shaddy, Virginia M. 1183
"The Shadow of Thy Wings"
    106

"The Shaker" 1184
Shakers 152
"The Shakers" 510
Shannon, James P. 1185
"Sharing the Fruits of Contem-
    plation" 63, 64, 106
Shaw, Agnes, O. S. B. 269
Shaw, R. 1781
Sheed, Frank 88
Sheed, Wilfred 1186
"The Shelter Ethic" 511
Shenker, Israel 1187
"The Shoshoneans" 512
The Shoshoneans (Dorn) 512
Shrady, M. L. 143, 144, 147,
    196
Shudō reishū no kompon 845
Shuster, George N. 1188-1191
Sibley, Mulford Q. 233
"Siete cualidades del arte
    sagrado" 914
"The Sign of Flowers" see
    "Ce Xochitl:..."
Sign of Jonas 91, 853, 1592,
    1593
"Signature: Notes on the
    Author's Drawings" 80
"A Signed Confession of Crimes
    against the State" 6, 513
"The Significance of the Bhaga-
    vad Gita" 190
"Signpost to Beauty" (Kountz)
    1088
"Silence" 106
Silence in Heaven 92-94, 148,
    801, 923, 1068, 1096, 1594-
    1607
Silent Life 95-98, 739, 788,
    796, 835, 836, 876, 917,
    983, 1608-1629
Silva, Ludovico 184
The Simple Steps to God
    (Father François de
    Sainte Marie) 155
The Sin of Sloth: Acedia in
    Medieval Thought and Liter-
    ature (Wenzel) 271
"Sincerity" 101-104, 106, 660
"Sincerity and the Muse" (Hall)
    1050
"Sincerity in Art and Life"
    (Owen Merton) 514
Sister M. Therese see Lent-
    foehr, M. Therese, S. D. S.

Sisters of Loretto at the Foot
  of the Cross 43
Sitwell, Sacheverell 348
Sivak, Denis 1192
"Six Poems" (Carrera Andrade)
  691
"The Sleeping Volcano" 106
Small, M. 1395
Smith, Huston 587
"The Social Catalyst" (Baker)
  948
Social Critic: A Study (Baker)
  see Thomas Merton:...
"The Social Dimension of Reli-
  gious Man in the Writings
  of Thomas Merton" (Kelly)
  1793
"Social Perspectives of Charity"
  36-38
"Solemn Music" 10
"Solesmes" 95-98
The Solitary Life 99, 515
Solitary Life: A Letter of
  Guigo 100, 145, 719
"Solitary Life in the Shadow
  of a Cistercian Monastery"
  918
"Solitude" 516
"Solitude and Love" 191
"Solitude Is Not Separation"
  63, 64
"Some Paradoxes of Julian
  Green" see "To Each His
  Darkness:..."
"Some Reflections on the Mo-
  nastic Way of Life" see
  "Vision of Peace:..."
"Some Reminiscences of
  Thomas Merton" (Kelty)
  1075
"Song" 106, 661
"Song for Nobody" 26, 662,
  663
"Song for Our Lady of Cobre"
  89, 885
"Song for the Death of Aver-
  roes" 26, 664
"Song from Crossportion's
  Pastoral" 89, 106, 665
"Song: If You Seek..." 26
"Song: In the Shows of the
  Round Ox" 26, 89
"Song of Purification" 681

"A Song: Sensation Time at
  Home" 666
"Sonship and Espousals" 517
"The Soul of Christ in the
  Eucharist" 41, 42
The Soul of the Apostolate
  (Chautard) 156, 695
"The Sounds Are Furious" 518
"South" 31
"The Sowing of Meanings" 89,
  106
"Sowing Thorns in the Flesh"
  (Marty) 1128
"Space Song" (Cortes) 702,
  703
Spanish translations 879-921
Speaight, Robert 1193, 1561
"Special Problems" 101, 102
Spidlik, Thomas, S.J. 297
"Spirit in Bondage" 60-62
Spirit of Man: Great Stories
  and Experiences of Spiritual
  Crisis, Inspiration, and the
  Joy of Life by Forty Famous
  Contemporaries 191
"Spirit Poets in Print" (Rayne)
  1170
"The Spiritual and Social Phi-
  losophy of Union" (Baker)
  see "Thomas Merton:..."
Spiritual Consciousness in Zen
  from a Thomistic Theological
  Point of View (Kishi) 519
The Spiritual Dialogue of East
  and West (Cuttat) 520
"The Spiritual Dimensions of
  Non-Violence" 30
"Spiritual Direction" 101, 102,
  521
Spiritual Direction and Medita-
  tion 101, 102, 755, 815,
  858, 1630-1637
"Spiritual Father in the Desert
  Tradition" 20, 522, 523,
  774
"Spiritual Life" 192
"The Spiritual Life" (Schlegel)
  1181
"Spiritual Reading" (Battersby)
  964
"Spiritual Revolution" (Bail)
  945
"Spiritual Roots of Protest"

see "Retreat, November
    1964:..."
Spiritual Summit Conference
    135, 165, 401
"The Spiritual Writer" (Lent-
    foehr) 1105
"Spiritualité psychédélienne"
    524
"Spirituality" (FitzGibbon) 1028
"Spirituality for the Age of
    Overkill" 525
"The Spirituality of Sinai" 22-
    24
"The Spirituality of Thomas
    Merton" (Hanlon) 1052
"Sponsa Christi" 4, 5
"Sports without Blood: A
    Letter to Dylan Thomas"
    103, 104, 667
"Spring Storm" 89, 103, 104,
    106
Springs of Devotion 132
Squire, Aelred, O. P. 1293,
    1489
Stark, Philip M., S. J. 1194,
    1195, 1276, 1317, 1367,
    1437, 1443
"Starlight and Non-Being" 113
"The State of Letters--A Let-
    ter from Thomas Merton"
    526
"Statement" (On Vietnam) 193
Steed, R. 1679
Steere, Douglas V. 16, 1268
Stein, Walter 88
Steinberg, Jean 215
Steindal-Rast, David F. K.
    1196
Stevens, Clifford 541, 1197,
    1198
Het stille leven 739
Stoerker, C. F. 1255
Stone, Naomi Burton 232,
    270, 277, 464, 468; see
    also Burton, Naomi
Stonier, Tom 267
Stork, P., Sister 1313
"Storming Heaven" (Speaight)
    1193
The Story of a Life (Paustov-
    sky) 527
The Story of Our Lady of
    Gethsemani (Burden) see

God Is My Life:...
Strange Islands: Poems 103,
    104, 1050, 1072, 1100,
    1109, 1119, 1140, 1638-
    1652
"The Strange Story of Frère
    Pascal" see "The Death
    of a Holy Terror:..."
"Stranger" 103, 104, 106,
    668
"The Stranger: Poverty of an
    Anti-Hero" 528
Stranks, C. S. 205
"The Strategy Is Love" (Sweeney)
    1202
"The Street Is for Celebration"
    529
"The Strife between the Poet
    and Ambition" 25
Strobridge, Robert G. 1506
Studies in Japanese Culture
    534
"A Study of Chuang Tzu" 113
A Study of Conversion and
    Community (Haughton) see
    Transformation of Man:...
A Study of Good (Kitaro) 530
"A Study of the Man and His
    Thought against the Back-
    ground of Contemporary
    American Culture" (McInerny)
    see "Thomas Merton and
    Society:..."
"The Study of Zen" 118
Stuhlmueller, Carrol, C. P.
    1199, 1250
Sturm, Ralph 1200
Styron, William 577
"Subject of Meditation" 101,
    102, 531
"Subliminal" (Sullivan) 1201
Sullivan, A. M. 1201, 1265
Sullivan, Kathryn, R. S. C. J.
    1479
Sullivan, M. 1259
Sullivan, Richard 1422
"A Summer at Gethsemani"
    (Stark) 1194
"Sundown" 82
"Sundown" (Cortes) 704
Suzuki, Daisetz Teitaro 118,
    200, 216, 288, 530, 782,
    1081

Swaminathan, K.   1374
Swartenbroeckx, P. , S. J.
   1527
Swedish translations   922-924
Sweeney, Francis   1202, 1578,
   1727
"Sweetgum Avenue Leads to a
   College of Charm"   669
Sweetman, M.   1486, 1627
Swenson, Mary   1203
Swenson, May   1509
Sykes, Christopher   1204,
   1290
"Symbolism: Communication
   or Communion?"   194, 532,
   533
"Symphony for a Sea Bird"
   113
A Symposium in Memory of
   Thomas Merton see The
   Cistercian Spirit:...
"Syria"   31, 77

"T. S. Eliot"   106
Tadashi, Kudo   844
Tadié, Marie   176, 755, 756,
   760, 764, 767, 768, 771,
   772, 774, 777, 778, 780,
   781, 783, 785-788, 1498,
   1523, 1525, 1694, 1698
Tagore, Rabindranath   446
"Taking Sides on Vietnam"   28
Tao   54-56, 113, 114, 790
"Tao for Tzu" (Fremantle)
   1037
"Talks with and about Thomas
   Merton: Monk, Man and
   Myth" (Morrissey)   1150
"Target Equals City"   105
Tasso, Bruno   823
Tatton, J. Meredith   1597
The Tears of the Blind Lions
   806, 1653, 1654
"Technique and Personal De-
   votion in the Zen Exercise"
   (Dumoulin)   534
The Technological Society
   (Ellul)   535
"Teilhard's Gamble: Betting
   on the Whole Human
   Species"   536
"Temperament and Meditation"
   537

"Temperament and Mental
   Prayer"   101, 102
Tèmpo di celebrazione   832
Tempo e liturgia   873
Le temps des fêtes   785
"Terror and the Absurd: Vio-
   lence and Nonviolence in
   Albert Camus"   538
"Tertullian and St. Cyprian on
   Virgins" see "The Face:
   ..."
"The Testing of Ideals"   36-
   38, 539
Thanh-Bàng   182, 925, 926
"Theology of Creativity"   106;
   see also "The Catholic and
   Creativity:..."
"The Theology of Prayer in
   the Spirituality of Thomas
   Merton" (Higgins)   1792
Théophane le Reclus   297
A Theory of Festivity (Pieper)
   see In Tune with the World:
   ...
"There Has to Be a Jail for
   Ladies"   26
"There Is a Grain of Sand in
   Lambeth Which Satan Can-
   not Find"   31
"There Is a Way"   82
Theses, 1787-1791   1795
Thimmesh, H.   1240
Thirty Poems   806
"Things in Their Identity"   63,
   64
"Thinking Out Loud" (James)
   1069
"This Is God's Work"   540
Thomas, Dylan   667
"Thomas James Merton, 1915-
   1968"   1060
"Thomas Merton"   1205
"Thomas Merton" (Cargas)   988
"Thomas Merton" (Casotti)
   1798
"Thomas Merton" (Evans)   1023
"Thomas Merton" (Hart)   1058
"Thomas Merton" (LasVergnas)
   1091
"Thomas Merton" (Van Doren)
   1220
"Thomas Merton" see "Pro-
   file:..."

Thomas Merton: A Bibliography (Dell'Isola) 929, 1099

Thomas Merton: A Biography (Griffin) 931

"Thomas Merton: A Growing Legend at St. Bonaventure" (Bannon) 962

Thomas Merton: A Different Drummer (Voigt) 936, 1795

"Thomas Merton: A Man for Our Times" (Dufresne) 1788

"Thomas Merton, a Man Revolted against Himself" (Kikama) 1084

"Thomas Merton: An Appraisal" (Stevens) 541, 1197

"Thomas Merton and No Man Is an Island" (Shaddy) 1183

"Thomas Merton and Poetic Vitality" (Kelly) 1073

"Thomas Merton and Society: A Study of the Man and His Thought against the Background of Contemporary American Culture" (McInerny) 1794

"Thomas Merton and the American Conscience" (Evans) see "Elected Speech:..."

"Thomas Merton and the Bangkok Conference" (Shuster) 1190

"Thomas Merton and the Franciscans" (McDonnell) 1121

"Thomas Merton and the Image of Man" (Hergott) 1791

"Thomas Merton as Father Louis" (Bamberger) 960

"Thomas Merton as Futurist" 1206

"Thomas Merton Backs Appeals of Conscientious Objector Here" 1207

"Thomas Merton Center Inaugurated" 1208

"Thomas Merton Center Planned at Bellarmine" (Nolan) 1153

Thomas Merton Documentary Film of the Bangkok Conference, December 9-10, 1968 1800, 1801

"Thomas Merton: estructura y análisis" (Delgado) 1007

"Thomas Merton Is Dead at 53: Monk Wrote of Search for God" (Shenker) 1187

"Thomas Merton, mon confrère, mon ami" (Kelty) 1076

"Thomas Merton, 1915-1968" see "In Memoriam:..."

"Thomas Merton: 1915-1968" (Evans) 1024

"Thomas Merton, 1915-1968" 542

"Thomas Merton, 1915-1968: An Appreciation of His Life and Work by One Who Knew Him" (Pallis) 1160

"Thomas Merton 1968: A Profile in Memoriam" (Stevens) 1198

"Thomas Merton on Camus" (Kikama) 1085

Thomas Merton on Peace 105, 1226, 1234, 1655-1662

Thomas Merton on Prayer (Higgins) see Merton's Theology of Prayer

"Thomas Merton on the Contemplative Life" (McGreggor) 1123

"Thomas Merton on the Peace Strike: Letter to Jim Forest" 543

"Thomas Merton: Outlines of Growth" (Dell'Isola) 1010

"Thomas Merton: Poet" (Sturm) 1200

"Thomas Merton RIP" (Davenport) 1000

Thomas Merton Reader 106, 1663-1672

"Thomas Merton Replies to a Perceptive Critic" 544

"Thomas Merton Resigns as Novice Master" 1209

"Thomas Merton: Saint-Scholar" (Belford) 965

Thomas Merton, Social Critic: A Study (Baker) 928, 1730-1737

"Thomas Merton Sponsoring American Affiliate of Pax" 1210

The Thomas Merton Studies
   Center   127, 1043, 1065
"Thomas Merton: The Dimen-
   sions of Solitude" (Lentfoehr)
   1106
"Thomas Merton: The Last
   Three Days" (Moffitt) 1144,
   1145
"Thomas Merton: The Man
   and His Meaning" (Morrison)
   1149
"Thomas Merton, the Public
   Monk" (Murray) 1152
"Thomas Merton: The Spiritual
   and Social Philosophy of
   Union" (Baker) 1785
"Thomas Merton: The Useful-
   ness of the Useless"
   (MacEoin) 1122
"Thomas Merton to Be Honored
   by Peace Prize" 1211
"Thomas Merton Today: Photo
   Essay" 1212
"Thomas Merton, Trappist:
   1915-1968" (Day) 1001,
   1002
Thomas Merton ... y envolvia
   en humo su cara y sus
   palabras (Belmonte) 1797
"Thomas Merton's Cables to the
   Ace" (Glimm) see "Exile
   Ends in Satire:..."
"Thomas Merton's Cables to
   the Ace: A Critical Study"
   (Flaherty) 1029
"Thomas Merton's Early Inter-
   preters" (Baker) see "An
   Image in the Making:..."
"Thomas Merton's Early Novel"
   1213
"Thomas Merton's East-West
   Dialogue" (Hart) 1059
"Thomas Merton's Mountain"
   (Burton) 982
"Thomas Merton's New Mexico"
   (Shannon) 1185
"Thomas Merton's Response to
   America, the Grim Reaper
   of Violence" (Baker) 949
"Thomas Merton's View of
   Peace" (Kikama) 1087
"Thomas Merton's View of
   Poetry" (Kikama) 1086

"Thomas Merton's World:
   View from a Monastic Win-
   dow" (Baker) 950
"Thonga Lament (Africa) 31
Thornton, Martin 206
Thoughts in Solitude   107, 108,
   180, 387, 750, 827, 842,
   863, 907, 1673-1693
Thrapp, Dan L.   1214
"Three Epigrams" (Cardenal)
   686
"Three Friends" 113
"Three in the Morning" 113
"Three Letters: To a Papal
   Volunteer; To a Brazilian
   Friend; To Dorothy Day"
   545
Three Muslim Sages (Nasr)
   546
The Three Pillars of Zen:
   Teaching, Practice, and
   Enlightenment   587
"Three Postcards from the
   Monastery" 89
"Three Saviors in Camus"
   547
"Three Sisters" (Cortes) 705
"Three Traditions of Christian
   Spirituality" (Noon) 1154
Thurber, James 608, 609
"Tibud Maclay" 31
Tiempos de celebración 915
"Time and the Liturgy" 85,
   548, 847
"The Time of the End Is the
   Time of No Room" 80,
   549, 550
"The Timeless Spirit and
   Counsel of the Saints"
   (Wolfe) 1229
"The Timeless Story" (Burger)
   976
Les titans 786, 1694, 1695
Tittiger, A.   1325
"To a Benedictine Studying in
   Germany" 88
"To a Brazilian Friend" see
   "Three Letters:..."
"To a California Priest in
   California" 88
"To a Contemplative Nun" 88
"To a Cuban Poet" 88
"To a Greek Writer" 88

"To a Moslem" 88
"To a New Convert" 88
"To a Papal Volunteer" 88;
    see also "Three Letters:
    ..."
"To a Priest" 88
"To a Professor of Humanities"
    88
"To a Quaker" 88
"To a Rabbi" 88
"To a Scholar" 88
"To a Severe Nun" 89, 103,
    104, 670
"To a Statesman's Wife" 88
"To a White Priest" 88
"To Alceu Amoroso Lima" 88
"To Alfonso Cortes" 26
"To Become a Monk" 106
"To Catherine de Hueck
    Doherty" 88
"To Daughters: To Study
    History" 10
"To Dr. John C. H. Wu" 88
"To Dorothy Day" 88; see
    also "Three Letters:..."
"To Each His Darkness" 80
"To Each His Darkness: Some
    Paradoxes of Julian Green"
    551
"To Edward Deming Andrews"
    88
"To Fr. Godfrey Diekmann,
    O.S.B." 88
"To Frank Sheed" 88
"To Friends of Victoria
    Ocampo" 88
"To Jacques Maritain" 88
"To James Baldwin" 88
"To Jean and Hildegard Goss-
    Mayr" 88
To Live Is to Love (Cardenal)
    157, 552
"To Mark Van Doren" 88
"To Merton, the Magician"
    (Yamasaki) 1231
"To Remember" (Peloquin)
    1162
"To Robert Lax" 88
"To Sister M. Madeleva" 88
"To Sons: Not to Be Numb"
    10, 671
"To Spanish Seminarians" 88
"To Study History" see "To

Daughters:..."
"To the Hon. Shinzo Hamai,
    Mayor of Hiroshima" 88
"To the Monastery" 106
"To: Thomas Merton. Re:
    Your Prophecy" (Marty)
    1129
"To Walter Stein" 88
Todd, Joyce 1215
Toelle, Gervase, O. Carm.
    1242, 1713
"Tomas Merton visto desde
    fuera de la orden" (Corts
    Grau) 998
"Tonight There Is a Showing
    of Champion Lights" 672
"Top of the Decade" 1216
"Toward a Theology of Resis-
    tance" 28, 105
"Toward the Parousia" 41, 42
"Towards a 'Monastic Therapy' "
    see "Final Integration:..."
Tower of Babel 25, 106, 109,
    110
"The Tower of Babel: A
    Morality" 103, 104
"The Tower of the Spirit" 113
Toynbee, Arnold J. 1127
"Tradition and Revolution" 63,
    64
"La tradition monastique et la
    réforme" (Allchin) 940
"Tradition occidentale" 553
The Tragedy of Father Perrin
    111
"Transcendent Experience" 118
Transformation of Man: A
    Study of Conversion and
    Community (Haughton) 554
"The Transformation of Man in
    Mystical Islam" (Meier) 555
"The Trappist Abbey: Matins"
    89, 106, 673
"Trappist Author to Receive
    First Pax Peace Prize"
    1217
"The Trappist Cemetery-
    Gethsemani" 89, 106
"The Trappist Cemetery:
    Gethsemani Revisited"
    (Berrigan) 967
"Trappist, Working" 89
Treasury of the World's Great

Diaries 195
"A Tribute to Flannery
   O'Connor" 556
"A Tribute to Gandhi" 30, 88,
   105, 141, 557, 819
"A Tribute to Thomas Merton"
   (Cameron-Brown) see
   "Seeking the Rhinoceros:..."
"A Tribute to Thomas Merton"
   (Peloquin) 1163
"A Tribute to Thomas Merton"
   (Saword) 1180
"Tropics" 89
"True and False" see "Non-
   Violence:..."
"The True Legendary Sound:
   The Poetry and Criticism
   of Edwin Muir" 558
"The True Man" 113
The True Solitude: Selections
   from the Writings of Thomas
   Merton 112, 1696, 1697
"Truth" (Cortes) 706
"Truth and Crisis: Pages from
   a Monastic Notebook" 559
"Truth and Violence" 560
"Truth and Violence: An Inter-
   esting Era" 18, 19
Trutter, Lambert, O. P. 1468
"A Tune for Festive Dances in
   the Nineteen Sixties" 674
Tunmer, C. 765, 789
"Tupuseleia" see "East with
   ..."
Turbessi, Guiseppe 212
Turco, Lewis 1591
Turner, Nat 577
Turning Point: Fateful Mo-
   ments That Revealed Men
   and Made History 159
"The Turtle" 113
Tusiani, Joseph 1218, 1284
"Tutto quello che ti tocherà ti
   bruccera. Thomas Merton:
   la sua biografia si chiude a
   Gethsemani" (Guidi) 1049
Twelve Poems (Pessoa) 730
"Two Articles by Thomas
   Merton" 83
"Two British Airmen (Buried
   with Ceremony in the
   Teutoburg Forest)" 25
"Two Celebrations" see

"Morte D'Urban:..."
"Two Chinese Classics" 561
"The Two Cities" (Bamberger)
   961
"The Two Cities of Thomas
   Merton" (Baker) 951
"Two Faces of Prometheus"
   see "A Note:..."
200 Contemporary Authors
   1060
"Two Kings and No-Form"
   113
Two Leggings: The Making of
   a Crow Warrior (Nabokov)
   572, 573
"Two Letters of the Late
   Thomas Merton: On the
   Future of Monasticism;
   Buddhist Monasticism and
   Meditation" 562
"Two Meditations for Our Mem-
   bers: The Priest in Union
   with Mary Immaculate" 563
"Two Moralities" 31
"Two Poems (Song of Purifica-
   tion, Memories of the An-
   cient World)" (Andrade) 681
"Two Poems Dedicated to
   Thomas Merton" (Kerouac)
   52
"Two Poems to a Dead Brother:
   Catullus and Thomas Mer-
   ton" (Stark) 1195
Two Questions on the War in
   Vietnam Answered by the
   Authors of Several Nations
   see Authors Take Sides on
   Vietnam:...
"Two Studies: The Presence
   of God" (Lentfoehr) 1107

Ugalde, Antonia 913
Ultimate Questions: An Anthol-
   ogy of Modern Russian Reli-
   gious Thought (Schmemann)
   450
"L'Ultimo Merton" (Festa) 1027
Ulysses (Joyce) 282, 457
"Unamuno" 564
"Unamuno y la vida monástica"
   (Arrayo) 564
"The Unbelief of Believers" 28

Uncle Tom 428
Underhill, Evelyn 446
Unicorn Folio 600, 637
"Union and Division" 63, 64
University on the Heights 160
"Unreal City" 106
Untermeyer, Louis 195
"Unwordly Wisdom" (Callahan)
  984
L'Uomo nuovo 833
"Urbanity and Grace" (Merwin)
  1140
"Urn with a Political Profile"
  (Cuadra) 713, 717
Urtecho see Coronel Urtecho,
  José
"The Usefulness of the Useless"
  (MacEoin) see "Thomas
  Merton:..."
"The Useless" 113
"The Useless Tree" 113
"Ut Sint Consummati in Unum"
  196
"L'Utilization de l'écriture
  Sainte chez Anselm de
  Canterbery" (Gregoire)
  565
Uw naaste als uzelf 747

Vader, A. 1640
Vallejo, Cesar Abraham 240,
  731, 732
Vallverdu Aixala, Josep 916
  919
Values for Survival see The
  Ecological Conscience:...
Valverde see Maria Valverde,
  José
Van Doren, Mark 88, 89, 106,
  1219, 1220, 1586
"Variations on a Theme" see
  "Elias:..."
Varieties of Unbelief (Marty)
  566
Vasques, Susan 865
Velarde, R. 1493
Verba Seniorum 115-117, 735,
  736, 1710, 1712
"Verbum Caro factum est?"
  4, 5
"Verbum Crucis" 4, 5
Verheissungen der Stille 801

Versfeld, Martin 553
A via de Chuang Tzu 874
Viana, Edmir, O.F.M. 862
Vida e santidade 875
Vida en el amor (Cardenal)
  183
Vida i santedat 916
A vida silenciosa 876
La vida silenciosa 917
"La vida solitaria al amparo
  de un monasterio Cister-
  ciense" 918
Vida y santidad 919
Vie et sainteté 787, 1698,
  1699
La vie silencieuse 788
"La vie solitaire a l'ombre
  d'un monastère cistercien"
  567
Vietnam 28, 105, 193, 445
"Vietnam--An Overwhelming
  Atrocity" 28, 105, 569
"Vietnam and Pacifism" 568
Vietnam: Lotus in a Sea of
  Fire (Nhat-Hanh) 139
"Vietnam: The Paralysed
  Critics" (Barnard) 963
"The Vietnam War: An Over-
  Whelming Atrocity" 569
Vietnamese translations 182,
  925, 926
"View from a Monastic Win-
  dow" (Baker) see "Thomas
  Merton's World:..."
Viglielmo, V. H. 530
Vinho dó silêncio 877
"Violence and Nonviolence in
  Albert Camus" see "Ter-
  ror and the Absurd:..."
"Violence and the Death of
  God: Or God as Unknown
  Soldier" 28, 105
"Virginidad y humanismo en
  los santos padres" 920
"Virginity and Humanism in
  the Latin Fathers" 570
"Virginity and Humanism in
  the Western Fathers" 54-
  56, 920
"Vision and Illusion" 106
"The Vision and the Poem"
  (Johnson) 1071
"Vision of Peace: Some

Reflections on the Monastic
  Way of Life" 571
The Visual World of Thomas
  Merton (Griffin) see The
  Hidden Wholeness:...
Vita e santità 834
Vita nel silênzio 835
"Vital Imperatives for Chester"
  10
Vitale, Philip H. 170
Vitalis, Dom 298
Viva Che! Contributions in
  Tribute to Ernesto "Che"
  Guevara 162
"La vocación monástica y el
  ambiente del pensiamento
  seglar moderno" 921
"Vocation and Modern Thought"
  20
Les voies de la vraie prière
  789
Voigt, Robert J. 936, 1795
Volpini, Valerio 1221
Vom Sinn der Kontemplation
  802
"Von den Wurseln des Krieges"
  803
Von Franckenstein, Clemens
  1051
Von Puttkamer, Annemarie
  1378
Von Wellsheim, Anita, Sister
  1222

Wallace, Welden 1223
Walle, Marthe van de 738
Walley, Dean 112, 1696
Walsh, Dan 106
Walsh, M. G. 1224
Walsh, Peter 1686
"War and the Crisis of
  Language" 105, 197
"War and Vision: The Auto-
  biography of a Crow Indian"
  572, 573
"War in Origen and St. Augus-
  tine" 81, 88
War within Man 198
"The War within Us" 60-62
Warren, Robert Penn 518
"Was Merton a Critic of
  Renewal?" (Andrews) 941
"Was the Death of Thomas

Merton 'A Blessed Fault?' "
  (Shuster) 1191
Wassmer, Thomas A., S. J.
  1611
"Watching among the ..." 89
The Waters of Siloe 854, 904
Watson, Katherine 1272
Watts, Alan 1225, 1706
Way of Chuang Tzu 113, 748,
  790, 874, 1037, 1225, 1700-
  1709
"The Way of Contemplation"
  904, 913
A Way of Spiritual Experience
  (Hasumi) see Zen in Jap-
  anese Art:...
"The Way to Peace" 112
"The Ways to Love" 106
"We Are Not Islands" (Lyons)
  1112
"We Are One Man" 63, 64
"We Have to Make Ourselves
  Heard" 574
"Weathercock on the Cathedral
  of Quito" (Carrera Andrade)
  691, 692
Webb, Geoffrey 1542, 1644
Weber, Richard, O. C. S. O.
  1226, 1227, 1306, 1504,
  1658, 1749, 1760
De weg van Tsjwang-Tzu 748
Weil, Simone 28, 105
Weisskopf, Walter A. 267
Wells, J. 1585
Weltliches Tagebuch 1939-1941
  804
Wenstrup, M., Sister 1503
Wenzel, Siegfried 271
"West" 31
"Western Fellow Students
  Salute with Calypso Anthems:
  The Movie Career of Robert
  Lax" 675
Whalen, James M. 1796
What Are These Wounds? 904
"What Contemplation Is Not"
  63, 64
"What Is Contemplation?" 63,
  64, 803, 904, 913
"What Is Liberty?" 63, 64
"What Is Meditation?" 101,
  102, 575
"What Is the Will of God?"
  36-38

What Ought I to Do? 115,
735, 1103, 1710, 1711
"What to Think When It Rains
Blood" 26
"When a Hideous Man..." 113
"When in the Soul of the Serene
Disciple" 89, 103, 104,
106, 889
"When Knowledge Went North"
113
"When Life Was Full There
Was No History" 113
"When the Shoe Fits" 113
"When You Point Your Finger"
(Cortes) 707
"Where Is Tao?" 113
"Where the Religious Dimen-
sion Enters In" 576
"Whether There Is Enjoyment
in Bitterness" 103, 104
"Whiske" 52
"The 'White Liberal' Myth"
(Jessey) 1070
"Who Is Nat Turner?" 577
"Wholeness" 113
"Why Some Look Up to Planets
and Heroes" 26, 676
Wienpaha, Paul 393
"The Wild Places" 199, 578,
579
"Wilderness and Paradise"
580
Wilderness and Paradise in
Christian Thought (Williams)
580
Wilderness and the American
Mind (Nash) 578, 579
Wilderness Theme in the
Second Gospel and Its Basis
in the Biblical Tradition
(Mauser) see Christ in
the Wilderness:...
Wilkinson, Gertrude, O. SS. R.
1762
Wilkinson, John 535
"Will a Narrow Lane Save
Cain?" 31
"William Blake" 106
"William Congdon" 581
Williams, George H. 580
Williams, P. Shirley 1746
Williamson, Claude C. H.
1460

Wills, Garry 1228
"The Wind Blows Where It
Pleases" 106
Windass, Stanley 175
"The Wine of New Life" 106
Winston, Clara 354
Winston, Richard 354
"The Winter's Night" 89
Wir Suchen Jesus den Christus:
Grundlegungen monastischer
Spiritualitat 805
"Wisdom" 89, 103, 104, 106,
677
"Wisdom and Initiation in
William Faulkner" see
"'Baptism in the Forest':..."
"Wisdom in Emptiness" 118,
200, 782
Wisdom of the Desert 106,
116, 117, 736, 781, 1104,
1712-1723
"With a Great Price" 106
"With the World in My Blood-
stream" 678
Witzman, H. 1755
Wolfe, A. F. 1230, 1559
"The Woman Clothed with the
Sun" 63, 64, 106
"The Woodcarver" 113
Woodcock, G. 1375
Woolf, Cecil 193
"Work and Holiness" 36-38
Word and Revelation (Balthasar)
582
Worland, Carr 1229
"The 'World'" 81
"World Is a Round Earthenware
Plate" (Cuadra) 713, 718
"World of Solitude" 112
"World of the Spirit" (Watts)
1225
The World Religions Speak on
the Relevance of Religion
in the Modern World 135,
165
"The World's Body" 106
"Worship" 41, 42
"Writing as Temperature" 583
Writing Degree Zero (Barthes)
583
"Written Next to a Blue Flower"
(Cuadra) 713
"The Wrong Flame" 63, 64

Wu, John C. H. 88, 124

Yamasaki, Jean 1231
"The Young Thomas Merton"
    (Deasy) 1004

Zaehner, R. C. 1232
Zahn, Gordon C. 105, 1233-
    1235, 1655
Zander, Valentine (Vera) 508
Zanni, Pietro 1236
Zaturenska, Marya 650
Zazen 393
Zeik, Michael D. 1237
Zen 54-56, 118, 124, 216,
    393, 404, 408, 423, 519,
    534, 585-587, 971
"Zen and Christian Mysticism"
    (Johnston) 584
Zen and the Birds of Appetite
    118, 790, 837, 841, 878,
    1724-1729
"Zen Buddhist Monasticism"
    54-56
"A Zen Catholic" (Zeik) 1237
Zen Catholicism: A Suggestion
    (Graham) 589
"The Zen Catholicism of
    Thomas Merton" (MacCor-
    mick) 1115
Zen e as aves de rapina 878
Lo zen e gli uccèlli rapaci
    837
"Zen in Japanese Art" 118
Zen in Japanese Art: A Way
    of Spiritual Experience
    (Hasumi) 585, 586
"The Zen Koan" 54-56, 587
"A Zen Philosopher" see
    "Nishida:..."
"The Zen Revival" 588
"Zen: Sense and Sensibility"
    589
Zen, Tao, et Nirvâna: esprit
    et contemplation en Extrême-
    Orient 790
Zen, Weg zur Erleuchtung
    (Enomiya-Lasalle) 590
"Zero Weather" see "Evening
    Song:..."
Znak Jonaska 853

Zukofsky, Louis 453, 591
"Zukofsky: The Paradise Ear"
    591